Teaching with Computers:

A Curriculum for Special Educators

Teaching with Computers:
A Curriculum for Special Educators

Gregory Church, M.S.
Computer Coordinator
Special Education Division
The Kennedy Institute
Baltimore, Maryland

Michael Bender, Ed.D.
Vice President of Educational Programs
The Kennedy Institute
Professor of Education
Johns Hopkins University
Joint Appointment, Department of Pediatrics
Johns Hopkins School of Medicine
Baltimore, Maryland

A College-Hill Publication
Little, Brown and Company
Boston/Toronto/London

College-Hill Press
A Division of
Little, Brown and Company (Inc.)
34 Beacon Street
Boston, Massachusetts 02108

Library of Congress Cataloging in Publication Data
Main entry under title:

Church, Gregory, 1960–
  Teaching with computers.

  "A College-Hill publication."
  Bibliography: p.
  Includes index.
  1. Special education—Computer-assisted
instruction. I. Bender, Michael, 1943–
II. Title.
LC3969.5.C48   1989   371.9   89-2783
ISBN 0-316-14246-8
Printed in the United States of America
EB

to my parents William and Mary Church for all their love, support, and
continuing encouragement

to the memory of my mother, Sally Bender, whose encouragement was
endless and who truly was a "Woman of Valor"

Contents

List of Figures and Tables

Preface

Teaching with Computers: A Curriculum for Special Educators presents special and regular educators and related staff members with guidelines for planning computer implementation and managing computers in educational settings. In utilizing this framework to design effective and relevant learning experiences, professionals, parents, and other advocates are provided with a context and an intuitive feeling for ways of developing and using computer technology easily and efficiently in educational settings.

The text presents a functional curriculum framework for developing computer learning activities and experiences appropriate to children and adolescents with learning problems. These learning problems are defined in the broadest sense to include all those factors that may interfere with the learning process, such as deviations in cognitive, physical, social, and emotional development. The integration of computer learning activities are conceptualized to include the basic-skill subjects of reading, writing, and mathematics.

What makes this resource specifically appealing to practitioners is its thoroughness in responding to questions that can occur daily as one works in developing a computer program. The authors have spent five years pilot-testing suggested software and strategies with teachers in actual classrooms and computer labs. Much of the content has also been presented for critical review at university and national conferences in an attempt to bring a practical and functional resource to its audience rather than new theories that have had limited testing.

Chapters 1 through 5 each conclude with a brief summary and some sample review questions and follow-up activities students may wish to pursue. Chapters 6, 7, and 8, beside providing a comprehensive listing of resources, are each supported by a glossary of reading, writing, and math terms respectively, enabling a person not familiar with some of the terminology in these areas to review specific definitions.

The authors believe this is a comprehensive resource that has material suitable for the novice as well as the seasoned professional. Its illustrations should provide clarity to the concepts presented in the chapters.

This book explores the many facets of customizing the computer for the special-education classroom. It is a resource guide that uses a nontechnical approach and is intended for those educators who wish to design and implement individualized computer technology for special-needs children.

Acknowledgments

The material in this book has been developed over a period of five years. It is an outgrowth of many curricular ideas developed at the Kennedy Institute's Division of Special Education and the Johns Hopkins University in Baltimore, Maryland.

The completion of this work would not have been possible without the assistance of a number of individuals and organizations. Foremost among these are M.E.B. Lewis and Eddie M. Denning, who are principal and assistant principal of the Kennedy Institute School programs. They are gratefully acknowledged for their excellent and thoughtful work in preparing the glossary section at the end of Chapters 6, 7, and 8. The students and teachers of the Kennedy Institute School deserve a special thanks for their consistent input and willingness to field-test much of the book's content.

A final acknowledgment is given to the following software publishers and distributors for their permission to report information about their programs: Britannica Software, Houghton Mifflin Company, Scholastic Software, Mind-Play, Spinnaker Software, StyleWare, Inc., and Sunburst Communications.

CHAPTER 1

Introducing Computers
in Today's Classroom

It has been several years since personal computers dramatically entered our work, school, and home environments, and it appears this rapid flood of new technologies will sweep us into the promises and pitfalls of the next century. For educators following in the wake of this technological inundation, there is unfortunately a bewildering problem of dealing with new technologies in terms of training, program development, implementation, and classroom applications.

Over the last several years there has been much speculation about the role of computers in education. Predictions that computers would take over many teaching functions encouraged counterclaims that computers could have only minimal impact since most teaching functions cannot be easily automated. To date, computer instruction in school settings has navigated a course between these two extremes. The concept of the computer as a novelty is rapidly fading (Scheffler, 1986). It now appears to be time to move toward evaluating and/or developing computer technology that acts as tools in teaching and in solving learning problems. As a result, there is a growing need for guidance on computer issues, methods, strategies, and tactics for managing the use of technology in education.

The advent of personal computers in school settings has provided a stage for an unprecedented period of growth and transition for education. The need for change and improvement will persist given the potential impact of emerging technologies on special-needs students. Making the decision to use computers can be an exciting and yet a complex process. In committing to the use of computers as a principal, teacher, parent, or advocate, one must first recognize the many implications associated with computer utilization.

Without first identifying potential issues involved with implementing computers, the planned benefits of technology often never come to fruition. In fact, failing to identify elusive issues can lead to short- and long-term problems for school programs. Problems can manifest themselves in administrator/staff relationships, role and organizational problems, decision making, or communications. Obscured issues can so adversely affect a new computer program, many such programs stagger and die in infancy. Current educational literature regarding the effectiveness of innovative programs seems to imply a high failure rate for any type of program that is innovative or attempts to produce much change (Berman and McLaughlin, 1975). Consequently, before embracing any new technology over more traditional practices, provide the opportunity for careful evaluation of proposed innovations in the school environment.

THE FIRST STEPS:
IDENTIFYING COMPUTER ISSUES AND PROBLEMS

Often, when you want to start a school computer program, the question arises: How do I begin? Let us start by defining some of the issues that affect the success of computer programs. These issues are forces or elements that impact on the proposed computer environment. These forces, to a large extent, influence and constrain the planning and development of school microcomputer programs. To be successful in embracing new technology, administrators and teachers must have an awareness of the variety of issues and must identify and describe these forces that act on the form and substance of proposed computer programs. Identifying these forces helps to assess and reduce the risks involved in any type of computer-program implementation.

Clearly, any type of assessment concerning the effects of computer-based programs on school settings will involve making insights into the substance of interaction between participating social groups, administrative policy, instructional methodology, curriculum, and school-resource bases. Bender and Church (1984) identified 12 factors that play a role in determining the success rates for computer-program implementation. Some of these factors include lack of knowledge of existing resources; unfamiliar jargon; resistance to newness and change; staff roles not clearly defined; and unclear performance standards. Often, when left unresolved these factors become barriers to successful computer-program implementation.

The variety and complexity of major program issues will depend largely on the size and scope of the proposed computer intervention program. For example, consider the impact of just a single computer implemented in a classroom versus in a resource-room setting. Does one implementation strategy require more teacher training, lesson planning, student access / scheduling, or security? Who has access to the computer? What kind of instruction will it support? The answers are never simple; however, identifying both obvious and hidden implications of the technology will help to minimize the pervasive effects that technology can often have on innovative computer programs.

RESISTANCE TO NEWNESS AND CHANGE

Implementing computers into a new setting introduces change. Proposed change challenges the status quo and tends to be threatening to a number of people. Similarly, an attempt to implement change can also be disruptive to school routine and debilitating to the staff members affected adversely by the process (Gorton, 1980). Change often implies that the present system and components are inadequate. Individuals may fear their skills diminished, personal pride reduced, or be concerned they may have to learn new skills. The extent to which computers will affect any of these aspects will depend in large part on the effectiveness of the people involved in planning for and implementing the technology.

Considering the knowledge required to develop a computer program, encouraging ideas and support throughout a school system can be a very effective procedure in overcoming the effects of resistance to technology. The following procedures can be helpful to those individuals planning to introduce technology into a noncomputer school environment. The purpose of these procedures is straightforward—to provide an open atmosphere in which participants have the opportunity to identify weaknesses in an existing system and collectively establish a basis for directing future implementation efforts.

Guidelines for Reducing Resistance to Microcomputers

I. Organize participants and identify school needs.
   a. Encourage all staff members potentially affected by the new technology to join in the planning process.
   b. Have the staff review the existing school environment (instructional objectives and methods, etc.).
   c. Identify all instructional and support areas that have problems or that have the potential for improvement or change.
   d. Evaluate the approaches through which technology might be helpful in improving or replacing identified problem area(s).
II. Acquaint the staff with the potential impact of technology.
   a. Discuss proposed technology approaches with the participants in order to gain an awareness of attitudes and feelings of staff members.
   b. Have the participants outline the benefits and disadvantages of the technology impacting on the identified problem areas.
   c. Have the participants identify the measures needed to implement the technology.
III. Develop a decision-making body for implementing the technology.
   a. Identify members with interest in the proposed project(s).
   b. Identify specific task groups and define responsibilities.
   c. Organize communications between task groups.

These guidelines represent only a preliminary effort in effecting the change process. You may or may not find them useful in further development efforts. They simply introduce the staff to the prospect of a technology intervention. Following these guidelines can provide a favorable implementation environment for the following reasons: (1) individuals who may be affected by the implementation feel like active and participating members in the change process; (2) the process provides an opportunity for participants to seriously critique existing programs and highlight various problem areas; (3) the process reduces the fear and anxiety associated with unexpected changes in procedures, policy, and job roles; and (4) the process provides a resource pool for new ideas on implementation approaches.

SETTING PRIORITIES FOR COMPUTER USE

Defining the use of microcomputer technology within special education environments requires the close support of administrators, teachers, support-services staff, and advocates. Together they face the challenges of transcending traditional curricula and instructional methodology with the intricacies of computer hardware and software in the effort to create an effective educational design. Too often, however, there are few objectives and little substance behind schools' initial computer programs, especially when curricula and software take divergent paths.

Approaches toward integrating computer-based educational programs at both the building and district level differ widely across school systems. Researchers have found it not uncommon for districts to implement computer instruction with no districtwide computer policy. Some of the most prevalent problems observed included: (1) lack of clearly presented goals for computer activities and (2) lack of implementation plans (Moskowitz and Birman, 1985). Similarly, Moskowitz and Birman noted that decisions at the district level often were not based on sound educational goals or supported with well-specified curricula. In addition, the planning and implementation of computer activities in many cases were supported by small groups of teachers called "computerists" (Sheingold, Kane, and Endreweit, 1983). These grassroots teachers have been responsible for initiating the development and coordination of computer activities in many school districts throughout the United States (Becker, 1983). Conversely, specialized administrative programs for developing and monitoring microcomputer-based programs were also being utilized (Bozeman, 1984). Further, in some cases planning for computer implementation has been constrained by obsolete state requirements and in other cases thrown to the wind under community pressures for keeping pace with other school systems (Moskowitz and Birman, 1985). Zuk and Stillwell (1985) contended that the pressure to implement computer literacy programs caused districts to have as their major priority the acquisition and placement of computer hardware before any formal training was given to teachers or before any curriculum development. It is these types of unidimensional programs that eventually fall prey to critics who are quick to point out that the novelty of computers is already waning.

Setting priorities for computer use, whether formulated from a district or building level, requires a framework for analyzing all components of the school environment. Within the context of determining priorities there must be an understanding of the essence or purpose behind computer utilization. Some examples of the kinds of justifications or needs behind new computer implementations may include: (1) administrative problems; (2) new instructional requirements; (3) new instructional techniques; and (4) comprehensive local or district-level improvements.

Administrative problems are typical of most school settings. The size and complexity of some systems may foster more problems than would smaller settings. However, administrative problems can be found at the district, building, or classroom levels. These problems may surface in school-records management; generating individualized educational programs (IEPs); or they may involve student scheduling or follow-up reporting. Essentially, this type of computer use involves some types of automation with the administrative process.

Education has always had to grapple with changing instructional responsibilities resulting from new educational mandates from federal, state, and local agencies. For instance, few of us would argue the impact Public Law 94-142 (The Education for all Handicapped Children Act, 1975) is having on the education system in terms of the instructional responsibilities for special-needs students. In fact, the situation is also well-documented in other countries such as Great Britain and Canada (Bunch, 1984; Csapo and Goguen, 1980; Welton, Weddell, and Vorhaus, 1984). A new requirement or regulation imposed on a school system will often require careful analysis of any modification(s) in order to support the school system in satisfying new laws. Computer use under these circumstances involves some new or innovative approaches to instructional management.

Today, especially with the continual changes in computer technology and software, the prospects of the computer supporting new instructional concepts seems bright (Rostron and Sewell, 1984 and Browning et al., 1985). From implementing schoolwide computer literacy programs, to providing computer information access by physically handicapped students, or even to providing a single computer to a classroom for remedial instruction, the use of computers as an instructional tool will be the likely result.

Finally, a new computer process might be appropriate simply because of a district's desire to improve the system. In some instances the reason for improvement may be tied to new administrative policies, eliminating or replacing years-old operating procedures, automating time-intensive procedures, cost reductions, faster reporting functions, or changes in curricula.

Frequently, however, reasons for implementing computer technology can be vague and poorly defined by initiators (Moskowitz and Birman, 1985). Educational research provides little objective data for specific insights into the correlative factors associated with the success or failure of planned implementation programs (Bozeman, 1984). However, in setting priorities for computer use, individuals should keep a number of factors in mind when determining computer usage.

Setting Computer Priorities:
Some Premises for Implementing Computers

1. The development paths of hardware and software must converge with those of curriculum development.

2. Computer policy should be developed to be consistent with appropriate local, regional, or state master plans.
3. Setting computer-program objectives and goals should precede any implementation efforts.
4. Initiators should always act with the support and cooperation of the administrative body.
5. Administration should always provide leadership roles for computer implementations.
6. Forced implementations efforts, whether caused by internal or external pressures, provide more problems than they solve.
7. Available resources should be balanced with proposed program goals. A phased implementation process should be encouraged when plans for computer usage are far reaching.
8. Implementation is easier to manage when the scope of proposed computer programs is implemented in a gradual manner.

DEFINING STAFF ROLES

Computers are inevitably going to induce instructional changes in the classroom. We are at a cultural turning point that is likely to produce significant changes in our society, which in turn will fundamentally alter our educational system. As new technologies apply new pressures to our educational system, it becomes necessary to evaluate the appropriateness of organizational roles and administrative and staff responsibilities. For example, the complexity of computer equipment and the expertise needed to implement, manage, and maintain the technology demand a variety of technical skills. Is it appropriate for a school to delegate such responsibility to a resource teacher with little or no computer training or a classroom teacher with daily teaching, planning, and behavior-management responsibilities? Should one teacher or group of teachers reduce their teaching responsibilities in favor of activities like computer hardware and software selection, computer maintenance, and computer programming? Similarly, in any integrative push of computer instruction with curriculum objectives, administrators, teachers and resource personnel might consider some of the problems associated with supporting the development of such endeavors.

Roles are expectations about the attitudes, beliefs, and activities appropriate to specific positions in an organizational setting and the context in which the organization operates. Roles relate to positions in the formal organization, not to people (Gross, Mason, and McEachern, 1958). Often, expectations can become problematic when activities change or the context of the organization changes. Role ambiguity is a major problem in school administration that would be greatly alleviated by more clearly defined written and definitive job descriptions (Vetter, 1976). Within traditional school settings, staff expectations that are not clearly defined or communicated represent a major source of misunderstanding and problems in school administration (Gorton, 1980). Conflicts may arise from disagreements over the evaluation of a situation, over values, goals, objectives, or over the choice of alternatives associated with changing the state of an organization (Schmuck and Runkel, 1985).

When the expectations of staff and those of administration are in disagreement, the potential for conflict increases dramatically (Hencley, 1960). Consider for a moment the potential administrative problems associated with staff roles as part of a computer-implementation effort. The administration has decided to implement microcomputer instruction for remedial purposes. What are the ramifications of expectations that are assumed or unwritten? Are administrators, teachers, or both responsible for decisions regarding changes in curriculum? Should teachers be required to have dual roles — teacher and technologist? On the other hand, should teachers specialize, needing knowledge in only certain types of software or hardware? Are teachers responsible for developing instructional computer materials along with traditional instructional materials? Should teachers be required to spend additional time outside the classroom maintaining and developing computer skills, classroom computer equipment and software? As part of any planning process, administrators should consider developing performance standards that support the efforts of new programs.

Certainly any proposed computer project will require some administrative definition of role responsibilities. The scope of job roles will depend on the size and complexity of the computer project. For instance, consider the role of a classroom teacher who wishes to improve the written expression of her/his class of students with learning disabilities. The school has only two computers, both of which are being used with secondary math classes. The special-education teacher wishes to augment individualized touch-typing and word-processing instruction within a self-contained classroom. The administration has seen very little student improvement in the upper-level math groups and is reluctant to invest any more funding in computers. The special-education teacher, after attending a number of computer workshops, has seen dramatic improvement in written expression through the use of computer technology. Considering the present school environment, what should be the role of the teacher? In addition to teaching responsibilities, should the teacher take on the role of computer advocate, innovator, implementor, or some combination of all these roles? In short, the breadth of staff responsibilities for any microcomputer project can depend on a variety of factors, including, but not limited to, a school's political climate, school or district resource base, goals of the proposed program, the instructional objectives of the computer program, and time-line for implementation.

Whether a new computer program targets a district, building, or classroom implementation approach, the reader can outline a number of general activities or responsibilities commensurate with the development of any type of school computer program. An outline identifying roles is helpful for visualizing the structure of a computer program; it helps you confront and solve problems of program organization. Construct a program outline by jotting down major responsibilities or roles, using a time-line approach. To be useful in developing staff organization, the outline should be informal and flexible. What the outline provides program developers is analogous to an architect's preliminary design drawings rather than a completed blueprint. The following outline of general activities can serve as a guide in developing role responsibilities for computer programs with varying demands and complexities.

General Roles for Computer Use

I. Setting the Stage for Computer Use
  a. Organize meetings with potential participants.
  b. Provide open discussions concerning school problems.
  c. Identify general school needs.
  d. Discuss available approaches.
  e. Highlight pros and cons with participants.
  f. Gain the support and commitment of participants.

II. Strategic Planning for Computer Use
  a. Establish a planning board.
  b. Establish planning policies.
  c. Identify resource bases.
  d. Review district and local master plans.
  e. Critique school needs and approaches identified in Stage I.
  f. Prioritize school needs with supporting solution approaches.
  g. Develop goals for computer implementation.
  h. Develop specific objectives form meeting program goals.
  i. Assign task groups to specific objectives.
  j. Develop time-lines and schedules.

III. Preliminary Ground Work for Computer Use
  a. Review similar computer projects in other school settings.
  b. Highlight project's successes and mistakes.
  c. Review current educational trends in project area.
  d. Review current hardware and software trends.
  e. Develop instructional objectives.
  f. Develop measurements for instructional objectives.
  g. Assess skill levels of staff in project's target area.
  h. Develop assessment of staff needs.
  i. Review school facilities for computer implementation.
  j. Assess need for improvement of facilities.
  k. Provide regular status reports of progress to teachers / participants.

IV. Training for Computer Use
    a. Identify available resources for training.
    b. Identify training needs to target staff members.
    c. Have target staff identify appropriate training objectives.
    d. Design training modules around skill needs identified in Stage III.
    e. Provide appropriate time frame for training.
    f. Evaluate the training process in terms of identified training objectives.
    g. Identify any needed follow-up training.
V. Implementation for Computer Use
    a. Have task groups identify unique characteristics or needs of their target student population.
    b. Develop computer-performance characteristics for target student populations.
    c. Identify vendor hardware, software, and peripherals appropriate to target student populations.
    d. Compare and evaluate different vendor product lines against your performance characteristics.
    e. Match vendor products with performance characteristics.
    f. Review product costs with available school resource base.
    g. Develop an implementation schedule.
    h. Implement computer use.
VI. Supporting Computer Use
    a. Monitor instructional procedures for consistency and continuity in curriculum content.
    b. Measure instructional effectiveness with models developed in Stage III.
    c. Develop feedback mechanisms for identifying problems with staff training, implementation scheduling, appropriateness of program objectives, and effectiveness of current policies.
    d. Evaluate and review procedures.
    e. Provide intervention strategies for dealing with inefficiencies.

EQUITY IN COMPUTER USE

In many school districts across the country, computers have permeated the instructional environment; resource rooms, computer labs, and classrooms abound with computer, peripherals, and software. By 1983 nearly 70 percent of all middle and junior high schools had one or more microcomputers; elementary usage also rose over 40 percent during the same period (Becker, 1983). However, the same study reported a variety of implementation approaches at both the elementary and secondary levels resulting in lower student access patterns for some schools. The study also identified different implementation philosophies among socioeconomic groups regarding computer-based instruction. Black, Hispanic and other minority elementary schools support computer-based instruction for below-average students in the belief that computer-based drills can improve student performance and help them catch up with other students. Conversely, low socioeconomic white schools prefer to use computers with above-average students in order to foster challenging independent work, which reduces the need for behavior-management by teachers (Becker, 1983). Are these appropriate implementation patterns for our students? Have these usage patterns caused disadvantages in the education of students with certain skill levels? As educators, we must identify these equity issues as part of our planning process, especially when trends with computer-based instruction are moving toward curriculum integration and there is an increased need of students for information access.

THE ADMINISTRATIVE FUNCTION

The initial decision to use computer technology in school settings has come from a variety of sources. For instance, classroom teachers have been responsible for many early implementation efforts (Becker, 1983; Sheingold, Kane, and Endreweit, 1983). Similarly, some utilization efforts have come from more traditional intermediary sources such as school boards, district planning councils, and advisory groups (Moskowitz and Birman, 1985). Developing a computer program requires the cooperation and involvement of many people. The administrator, teacher, or advocate should not attempt to introduce or implement a proposed computer program single-handedly. The dynamics of educational change has shown that the cooperation, support, and leadership in introducing change can come from many sources (Goodlad, 1975). However, it is important to recognize that the administration and the principal are key figures in any implementation process (Demeter, 1951). The support for such innovations, if they are to be successful, requires the cooperation of these individuals.

Granted, decision making occurs in a variety of settings and is initiated by teachers, principals, or large advocacy groups. But an administrative body must understand the importance of leadership in developing computer-based instructional programs. Further, making effective decisions is vital for continued success as an administrator. For many practitioners, work experience and intuition blend themselves into an effective decision-making instrument. Although experience and intuition can effect favorable results in the decision-making process, they alone are seldom sufficient in making effective decisions (Gorton, 1980). An administrator having little or no experience in the use of computers would be hard pressed to make computer-utilization decisions based on intuition alone. As a result, the decision process must be supported by analysis. Such analysis would include the utilization of relevant information sources, access to experts in the field, and decision-making models.

The following sections can help administrators facilitate the decision-making process for computer-based instructional programs. Figure 1-1 illustrates the process; the following sections describe the process in detail.

- *Educational environment.* For us, the educational environment consists of the many educational components of a school's program environment. These educational components collectively provide the means for planning and implementing educational directives. For example, some of these components include educational mandates; administrative policies and procedures; individual student needs; instruction; staff responsibilities; training needs; and curriculum. All these elements together provide a framework for our educational system.

   Impacting these educational components are various structural and situational variables that act as possible change agents for education. Making decisions about computer utilization evolves out of the realization that our educational environment is dynamic and is influenced by many structural and situational variables—structural variables such as emerging computer technologies that automate and model difficult or complex tasks, and situational variables that change instructional requirements or produce new educational demands for special-needs children. As these variables begin to apply pressure on the existing educational system, questions and issues arise regarding the future direction of educational planning. Hence, careful program evaluation becomes imperative in the decision-making process for computer-based instruction.

- *Awareness.* This step in the process allows the administrator to define those educational components that may require program evaluation or analysis. Similarly, the administrator must identify those structural and situational variables that may have impacted a school's process, function, or continuity. In order to make effective decisions regarding the use of computers, an administrator must first qualify the questions, issues, or problems that require such decisions. The process should not be governed by assumptions about "computerized instructional panaceas," school-community pressures to keep pace with technology, or hurriedly made student- and instructional-need diagnoses.

   Provide an opportunity to investigate and analyze the educational environment and to develop an awareness of the impact that variables have on the school program. Do this through a questioning process:

   1. Has the educational environment experienced change resulting in new educational needs? Do these changes require new educational planning or decision making? Have new structural or situational variables affected the instructional environment? What are the characteristics of these structural and situational variables? Can traditional methods accom-

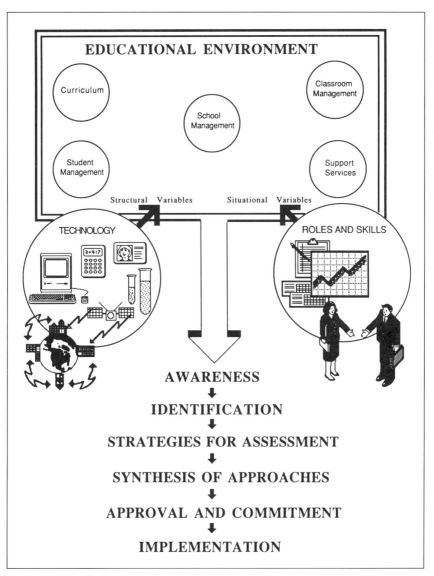

Figure 1-1. The decision-making process for computer implementation.

plish the needed change? Can computers be used as a tool to augment the change process? Are there any personal biases?

2. How can computers improve the exisiting school program? What

sources of information are available to provide insight into their potential use? In what school settings are they most beneficial? Which staff members are affected by the potential use of computers? What student groups are affected by the use of computers? Will the use of computers affect existing administrative policies, procedures, or responsibilities?

3. Who is experienced enough to make decisions on computer use? Who should be involved in the decision process? Does the decision to use computers require a time-line for school implementation?

- *Identification.* After the administrator attains some insight into the educational environment and the relationships between educational components and changing structural and situational variables, the identification step provides the opportunity for developing alternative methods for addressing identified needs areas. As an administrator, use the awareness step as a catalyst for identifying alternative courses of action. Will traditional innovations provide adequate means for producing a desired outcome? Can computers support a more effective solution, or will some combination of traditional and computer efforts produce the most effective solution? Depending on a school's resources, courses of action can often be limited in scope and may result in few alternatives. Similarly, access to timely information, large resource bases, or sound analysis can provide a creative environment for planning new approaches. Nevertheless, whatever the situation is in a school setting, it is advisable to generate as many alternatives as possible. This provides the decision maker with more flexibility as structural and situational variables induce continual changes in the educational environment.
- *Strategies for assessment.* The strategies step provides a framework for assessing the feasibility of alternative courses of action. In attempting to assess various computer-implementation alternatives, the educator must realize that precisely forecasting the impact of computer technology on the school environment may not always be reasonably likely. For example, a group of children may react differently to computer instruction from what was anticipated; or staff training may not be adequate for meeting computer competency skills; or the school's estimated resource base (hardware, software, knowledgeable staff, etc.) may be insufficient for completing computer-program objectives.

The educator, regardless of technical proficiency, can evaluate various computer alternatives using a variety of techniques and methods. Many of these techniques will be discussed later in Chapter 2. For now, let us assume these techniques are not prescriptive models but descriptive assessment vehicles for focusing the questioning of computer-utilization alternatives. Any decision-making approach to computer usage should highlight important questions that take into consideration instructional program objectives; potential impact on target populations and support staff; competency levels; knowledge bases; school resources; policy and procedures support; and leadership roles. As previously noted, the administrator should realize feasibility assessments does not involve choosing right or wrong alternatives or using the assessment model to automate the decision-making process for the administrator; feasibility assessment simply directs or focuses the assessment process on specific aspects related to various alternative courses of action.

• *Synthesis of approaches.* Because of the variety of implementation patterns that are available for computerized instruction in schools and classroom settings, the decision of supporting one approach over another can be difficult. Often one alternative implementation approach may be very appropriate within an elementary environment, but the same approach across various instructional settings may have limited usefulness for meeting various instructional objectives at the secondary level. While the usefulness of one computer-implementation approach may play a major role in specialized classroom settings, a combination of alternative programs may be more appropriate or effective for other school situations. The synthesis of approaches step provides the opportunity for some creative thinking and allows the administrator to reexamine assumptions about implementation approaches. This phase will filter out those important characteristics or aspects of various program alternatives that have the most utility in meeting the needs of the educational environment. A decision for computer use may surface through one alternative approach, or a course of action may be assimilated through various components of multiple alternatives.

• *Approval and commitment.* Once the administrator has made the decision to implement computer technology, the approval and commitment step becomes critical in securing acceptance and supporting such initiatives. Supporting the process of computer-based instruction requires some preliminary procedures in order to initiate action. For example, primary to the success of any computer-implementation process is gaining creditability as decision maker(s) and the ability to obtain approval of decisions from the staff; developing administrative policy and procedures that support future directives; and organizing a framework for future staff and resource support. The support and success for any computer-based instructional program will depend on the ability of the decision maker to use this phase in the decision-making process as a vehicle for reducing negative effects associated with the change process. As previously mentioned, negative effects can vary from initial groundwork development, such as staff resistance, to change or implementation problems, such as a poorly coordinated school development plan.

• *Implementation.* Only after the administrator has accomplished the objectives of these steps of the decision-making process should a concerted effort be made to implement computerized instruction. The decision-implementation step sets the stage for basic activities that are fundamental to any type of computer-implementation program. Depending on the scope of the computer-implementation decision, the administrator's responsibilities will vary from one program to another. For example, an administrator may only need to provide program objectives and monitor program progress if a school has an existing computer program supported by experienced staff and computer equipment. On the other hand, if the decision to use computer-based instruction is new to a school environment, administrative responsibilities can include designing and implementing an extensive computer-utilization master plan; obtaining and organizing a variety of resources; providing training for large numbers of staff; redefining roles; or even developing new curricula. Although administrative responsibilities can and will vary across school computer programs, the following list of basic implementation steps apply to most situations:

1. *Initial planning.* Develop general computer-program goals. Support these goals with specific instructional objectives. Similarly, develop administrative procedures that coordinate and facilitate these goals and objectives.

2. *Organizing the participants.* Identify potential participants based on the following criteria: (a) individuals impacted by the computer project and; (b) individuals with appropriate technical and support skills and past experience with similar projects.

3. *Organizing the resources.* In the identification of resources, it is necessary to consider three levels of support: (a) human resources—sources of technical information support; (b) equipment resources—tools for actual use and applications development; and (c) funding resources—initiating and developing support sources.

4. *Scheduling the process.* Identify and prioritize specific planning sessions that are relevant to the computer implementation. These planning sessions should be sequenced jointly with the development of program objectives. Finally, in scheduling these sessions, consider role responsibilities, interests of staff, timely computer and instructional information, and a presentation framework that can be expressed in an orderly and meaningful manner.

5. *Monitoring the program.* In order to support decisions, the administrator should provide mechanisms for giving instructions, communicating task responsibilities, coordinating various concurrent jobs, and documenting activities through reporting functions.

6. *Evaluating the program.* The administrator should provide for an evaluation process (formative and summative) that addresses the adequacy of the planning process, project objectives, etc. Formative evaluations measure the planning processes, and summative evaluations evaluate results or outcomes of the planning process.

IDENTIFYING COMPUTER RESOURCES

Another very basic concern facing those educators wishing to develop computer-based instructional programs is resource support. Issues of resource support continually surface as major obstacles in developing and supporting the growth of school-based computer programs. Typical comments from the field include: "There aren't enough computers to go around"; "There's just not enough special education software available for my kids"; "Who can I ask for special information on classroom software?"; "What kind of computer training do my teachers need?"; "I heard about a great software package last week for my children. I just don't know what I need to run the program on my classroom computer!"; "We have very limited funding. What's the best computer for our children?"

Very often, the lack or shortage of available resources is identified as a major factor curtailing the growth and development of computer-based instructional programs. Without question, limited resources will always be a factor in planning the direction, size, and scope of any school computer program. However, it is not uncommon for innovative programs to fail in school systems even with large amounts of resource support. Conversely, many school systems have developed exceptional computer programs with small budgets and very limited resources. Why are some schools so effective in developing such in-depth and responsive programs with such few resources? Clearly, the amount of available resources to a school does not by itself determine the success or failure of a computer program. The answer to the problem of resource support depends to a large degree on one's ability to recognize resource need in light of the current computer goals and objectives; reviewing existing internal and external resources; and identifying and accessing outside resources. The lack of knowledge about the variety of existing resources and the means of accessing these resources will have short- and long-term consequences on the potential development of computer programs, as well as on the alternatives available to individuals, due to functional changes in planned growth, unanticipated instructional developments, and changing student needs.

An essential part of any computer-development activity is the identification, evaluation, acquisition, and recruitment of the resources needed to attain the desired instructional objectives. In developing a resource pool for any computer program, it is necessary to consider three levels of resource support: (1) human resources; (2) equipment resources; and (3) funding resources. The needs associated with each resource level will vary depending on the computer project's objectives and the dynamics of the educational environment in which the particular computer project will be implemented.

• *Human resources.* First, we can define human resources as sources of technical information support, technical "hands-on" support, administrative and leadership support, and advocacy support, all of which provide a knowledge base for training, planning, implementing, managing, and maintaining computer utilization efforts. Some examples of these resources include professional associations; parent groups; resource and teaching staff; colleges and universities; local user groups; consulting firms; local, state, and federal education agencies; public and private sector agencies, etc. The value of these resources should not be overlooked. For instance, university support can provide assistance in training and research, or provide a source of prospective staff members. Local education agencies (LEAs) can facilitate the dissemination of information on existing hardware and software and their effective uses; or even provide workshop or training support for computer programs.

• *Equipment resources.* This level of resource support provides the tools for developing instructional applications. Most obvious of the equipment resources are computer hardware, software, and peripherals. These are the traditional sources of support. However, there are a variety of complimentary equipment resources that augment the effectiveness of traditional resources.

Today, with the abundance of software and hardware packages on the market, there exists a real need in schools for a formal mechanism to provide a "bridge" between new technologies and computer-using teachers and staff. This bridge is often referred to as an information center, support center, or resource center. The major functions of such a center include user assistance, software and hardware evaluations, instructional consulting, and sometimes training.

Computer hardware, along with its own floppies and hard disks, should be viewed as a security risk. As a result, equipment resources should include electrical protection, security and privacy safeguards, and appropriate environmental facilities that support instructional activities.

Lastly, many school systems overlook the communications networks and support materials that provide a school environment with a flexible and responsive educational program. There are a variety of other tools available for use including voice and data communications, text and messaging, information retrieval, image transmission, and monitoring and control systems.

• *Funding resources.* Finally, the funding resources, such as public and private sector grants, fund-raising activities, and associated flexible funds, provide the means for initiating and obtaining the knowledge and tools necessary for undertaking computer-based instructional programs. There never seem to be enough of these resources available for accomplishing all the agreed-upon program objectives in a school's agenda. In allocating funding support, it should be emphasized that certain resources will require different levels of funding throughout the life of a school computer program. Both short- and long-term fiscal planning should reflect this changing level of resource support.

In developing insights into funding allocations, which include short-and long-term costs projections, consider the interrelationships of the needs of knowledge and tools during the life cycle of computer program. For example, during the first years of implementation the major costs will be for the installation of the hardware base; these costs will be much higher than for other equipment resources such as software. However, as a computer program experiences growth and expands the scope of instructional programming, software costs will increase dramatically—often outstripping the cost of hardware by two or three times. As a result, new instructional demands will require a shift in funding for computer-based instruction. Consequently, because of the dynamics of various resources, funding support should be planned, developed, and adjusted in accordance with functional changes, unexpected growth, changing instructional objectives, and new and/or follow-up training needs.

A CHANGING TECHNOLOGICAL SOCIETY AND ITS IMPACT ON EDUCATION

Every day we are seeing more and more evidence of microcomputers and the associated technology interlacing its presence into many aspects of our daily lives—home, work, education, and leisure activities. Regardless of the trends, however, the requirements of our information-oriented society, which is based on scientific technology, demand responsive instruction and training in schools and universities. Figure 1-2 describes a variety of technological and societal factors impacting the educational environment.

Central to questions regarding the future of technology in education are the assumptions we make about the future characteristics of our society. Technology has moved our society out of the industrial age into the information age. Progress has been made in telecommunications, networking, automation, and media integration. Technology has made societies and culture interdependent through the ability to communicate at a long distance. Traditional methods of thinking about the electronic media have become blurred. Communications have become integrated—phone lines are connected to televisions and computers; radio stations are sharing data with computers; movies are beamed into homes through microwave or viewed by videodisc; and many televisions are becoming on-line electronic newspapers. Most of us would agree that computers have helped improve our society's capacity to collect, store, analyze, process, and disseminate information.

If we think about the goals of our educational system, we can also see how information provides a connecting thread to our instructional system; writing, reading, speaking and listening, mathematics, and science are all components of the educational environment that use, analyze and dissemi-

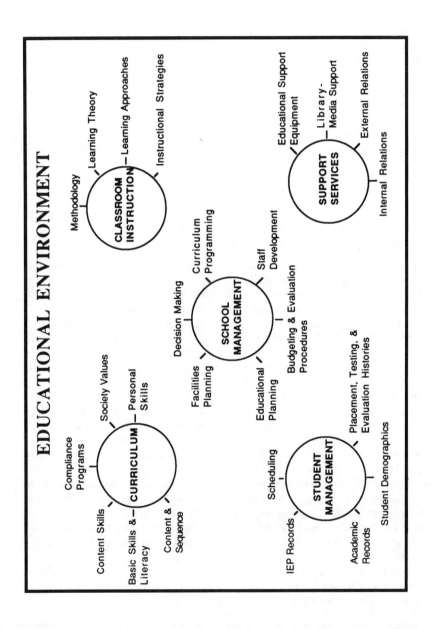

TECHNOLOGY

- Provides users with tools having broad functions.

- Will integrate diverse sources of information.

- Increases sources of information.

- Provides timely information to users.

- Will increase user interactions.

SOCIETY ROLES AND SKILLS

- Users will apply tool functions to various problem situations.

- Users must develop self-directed skills for information access.

- Users must develop organization and information management skills.

- Users must develop strategies for decision making.

- Users must develop cooperation skills.

Figure 1-2. Technological and societal factors impacting the educational environment.

nate information. Information and the ability to use it as a tool are key factors to the future relationship of computers and education. Societal demands for managing information, applying this information under various job situations, and using appropriate problem-solving methods with various sources of information will require changes of the content of existing school curricula. These changes will inevitably raise new questions for our educational system. For instance, what are the equity issues if some educational programs are slow to react to changing societal demands and students are expected to perform in a variety of job roles given inappropriate or limited skills for accessing, managing, and applying information?

Also, the demands of an information society will foster new roles for the educator, student, and parent. Consider for a moment changes in traditional curriculum and teaching methodologies. What impact will they have on the future training of educators, certification issues, or the appropriateness of classroom skills of teachers already in the field? How many school systems are actively pursuing efforts to facilitate, and support educators in, the process of changing current educational methods and behaviors in light of the future trends of our society? If education is to be responsive to the demands of an information society, the future needs of our students must be translated into a responsive instructional program.

Student needs will grow in many directions as technology impacts our society. Eventually, almost all students in this country will be in direct contact with computers. Already our society shows much evidence of a rich computer environment. As the information age brings people, ideas, and values together through communications, the role of the student will change. Students must be responsive to an increase in new information, i.e., address accessibility issues, filter through large volumes of information for specific needs, and manage a diversity of information sources. Similarly, communication and information exchange will provide opportunities for interactions between large and diverse groups of people. This process will involve cooperative problem solving and require a variety of management strategies for planning, organizing, and idea processing. Traditional student skills, including reading, writing, and mathematics, must be augmented because of these future needs.

DEVELOPING COMPUTER COMPETENCY SKILLS

The training needs of professionals in education are vast and often overwhelming. With the advent of microcomputers in the classroom, the training needs of educators have become a central issue for many school systems across the country.

Microcomputers have the ability to become powerful instructional resources. For administrators, however, there is unfortunately a bewildering problem of dealing with this technology in terms of staff training.

Zuk and Stillwell (1984) describe many school districts planning and implementing computer literacy programs with the first priority the acquisition and placement of hardware—preceding any concentrated teacher-training activities. In a national survey conducted by Educational Research Services, Inc. (1982), 24 percent of schools reported that their computers were not being fully utilized due to inadequate staff training. Similarly, this report indicated that over 20 percent of the respondents had "misunderstandings about computer capabilities." The study also asked respondents what was the most important feature for developing successful microcomputer programs, and nearly 44 percent of the respondents selected "staff training" as a key factor in developing computer programs. Other studies support this issue concerning the need for computer training. A study by Robinson and Protheroe (1985) explored the attitudes and perceptions of teachers, using a list of "skill needs" for the classroom. The highest ranked "need" was in the use of computers (46 percent). Stevens (1982) in another attitudes study, which surveyed preservice teachers in 1979 and again in 1981, found higher anxiety levels regarding computer usage in the 1981 sample, suggesting that many new teachers are feeling more pressures to become computer literate.

Griswold (1983) and Egan, Bowers, and Gomez (1981) have identified individual differences in teachers that may affect an individual's motivational level and ability to learn about computers. The Griswold study found that education majors with field-independent cognitive styles had higher test scores on technical knowledge than education majors with field-dependent cognitive styles. The study also found that educators with internal locus of control had higher levels of computer awareness than those with external locus of control (measured with Rotter's scales). The Egan study found that reading skill, spatial memory, and age correlate with performance on the use of some computer activities.

Unfortunately, there is little agreement among proponents of staff training as to what computer competencies should be included as part of in-service training programs (Bruwelheide, 1982; Fellmy and Nicholson, 1985; Hoth, 1985). For many years now, computer-literacy programs have focused their energies on teaching technical computer-programming classes. Many questions have been raised regarding the training emphasis on computer programming rather than on instructional-applications development (Diem, 1984; Sandoval, 1984). Such training issues include the need for instruction that supports those teachers wishing to teach about computers (Moore, 1984) and those who wish to use the technology as an instructional vehicle (Rogers, Moursand, and Ence, 1984).

However, the demand for end-user computer-programming skills will decrease dramatically over the next decade. A combination of new intelligent hardware and software will be the major change agent for decreasing the need for computer programming and increasing the demand for teaching skills that emphasize instructional uses of computer technology. Today, for example, computer users are developing many of their personal-computer applications—instructional shell programs, authoring systems, and authoring languages are only a few examples. Still, many of these instructional tools require some technical skill to master and use effectively. However, future uses of computer technology will be characterized by users who will design and implement most applications using nontechnical approaches, such as interactive voice conversations with the computer or simply a handwritten outline of a lesson with which the computer will write the instructional program. Similarly, these "smart" programs will create instructional environments that use advanced interactive graphics, video, voice, and communications networks for presenting and disseminating instructional information.

As a result, the computer training emphasis for classroom instructional use must shift away from knowing the "bits, bytes, and the assorted technical nuts and bolts" of computer technology toward developing knowledge that supports the idea of using technology tools as the instructional vehicle for the classroom. This knowledge should provide the teacher with skills for integrating technology tools into practical instructional applications that are used in a responsive and nonthreatening instructional manner. Teachers wishing to use computers as an instructional tool need to know what capabilities computers have, how these systems can be implemented in a variety of educational settings, and what technical and material resources are required for supporting computer-based instructional programs.

As a result, those educators wishing to implement programs utilizing computer technology should consider what constitutes computer competencies within the context of their programs. Similarly, the research also suggests that scope and breadth of computer training provide multiple learning paths for individuals, supporting different needs of the teachers through different training approaches.

SUMMARY

Professionals, when considering the implementation of computer technology, must recognize and deal with computer issues. This chapter highlights for the reader some of the major issues concerning the planning and use of technology in education. Some of these issues include resistance to change, setting priorities, defining staff roles, administrative responsibilities, developing resources, and student equity. These issues, without proper attention, often develop into major barriers to successful computer implementations.

As a result, these issues and others the reader may consider require planning frameworks that identify these issues and establish purposeful actions to eliminate or reduce the effects of these issues on the school's program. Chapter 2 will provide the educator with a number of planning frameworks for dealing with these and other computer-planning issues.

The following are sample review questions and some follow-up activities students may wish to pursue. These activities can be used to further develop the concepts and practical applications presented in this chapter.

REVIEW QUESTIONS

1. Why are computer issues and problems important to educators when planning, designing, and developing school microcomputer programs?
2. Who should be involved in identifying technology issues, and why are they important players in the process?
3. Why is the educational environment important in making decisions about computer utilization in instructional settings?
4. What is the difference between structural and situational variables with respect to the educational environment?

SUGGESTED FOLLOW-UP ACTIVITIES

1. Contact a local school using computers and list the major computer-planning issues identified by the school.
2. Contact two different schools using computers and identify and rank their computer-program priorities.
3. Contact a principal of a local school using computers. Identify and list the roles and responsibilities he/she may provide, if any, for teacher using computers. Secondly, contact a teacher in the same school and identify and list his/her perceived roles and responsibilities as a computer-using teacher. Compare both lists. Do both sets of roles match? Are there any role discrepancies? Why are there discrepancies?
4. Contact a local school using computers and identify those resources that limit or constrain the growth and development of the micro-computer program.

CHAPTER 2

*Planning for
Computer Implementation*

During the past 10 years, teachers, administrators, and parents have been witness to the deluge of all types of microcomputers, peripherals, software, and assorted electronic gadgets into schools and classroom settings. Too often in education, there is a rush to embrace ideas that are new without careful analyses (Hofmeister, 1981). Initial positive results are often tempered with long-term realities. Poor information and preparatory planning, few integrative educational objectives, and little direction or substance behind short- and long-term computer implementation strategies have left many school programs vacillating in technical inadequacy and educational inconsistency. For many school programs, the primary focus has been on hardware and software literacy for both students and teachers. With the emerging educational emphasis shifting toward an integration of computer technology and curriculum, the planning process will need to be linked more closely with educational goals.

The previous chapter identified some major issues that teachers and administrators should consider before attempting the implementation of computer-based educational programs. These issues, and others you may identify, are important for a number of reasons. First they provide an awareness of the potential problems that may exist for technology in educational environments. Second, ascertaining an awareness of potential problems actually provides a capacity to measure the unknown variables within school settings. And finally, identifying technology issues provides a mechanism for monitoring the current school environment and gives the administrative staff planning direction and insight into the action required for planning future computer-program activities.

Chapter 2 will build on the issues presented in the previous chapter, again using education and technology issues as a framework for designing and developing effective planning procedures for computer-based instructional programs. Teachers, administrators, and parents should use these procedures as guides for organizing, planning, and implementing school and classroom computer-based instructional programs. The following sections review current planning theory and document a variety of procedures and activities that may facilitate the planning process.

PLANNING FRAMEWORKS FOR COMPUTER IMPLEMENTATION

As we see evidence of the growing power and flexibility of new microcomputer systems, with larger computer memories, faster and more powerful computer architectures, advanced graphics, friendlier user-interfaces, and more intuitive software (natural language processing and artificial intelligence packages), the degree and rate of change is causing many schools to adopt more responsive planning measures. This increased demand for short- and long-range planning coupled with the difficulty in developing and updating such plans, have generated much interest and debate in this area.

There are currently a variety of planning approaches available to educators. The planning approaches presented here embody different methodologies and operational techniques. Some of these approaches assimilate a long-term planning framework; others focus on defining specific needs; some plan by objectives; and others appear not to have any directed planning approach. The reader should keep in mind that educational studies have not demonstrated any one particular method to be superior. To many this would seem only to complicate the planning process. However, depending on the school environment and the issues involved in the computer-implementation process, components of some or all of these planning approaches may have relevance to your current educational setting. Finally, the reader should keep in mind that these planning models represent stylistic tools through which individuals can structure their thinking process within the context of a problem-solving atmosphere.

STAGES OF GROWTH PLANNING MODEL

Richard Nolan and Cyrus Gibson presented a very descriptive planning approach in the *Harvard Business Review* in early 1974. Although written almost three years before the advent of educational microcomputing, "The Stages of Growth Model" presents a planning framework that even today accurately describes the development of computer technology in education. Even through this framework is based on a business model, with little modification the framework represents the general growth trends of computers in many schools and classrooms across our country. You may experience some or all of these stages in your school setting. However, it is interesting to note the importance of effective short- and long-term computer planning at later stages of this planning framework. Without such planning, school systems may waver indefinitely in one or more of these stages, hampering future development. Consider for a moment internal and external school resources; the availability of such support in any school or organization is limited. Entitlement funds, available training time, funding for equipment, or access to timely information are only a few examples of the seemingly endless types of scarce resources. As a result, both short- and long-range planning can play a central role in assessing feasibility and need; acquiring adequate resources; developing a timetable for their use; and most importantly, directing the educational use of computer-based instruction.

Here is a modified outline from "The Stages of Growth Model" (Nolan and Gibson, 1974):

Stage 1: *Early success.* This stage represents initial implementation activities of microcomputer technology. School and teacher experiences during this stage can be characterized by some experimentation, awkward and/or poorly adapted use, and generally some initial classroom success.

Stage 2: *Proliferation.* During this stage teachers are motivated by early successes, and general interest grows as new hardware, software and peripherals are introduced into the classroom. During this stage computers are used in a variety of instructional settings. This stage provides a learning environment for both students and teachers.

Stage 3: *Administrative direction.* This stage becomes necessary as costs due to experimentation rise. Cost-benefit analysis and justification policies must be installed in order to control the variety of implementation approaches and to reduce resource waste and/or duplication.

Stage 4: *Integration of computer use.* During this final stage, the use of computers is directed by administrative planning and integrated into school curricula. Careful planning is required if instruction is to be systematic and based on sound pedagogy.

To some individuals the stages of this planning approach may seem to describe a natural growth pattern of computers in the implementation environment. To others, this may seem in some sense an unwieldy approach to computer implementations. However natural or unwieldy the process may appear, the model stresses the importance of long-term administrative direction in order to support the development of computer-based programs.

McFarlan and McKenney (1983) support this planning approach with a very similar model. This planning example, although very similar, illustrates that such an approach can foster innovative programs. Such an approach also supports the opportunity to experiment with computer technology and discover effective uses through hands-on learning experiences. This experimenting is said to provide the user with unique insights into the potentials of the technology. The four stages of the McFarlan and McKenney model include:

1. *Identification and initial investment.* During this stage educational decisions are made to experiment with computer technology. Experimentations are key activities during this stage.

2. *Experimentation and learning.* This stage is also characterized by much classroom experimentation. A trial-and-error atmosphere is a key factor to this model, because too much administrative control during early experimentation can stifle computer-applications development.

3. *Administrative control.* This stage requires some administrative direction as computer applications develop and require additional resource support.

4. *Widespread technology transfer.* This stage provides strong administrative support and planning as curriculum and computer instruction develop across grade levels.

SYSTEMS PLANNING MODEL

Systems planning models are based on the philosophy that an organization and its complex component parts operate as a functional unit or a coherent whole within the context of an external environment. Similarly, such an organization is goal- or purpose-driven. For example, the school unit would include many constituents such as curriculum, administration, classroom instruction, and classroom management. These parts together facilitate the goal of educating students. The external environment of the school unit may include the business community or current trends in computer technology. In addition, systems planning models stress the regular interaction of a unit's components. In a school setting we would see examples of this interaction on a daily basis as with administrator-staff relationships; or with teachers developing content for individualized instruction; or with individualized education programs (IEPs) and special needs students. Finally, the systems planning framework attempts to identify external variables found in the external environment and internal variables found within the organizational system, define the interaction of these variables, and measure the effects of such interactions on both the organization and the external environment. School-community relations would be an example of this type of interaction.

Planning and Design Approach

Gerald Nadler (1981) describes a systems planning model that addresses the interaction of internal organizational variables and external environmental variables as a framework for planning change. The planning and design approach (PDA) model, as a planning tool, embodies a number of concepts that may be helpful to educators planning microcomputer-based instructional programs. These concepts, PDA's conceptual framework, are itemized in the following list along with the authors' brief description of their relevance to computer-based instructional planning:

1. *Time-line perspective.* This concept implies a planning strategy that is future-oriented or long-term—one that envisions an ideal or perfect future system. As educators plan computer intervention, the realization that computer technology is rapidly changing leaves many questioning hardware and software instructional utility in the classroom. Hence, PDA's long-range planning perspective encourages educators to utilize current proven technology and at the same time idealize future patterns of computer use. Such future perspectives can help educators measure the breadth of future computer potentials.

2. *Purpose-oriented strategies.* This concept can be defined as a planning perspective that develops activities based on a long-term strategy. Hence,

using the example of planning a computer program, PDA's purpose-oriented strategies direct the planning process toward specific instructional orientations and educational goals. The result is that a plan precisely describes activities, roles and objectives that support long-term educational goals. For example, consider a long-term educational goal of integrating computers into a district's curriculum. Should planning activities be short-term, concentrating on implementing computers in a few classrooms for the singular purpose of microcomputer programming or literacy, or should planning activities be directed toward a schoolwide instructional program that emphasizes computer–curriculum integration? The PDA model continually provides the opportunity to question such planning activities, monitoring progress toward a long-term purpose or educational goal.

3. *Prescriptive systems approach.* Using the system concept of individual organizational parts functioning collectively toward one or more important goals, we can define the prescriptive systems approach. Applying this analogy of individual parts functioning together for a common purpose, one can see that each part has distinct functions and responsibilities. As such, these parts may require different prescriptive actions based on problems caused by the external educational environment. As conditions or needs change, the prescriptive systems approach encourages new plans that reflect the original purpose of the program. This process can be helpful to educators as comprehensive computer plans change due to changes in services, needs of special populations, or changes in curricular content.

Nadler's PDA model contains five phases or steps that are part of the planning process. These planning steps include the following:

1. Define a planning goal.

   • Encourage multiple goal statements.

   • Iterate more specific goal statements.

   • Generate a broad comprehensive goal statement.

2. Identify ideas for a solution.

   • Encourage multiple solution ideas.

   • Identify feasible solution ideas.

3. Identify an ideal plan.

   • Introduce feasible solution ideas.

   • Generate multiple plans based on solution ideas.

   • Focus in on an ideal comprehensive plan.

4. Detail the ideal plan.

   • Reintroduce the broad goal statement.

   • Detail the ideal comprehensive plan.

   • Gain commitment for the ideal plan.

5. Implement, evaluate, and refine.

   • Implement the ideal plan.

   • Monitor the process and progress of the ideal plan.

   • Compare progress with the goal statement.

   • Refine the ideal plan.

THE ORGANIZATIONAL ELEMENTS MODEL

Roger Kaufman (1977, 1979, 1980, 1982, 1983, and 1984) describes a planning approach that does embody many formal systems model concepts, including the consideration of both internal and external needs. However, the organizational elements model is interpreted differently in terms of its outcomes and process. Kaufman's model places great emphasis on outcomes or products of an organization and their impact(s) on society. For education, the concept could be applied to the skills students learn in the school environment and to what degree these students and skills impact the present and future workplace. As part of the planning process, major emphasis is placed on developing an "external-needs" assessment. Kaufman describes this needs assessment as identifying and describing the implementation environment in terms of "what is and what should be,"—a process Kaufman refers to as identifying performance "gaps." Educators developing computer intervention programs can apply this planning concept in a number of different ways. Applications of the gap concept are described in the paragraphs that follow.

In a very practical sense, the concept of a gap can be applied to student academic performance and/or IEP development for special-needs students. Examples of gap identification may include focusing in on weaknesses in academic performance and developing short-term instructional objectives for students, including, but not limited to, computer-aided instruction (CAI) or computer-managed instruction (CMI).

Again using staff training as an example, gap identification may even include supporting staff development activities related to trends in computer technology. Needs assessment may identify shortcomings in teacher-training programs for hardware and software setup, applied uses of technology, or hardware and software evaluation techniques.

As a final example, in classroom and school management one can use the gap concept for the identification of weaknesses in student record keeping, scheduling, or tracking meetings with parents, counselors, or evaluators. Computers may be helpful in closing classroom and administrative support gaps.

Kaufman's organizational elements model (1984) applies seven basic formal planning procedures. These procedures are used to identify and define needs and also implement planning solutions to those needs. These procedures include the following:

1. Identify problems based on external needs.
2. Generate solution requirements and identification of solution alternatives.
3. Select solution strategies.
4. Implement strategies.
5. Evaluate strategies.
6. Isolate needs that require revision.

CONTINGENCY PLANNING THEORY

Contingency planning approaches are based on monitoring and analyzing both internal and external variables in the school environment. This planning approach relies on data and information collection, which provides a basis for the primary focus of contingency planning models—the anticipation of future events. The contingency planning process considers unforeseen events that may or may not occur over both short and long periods of time. Deliberate forethought into possible future problems during the planning process is the prominent feature of this approach. Steiner (1979) describes a contingency planning framework that identifies and quantifies the environmental variables found within a program setting. The environmental variables are quantified based on both statistical measurements, such as probability estimates, and subjective assumptions made by planners about future events. Once assessments are made on the probability of future events, the contingency planning process can accommodate alternative approaches that address any potential problems.

As a computer planning approach, contingency strategies can reduce uncertainty in the planning process. Administrators can use contingency planning strategies to plan concurrently for present and future technology trends in a variety of school microcomputer settings.

For example, planning for both present and future changes in computer technology can offer many advantages to the school environment. Many traditional software packages that provide data-base capabilities (a means of organizing information) require an extensive understanding of computer syntax, computer-data relationships, and often require learning a computer programming language. As a result, developing computer applications can be an arduous task for many nontechnical users. However, by monitoring current and future trends and developments in software, schools can take advantage of new opportunities for developing responsive information-oriented educational software. New trends in software that embody the "hypermedia" concept, such as *Guide, Zoomracks,* and *HyperCard,* can be defined as interactive information systems by which nonprogrammers can create and organize text, data, pictures, music, sound, voice, video, and animation through easy-to-use nontechnical procedures.

Similarly, as the present base of school computers and software begins to age and become less cost-effective, schools must provide short- and long-term planning that provides for consistent resource support for replacing and updating "old" technology. Hence, by planning for unforeseen events, contingency planning can offer many advantages to educators planning instructional programs in light of changing technical environments.

The following framework is adapted from Stiener (1979) as a guide to the contingency planning process.

1. Identify internal and external variables.

   - Collect information on key program variables.

   - Identify problem areas.

   - Identify the needs of the program.

   - Develop a needs assessment of current and future program demands.

2. Develop program goals and objectives.

   - Gain commitment for program.

   - Identify current and future planning priorities based on need.

   - Develop goal statements for current and future directives.

   - Support current and future directives with specific objectives.

3. Implement program plan.

   - Provide resource support.

   - Schedule implementations.

   - Training.

4. Support program activities.

- Monitor process and progress based on internal and external variables.

- Re-examine present and future needs.

- Determine need for contingency plan.

- If contingency planning is needed, repeat process.

The contingency planning approach is repetitive in terms of process. Hence, a planner may cycle through the above steps many times during the development, design, implementation, and maintenance of instructional microcomputer programs.

PROJECT PLANNING

The project planning model is a variation of traditional systems development techniques. Introducing microcomputers utilizing this planning approach involves the use of "cautious" school computer projects. Each computer project is an incremental project in a larger group of projects under the direction of a three- to five-year school plan. Similarly, each project is designed to make only small incremental changes within the school setting, thereby reducing staff anxiety associated with major organizational changes. Also, this model is applicable in both large and small school settings where knowledge, funding, and experience with introducing new computer technology is often limited.

By developing cautious short-term projects, the risk associated with these development efforts is greatly reduced. Project planning seeks to accomplish the main goals of an overall computer school plan, but its framework consists of a series of short, high-chance-of-success projects. Therefore, most short-term projects under the direction of a long-range school plan should last no longer than four to nine months. For example, training a small staff group at one time to use microcomputers does not require a lot of extensive administrative planning. Also, due to the short length of projects, only proven technology should be used. This greatly increases the likelihood of microcomputer program success. As a final example, by identifying high-priority problem areas and concentrating short-term efforts on these needs, resources can be applied more effectively, given their limited supply.

The project planning approach involves the following four basic steps as part of the planning model:

1. Develop long-range planning goals.

   - Identify problems.

   - Develop short- and long-term planning needs (school plan).

2. Identify and develop planning efforts.
   - Determine high-payoff areas for implementation.
   - Develop efforts as a basis for long-range planning.
   - Prioritize efforts based on needs.

3. Develop project approaches.
   - Define a series of short projects (four to nine months long).
   - Match short-term projects with the school plan.
   - Provide project justification.
   - Schedule projects.

4. Implement projects.
   - Match projects with proven technology.
   - Provide implementation support.
   - Evaluate projects.
   - Add projects when the school plan requires such enhancements.

The preceding planning frameworks offer educators a variety of approaches for planning computer programs. Similarly, these planning models and others the reader may identify can be used independently or used in conjunction with other frameworks as tools for implementing computer programs. The planning approaches a school may choose to use will depend on a number of different factors, such as the complexity of the computer project, administrative decision-making style, styles of leadership, or the formal and informal character of the school environment.

These planning guides can help address many of the issues identified in Chapter 1, such as shifts in curriculum content, changing instructional needs of special-needs students, short- and long-term teacher-training needs, and changes in student demographics. Many of these issues can be addressed by the planning frameworks through the use of need assessments, goal development, defining objectives, developing short- and long-range plans, and various evaluation procedures.

The following sections provide an opportunity to address in detail some basic planning tools or guides that can be generalized for a variety of computer planning approaches. These guides are useful for developing planning frameworks for computer-based instruction.

COMPUTER IMPLEMENTATION: PLANNING TOOLS

In the previous section, a number of computer planning frameworks are outlined for developing instructional microcomputer programs. These frameworks or models provide the reader with a variety of choices for implementing computer technology in school settings. Similarly, these models provide some general planning steps for directing the movement toward computer use in schools.

This section provides the reader with specific planning tools for carrying out the processes of the planning models described in the previous section. Planning tools can be defined as those procedures that enable the planner to analyze a problem situation within the context of the educational environment. Accordingly, planning tools provide the following functions: (1) allow collection of data from the educational environment; (2) analyze the data; (3) develop the data into information; and (4) use the information to promote the growth of a knowledge base about a problem within the context of the educational environment.

Consequently, planning tools provide professionals who are responsible for developing computer programs with a number of data-collection techniques and statistical methods for solving instructional computer planning problems.

THE KNOWLEDGE BASE

Central to any planning approach is the need for knowledge. This knowledge is generally used in identifying and analyzing problems within a school's computer implementation environment. This is especially true when implementing computer technology in educational environments where the capacity for change can greatly affect existing educational components in the school or classroom setting. In order to develop effective planning, the knowledge base must be broad enough to cover a variety of issues that have the potential for affecting the school setting. Figure 2-1 illustrates the development of a knowledge base. This knowledge-base model expresses the view that planning microcomputer projects evolves out of a process in which planners gather and filter data, identify and develop information, and generalize selected information into specific knowledge about problems in the educational environment in order to solve specific computer planning problems.

- *Data collection.* As the model demonstrates, developing knowledge for the planning process involves collecting data from the educational environment—specifically, data about the situational and structural variables (see Chapter 1, Figure 1-1) that impact the computer implementation setting. The data-collection phase of the model represents the gathering of "raw data." The concept of raw data can be defined as measurements of variables from the educational environment. For example, a pool of collected data might include the numbers of computers in a school, the number of teachers in a school, or the number of software packages in a school's software library. These data quantities by themselves don't provide information to the

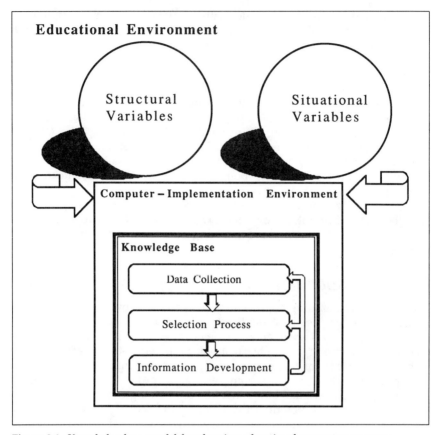

Figure 2-1. Knowledge-base model for planning educational computer programs.

planner. These measurements only take on meaning or provide information when put in the context of a specific problem statement. Hence, in the data-collection phase these data are termed "raw data."

The data-collection process involves gathering two types of raw data. These two types of raw data include first-hand data (primary data) and second-hand data (secondary data). First-hand data are gathered from original sources, for instance, through surveys, interviews, or direct observation. Second-hand data are obtained through sources other than original sources; these are data collected and distributed by other sources. Census information is an example of a secondary-data source.

• *Information development.* The information-development process captures both first-hand and second-hand data. After data capture, the information development provides a number of statistical methods for analyzing raw data.

The first step in the information development process involves the aggregation of collected raw data. The process assembles different data fragments into a logical collection or sum of data for analyzing certain questions. Second, information development provides the opportunity to manipulate raw data. This process provides the planner with the freedom to control or manage data by any matched orders or conventions deemed necessary for analyzing problems. This process is required for any problem-solving activity that attempts to develop some level of knowledge about a situation.

- *Selection process.* Finally, the selection process filters out extraneous information and provides decision makers with grouped information developed from the information-development phase. Also, the selection process may require additional data collection in order to obtain more information for planning purposes. The selection process allows planners the ability to formulate knowledge bases from collections of specific information sets obtained from previous steps of the knowledge base model. This level of the process focuses all the information on the problem. As a result, the planner can use this knowledge to develop perspectives or approaches that may be helpful in developing solutions to the problem.

COLLECTING DATA FOR COMPUTER PLANNING

In gathering both primary and secondary data for planning purposes, avoid making systematic errors often termed "bias" data or data that don't accurately represent the situation in question. Both primary and secondary data can become bias, however. Secondary data are often considered more likely to contain bias due to interpretation and collection techniques. The way to reduce bias in primary data is to follow strict data-collection techniques. Bias in secondary data can be reduced by using standard sources with proven track records.

There are practical limits to the amount of data collection required in the planning process for setting up computer programs. Any school environment will experience diminishing returns as data-collection costs increase beyond the practical justifications for certain projects.

Techniques for Data Collection

The following procedures are general-purpose information-gathering tools that may help in the planning process. These techniques can identify computer issues or problems teachers may have in the classroom setting.

Carnegie Quarterly (1985) reports that many teachers still feel that microcomputer instruction is a passing fad, following many defunct teaching approaches of the past. Similarly, Scheffler (1986) identifies this prevalent skeptical attitude among educators toward computers in education. Often resistance to change or even unjustified perceptions of educational computing as a novelty or fad can only hinder a school's long-range planning process. Hence, self-surveys and/or interviews can be used to identify these feelings and attitudes toward technological change.

Survey data-collection techniques are often in the form of questionnaires sent to respondents through the mail or survey forms handed out to staff. Expect return rates to run at about 40 to 60 percent using this method. Make the number of questions small and the questions themselves nontechnical in nature. Interviews can be face-to-face or by telephone. Although a very accurate data-collection technique, the process is very expensive for large school environments. Similarly, such techniques require a great deal of staffing and scheduling work.

Lastly, observation or inspection can be used to collect data for those instances when human contact is not required or is not appropriate. For example, suppose a school wishes to determine why students are having problems with a particular software package. We could interview the teachers. But given a large class of students and the demands of teaching, a teacher may be hard pressed to accurately chart both content problems or student/computer processes problems. Observation may identify the need for additional mechanical process directions for using the computer program. Similarly, after inspection, the software instructions and feedback may need to be improved or augmented, as in multisensory instruction (adding computer speech or graphics demonstrations) for concept development.

DEFINING COMPUTER PLANNING QUESTIONS

Questions are an integral part of the data collection process. They frame a range of information that may be required as part of the computer planning process. There are three basic types of measurement structures used in surveys or interviews. These measurement structures consist of nominal, ordinal, and interval scales. The following paragraphs give some examples of each type, then structure each of the measurement scales in the context of a computer planning survery.

• *Nominal scales.* These measurement scales define data items as logical categories, or sets, with no inherent order among items within a set. Hence, allowable responses to a question must be mutually exclusive and accurately represent all levels of differentiation regarding the problem. Some examples of nominal scales include:

Student sex:	Female, male
Computer manufacturer:	Apple, Atari, Commodore, IBM, Tandy
Computer Type:	Apple II +, Apple IIgs, PS/2, C-64, Amgia

- *Ordinal scales.* These measurement scales rank data items in order. Typical survey questions rank data items as 1,2,3,4—1 being most important and 4 being least important. For example, suppose a question asks a group of teachers to rank in order of importance the use of funding for computer equipment next year. If it can be ranked, such measurement scales may be useful to the computer planning process.

Sample Question. The school is planning to use $1,500 for new computer equipment next year. We would like some teacher input on the priority of computer purchases for next year. Please rank in order of importance the use of the $1,500 for equipment purchases. (1 = most important; and 4 = least important.)

a. New dot matrix printers for the computer lab ⎯⎯⎯⎯
b. A new 1200 baud modem for each class ⎯⎯⎯⎯
c. New 3½-inch disk drives for each class computer ⎯⎯⎯⎯
d. New color monitors for each class computer ⎯⎯⎯⎯

- *Interval scales.* This set of measurement scales is the most common set of tools used for developing questions. These scales measure data items in terms of some quantity often expressed in numbers. Some examples of interval scales are the number of computers in Mr. Hill's class; years of special-education experience; student test scores; or hours of computer use.

Because surveys must be modeled after one of these scales (except in the case of open-ended questions), it is important to recognize that each scale has practical limits for the kinds of analysis that can be performed on a question. Hence, all questions must be unambiguous in their scale type.

Finally, let us illustrate the use of these scales in a problem framework. After repeated staff complaints about having little or no instruction time in the school's computer lab, a principal wishes to determine if there is a problem with teacher usage patterns in the school's computer lab. As a result, a questionnaire is developed to measure teacher usage patterns in the computer lab. The following four questions are part of the questionnaire to be used in a survey:

Sample Questions.

1. How often is computer lab equipment broken during your instruction time in the computer lab?

_____ Frequently; _____ Occasionally; _____ Never
(Ordinal)

2. Do you require repeated schedule changes in order to use the computer lab?
   _____ Yes _____ No   *(Nominal)*

3. How many times in the past six weeks have you had scheduling conflicts with other classes regarding instructional use of the computer lab?
   _____ Number of times   *(Interval)*

4. How often is the computer lab available to your class for instructional use?
   _____ Frequently; _____ Occasionally; _____ Never
   (Ordinal)

SELECTING SAMPLES FOR COMPUTER PLANNING

In most school settings it is unnecessary, too expensive, or too time-intensive to sample everyone regarding computer planning problems. However, the planner should clearly define the target population in question. Target populations can include teachers in a computer literacy program; a special-education class with computers in the classroom; schools or districts with computer programs; or colleges and universities with research programs. Usually, an outline is first developed in order to define the population and its characteristics. Secondly, a properly chosen fraction of the target population is used to represent information about the whole population. Due to cost, time, and staff constraints, fractional sampling is often the only feasible way to sample a large comprehensive population. What follows are four general sampling alternatives available to educators planning computer-based instructional programs.

1. Simple random sample. All sampling techniques have their fundamental origins in simple random sampling. A simple random sample provides the opportunity for every member of the target population to have an equal opportunity for every member of the target population to have an equal chance of being chosen for the sample.

Suppose the administration wants to sample the types of reading software being used by 100 various teachers in, say, elementary classrooms. First we would outline or list these teachers. We would pick at random, say, 10 teachers. In order to make random choices, the reader may wish to use a random number table available in any statistics book.

The first teacher chosen would have a 1 percent chance of being picked ($\frac{1}{100}$ = 0.01 × 100 = 1%). Assuming one doesn't replace a new teacher for the first teacher chosen (simple random sampling without replacement), a second teacher chosen at random would have a 1.01 percent chance of being picked ($\frac{1}{99}$ = 0.0101 × 100 = 1.01%). However, one should not be concerned about very small probability changes in the sample, because our population of teachers is very large.

2. *Systematic sampling.* A systematic sample will randomly select a data item at a specific interval. For instance, in the previous example we may wish to sample only five teachers. As a result, we would divide 100 by 5, obtaining 20, which we would use as our interval. (We must use whole numbers; we can't easily sample 20.7 teachers.) Thus we would sample every twentieth teacher in the population. Determining a starting place is very important. To begin, use a random number table to determine which of the first 20 teachers will be the starting place. Let us say that teacher number 13 is randomly selected; hence, we would begin at teacher 13 and choose every twentieth teacher until we have our sample size of five. Our sample would include teachers 13, 33, 53, 73, and 93.

3. *Stratified sampling.* This sampling technique allows planners to obtain representative samples from populations in question. For example, educators may be interested in obtaining information regarding equity issues as part of a student computer literacy program. In some districts 80 percent of the students are white, 15 percent black, 11 percent Asian, and only 3 percent Hispanic. A small simple sample could easily contain no Hispanics and an underrepresentation of black students. Stratified samples define separate groups as lists that are homogeneous, and take simple random samples from each student group. Similarly, the size of the stratified sample may be proportional or disproportional to group size, depending on the type of information required for planning.

4. *Cluster sampling.* The cluster sample is similar to the stratified sample technique, but each group sampled is heterogeneous. This approach allows the planner to keep the sample size small, reducing funding, expenditure time, and staffing costs while ensuring that the population being sampled is representative. As an example, suppose the survey on computer equity used a cluster approach. The plan would involve the selection of clusters of students within schools of the district so that the population in each cluster represents a balanced cross section of the district population. Sample size is dependent on the importance and variety of the information and the size of the population in question.

USING DATA TO DEVELOP A KNOWLEDGE BASE FOR COMPUTER PLANNING

This section will introduce some basic planning analysis approaches that may be helpful in developing knowledge about the problem environment. The techniques to be discussed are helpful for doing many types of data analysis. However, for those planners who wish to do more complex data analyses, other techniques or methods may be required for data analysis.

Surveys, interviews, and observations provide the planner with the ability to collect raw data. Collecting data is the first step in developing a knowledge base for computer planning.

The data-collection techniques (surveys, interviews, observations, etc.) are usually for collecting raw data consisting of both biased and/or unbiased data. This biased or unbiased data are often in a form that requires aggregation and manipulation and may or may not represent the information that the planner requires.

The following techniques provide the planner with a number of planning tools that help aggregate and manipulate raw data into information. These techniques use very simple statistical and graphic methods for organizing and analyzing large amounts of data. These techniques allow the planner to look at specific variables that may have some relevance to the problem.

Frequency Distribution

A frequency distribution allows the planner to review the characteristics of variables found in a collection of raw data. Frequency distributions analyze data variables that are typically gathered through data-collection techniques such as surveys, interviews, or observations. A frequency distribution displays the variety of responses to question variables and shows the frequency of those responses.

As an example, the problem concerning teacher usage with respect to a school's computer lab will be used to illustrate the concept of frequency distributions. The following frequency graphs display teacher responses to the questionnaire developed by the principal wishing to gain insight into problems associated with the school's computer lab. Figures 2-2, 2-3, and 2-4 show examples of frequency distributions from three questions on the questionnaire. The vertical scales on the left side of the graphs indicate frequencies of teacher response. The horizontal scales indicate the distribution of possible responses to the measurement scale.

Figure 2-2 graphs the frequency of the data variable (broken equipment) with respect to the ordinal measurement scale (frequently, occasionally, and never). The question asks "How often is computer lab equipment broken during your instruction time in the computer lab?" The frequency distribution shows the variety of variance to the data variable (broken equipment).

Figure 2-3 also shows a frequency distribution of the data variable (the need for new scheduling) with respect to the nominal measurement scale (yes and no). The question asks "Do you require repeated schedule changes in order to use the computer lab?" Yes or no are the possible responses. This frequency distribution shows the frequency of yes and no responses to the variable (schedule changes).

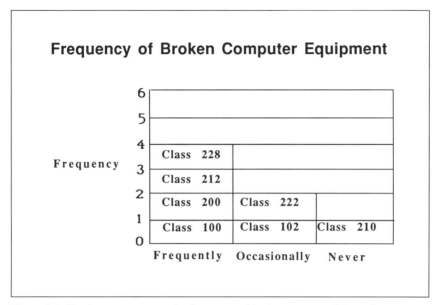

Figure 2-2. Teacher responses on the frequency of broken computer lab equipment.

Figure 2-3. Teacher responses on the frequency of computer lab scheduling conflicts.

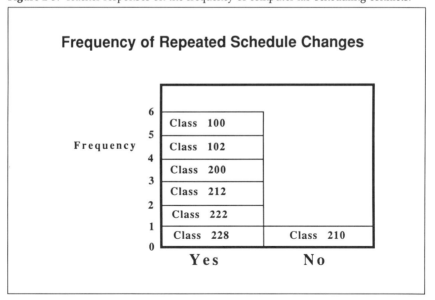

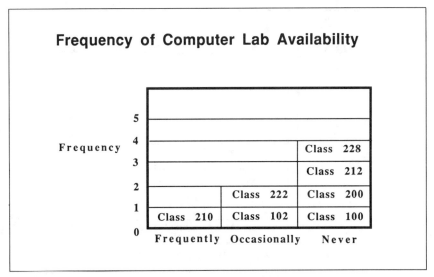

Figure 2-4. Teacher responses on the frequency of computer lab availability.

Finally, Figure 2-4 displays the frequency distribution of the data variable (computer lab availability) to the ordinal measurement scale (frequently, occasionally, and never). The graph illustrates the frequency distribution of classes responding to the variable (computer lab availability).

Central Tendency Statistics

With the additional planning tool technique of central tendency statistics, the planner can further study the data in the frequency distribution. For example, a distribution of responses can be averaged through the use of central tendency statistics. These statistical techniques include the *mean, median,* and *mode.*

The mean of a question variable refers to a numerical average. It is obtained by summing all of the response scores and dividing by the number of responses. For example, Figure 2-5 is a frequency distribution of teacher responses (identified by classroom number) to the question "How many times in the past six weeks have you had scheduling conflicts with other classes regarding instructional use of the computer lab?" As a result, the mean for the variable (number of scheduling conflicts) in Figure 2-5 is 6 + 4 + 9 + 1 + 5 + 4 + 10, or 39, divided by seven classes, which is an average of about five schedule conflicts per six weeks.

The median of a distribution is the point in the scale where the variable in question is divided into two groups of equal units. Let us use the following

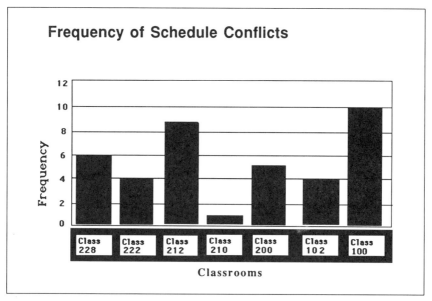

Figure 2-5. Teacher responses on the frequency of computer lab schedule conflicts.

example to illustrate the median concept. In the case of a district wishing to determining the median cost of new computer equipment during the school year for the district's five schools, and given the individual costs for each school as $3,500, $4,300, $4,500, $5,000, and $5,200, a median cost would be $4,500 dollars for computer equipment purchases. The reason is $4,500 divides the group of five schools into two equal parts of two below $4,500 and two above $4,500.

The mode is the most frequently occurring value for a variable in a distribution. In Figure 2-5 the schedule conflict variable has a mode of 4. However, in the previous example of equipment cost there is no mode, which is not uncommon in survey data.

Cross Tabulation of Frequency Distribution

An important task in gaining knowledge about problems is being able to study the interrelationships between question variables. Cross tabulations of frequency distributions, specifically two-way frequency distributions, provide a technique for exploring variable relationships.

We will now reexamine the question concerning problems in the computer lab. The principal's initial purpose was to develop some insight into questions regarding teacher usage patterns in the computer lab, as well as the

**Table 2-1. RAW DATA ON BROKEN
EQUIPMENT AND SCHEDULE CHANGES**

	Classroom						
	228	*222*	*212*	*210*	*200*	*102*	*100*
Broken equipment	F	O	F	N	F	O	F
Schedule changes	Yes	Yes	Yes	No	Yes	Yes	Yes

Key: F = frequently; O = occasionally; N = never.

**Table 2-2. CROSS-TABULATION OF
BROKEN EQUIPMENT AND SCHEDULE CHANGES**

Schedule changes		Frequently	Occasionally	Never
	Yes	4	2	
	No			1

Broken computer equipment

relationship of computer lab availability to equipment breakdowns. Table 2-1 lists the combinations of data jointly on the variables of broken equipment and schedule changes. The data in Table 2-1 were joined from the individual data found in Figures 2-2 and 2-3.

Looking at Table 2-1 with respect to schedule changes, one can see that there are six "yes" responses and one "no" response. The broken equipment data are nearly all different. The relationships between this data can be best displayed using a cross tabulation of both the broken equipment and schedule change variables.

Table 2-2 represents the relationship between the two variables, broken equipment and schedule changes. The data in the table suggest a clear pattern between broken computer equipment and the need for teachers to make regular changes in the computer lab schedule to accommodate problems with broken computer equipment.

Similarly, Table 2-3 compares raw data concerning the variables of broken equipment and computer lab availability. The data in Table 2-3 were collected by aggregating the data found in Figures 2-2 and 2-4. Again, looking at Table 2-3 one can see the relationship between these two data sets is not very pronounced, so a second cross tabulation is used to display any relationship between the two data variables.

**Table 2-3. RAW DATA ON BROKEN
EQUIPMENT AND COMPUTER LAB AVAILABILITY**

	Classroom						
	228	*222*	*212*	*210*	*200*	*102*	*100*
Broken equipment	F	O	F	N	F	O	F
Lab availability	N	O	N	F	N	O	N

Key: F = frequently; O = occasionally; N = never.

**Table 2-4. CROSS TABULATION OF
BROKEN EQUIPMENT AND LAB AVAILABILITY**

		Frequently	Occasionally	Never
	Frequently			4
Broken equipment	Occasionally		2	
	Never	1		
		Frequently	Occasionally	Never

Computer lab availability

The cross tabulation shown in Table 2-4 allows the user to manipulate the two data sets into a clearer form for presentation and evaluation. Again, by using cross tabulations the table shows a fairly strong correlation between the frequency of broken equipment and computer lab availability.

These procedures allow the planner to see a trend of correlation between data variables. As is seen in Table 2-4, the frequency of numbers are scattered from the lower left to the upper right of the graph. What can one conclude from the analysis? Is there a problem? If so, what is the problem? Can the survey data and the analysis provide some answers to the contributing causes of problems with the computer lab? There are no formulas for interpreting the analyses. The preceding planning tool, cross-tabulation of frequency distributions, can help the user narrow potential interrelations of different data variables. Secondly, cross tabulations give the user the ability to observe interrelations found in the data. Finally, this technique can provide planners with general indicators for evaluating decisions regarding planning policy implications. Even within the confines of the limited set of questions and the small sample, one can say that equipment problems may have an effect on computer lab availability, and that to some extent schedule changes result from broken equipment in the computer lab. Hence, the principal may wish to further explore the equipment problems in the computer lab as part of the school's computer planning process.

Historical Record Monitoring

Lastly, a very useful information gathering technique that can be used in a variety of settings is simple historical record monitoring, which captures data on a variety of computer planning variables. Some of these variables might include such things as student computer instruction, computer hardware use, frequency of instructional software package use, frequency of hardware problems, or usage of computer supplies. The examples are endless. What is important is that the planner have the capability to access this raw data and use it in an appropriate information framework for solving computer planning problems.

A historical record monitoring system consists of four basic steps or procedures: (1) establishing a performance norm; (2) determining a deviation from the norm; (3) determining procedures for collecting and comparing performance data; and (4) establishing a means of extrapolation.

The first step in developing historical records is to establish what function or data set over time are to be monitored (e.g., student/computer interactions, scheduling, processes, etc.). Similarly, the function should have some performance standard or norm that can be measured against (e.g., usage, expenditures, number of students or computers, etc.). In fact, historical recording may be used to develop a distribution of measures for a function, and in turn this distribution may determine a common long-run performance standard or expected value. The second step of the process involves the establishment of a deviation from the norm—either above or below the norm. Third, the planner should determine a schedule and procedures for collecting data and comparing it with the performance standard. The last step involves extrapolating the performance of the data. This method assumes that historical data contain a stable pattern; as such, a trend or seasonal cycle will continue in the future. Extrapolation methods are also referred to as time-series methods.

As an example, consider a historical record that attempts to monitor computer equipment breakdowns in a large school district. The administration wishes to determine a norm or performance standard for computer equipment breakdowns. The administration would find it very useful to plan future computer maintenance budgets in a more predictable fashion. As a result, data will be collected on the number of computer breakdowns per week for the entire school district (36 weeks per school year). As an example of the weekly charting, Figure 2-6 shows a historical record of

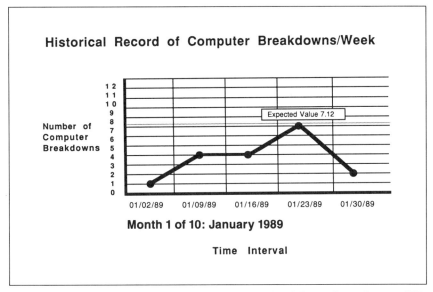

Figure 2-6. Historical record of school district computer breakdowns during January 1989.

computer equipment breakdowns over a five-week period in January of the 1989 school year. This historical data can provide administrators with a very practical way to determine the overall district computer-maintenance picture for the school year based on historical trends.

Table 2-5 provides a distribution of (1) the number of computer breakdowns; (2) the frequency of weekly occurrences for that breakdown; (3) the probability of the breakdown occurrence (obtained by dividing the second column by the total number of weeks the record was kept [36]); and (4) the computed expected value for weekly computer breakdowns.

One can define expected value as the weighted average of the outcomes from a set of data. In this case, the set of data is the number of weekly computer breakdowns for the 1988–1989 school year. Similarly, the random variable is simply a variable (weekly computer breakdowns) that can take on different values over a period of time.

To calculate the expected value of the random variable (weekly computer breakdowns), we multiply each value that the random variable takes on by the probability of occurrence of that value and then sum these products (see Table 2-5). The total in the fourth column of Table 2-5 tells us that the expected value of the random variable weekly computer breakdowns is 7.12. This means that the administrator can predict, over the long run, an expected weighted average of 7.12 weekly computer breakdowns for the school district. Thus, with this information the administration can plan an

Table 2-5. PROBABILITY DISTRIBUTION OF WEEKLY COMPUTER BREAKDOWNS

Number of computer breakdowns	Number of weekly occurrences	Probability of occurrence (Column 2 divided by 36)	Expected value for computer breakdowns (Column 1 × Column 3)
1	1	.028	.028
2	1	.028	.056
3	1	.028	.084
4	2	.056	.224
5	4	.111	.555
6	4	.111	.666
7	5	.138	.966
8	8	.222	1.78
9	4	.111	.999
10	3	.083	.83
11	2	.056	.616
12	1	.028	Expected .336
	Total 36	Total 1.00	Value 7.12

appropriate maintenance budget based on the expected value produced from the historical record monitoring technique.

Finally, what does this analysis provide to the planner? Does the principal have a computer lab problem? Did the survey provide the right information to the principal? Can the information provide other possible hypotheses concerning teacher problems with the computer lab? Can the computer breakdown information provide district administrators with insight into the budget-planning process?

The reader should consider that mathematical calculations used exclusively in studying a problem situation will not provide all the answers to computer planning needs. These procedures aid the planner by framing the potential relationships between survey, interview, and observation data. Therefore, by organizing data in clear, manageable frameworks these techniques provide the planner with knowledge that can be used in developing computer planning policy.

DEFINING PLANNING GUIDELINES

Central to planning computer programs is asking the right questions about the school's implementation environment. In most educational environments—either because of limited resources, changing demographics, or new educational mandates or methods—schools face changes in educational requirements. Changing educational requirements can foster new problems or needs for school systems.

Given the dynamics of the educational environment, computers can be used in a variety of ways to augment a successful change process in school settings. For instance, computers can be used as a direct intervention tool for instruction; as a support tool for supplementing classroom instruction; as a diagnostic tool for testing students; or in a support role for the development of new curriculum, classroom and school management, communications, or even in modeling innovative instructional design approaches.

The variety of computer implementations will vary depending on the types of needs identified by committees or task groups, as well as the ability of these groups to apply proven technology to existing school problems. How well educators are able to anticipate, understand, and consider the consequences of computer technology or identified school problems is a major concern in determining planning policy.

As a result, professionals must select a questioning approach that provides appropriate information about the problem environment. The following basic planning guidelines involve a combination of analysis, judgment, and perhaps intuition in order to attain short- and long-term program objectives.

DEVELOPING GOALS FOR COMPUTER IMPLEMENTATION

In most school planning situations that are intended to serve the needs of many student groups, the task of developing goals and objectives is by no means a straightforward process. The broad range of educational goals that a school embraces is as diverse as the values and ideas of the society the system attempts to serve. We see that the differences within student populations require that the overall goal to provide appropriate education must be divided into a series of subgoals that define to whom the education is directed—infants, children or adults. Furthermore, since education has many attributes, an educational goal must be divided according to what aspects of education are to be addressed—special education, early education, vocational education, secondary education, and the like. Hence, the need for goals to be expressed as specific need statements is mandatory for developing any effective computer planning approach.

The first step in the development of program goals is the formulation of goal statements. This step will embody the future direction of the planning processes. Developing program goals will furnish a centerpiece for structuring problem definitions around specific goal statements. It provides a set of boundaries or constraints on the implementation environment. For example, if a school system plans to implement computer technology in a special-education setting, is it then the responsibility of the school system to provide computer access to all groups, including disabled and nondisabled populations?

Determining the content of goal statements involves developing an awareness of the educational environment and developing information on the structural and situational variables found in that environment. This in turn will lead planners toward manageable procedures for the analysis of problems in the school environment. Goal statements must be specified in terms of what school needs are to be addressed, as well as which school populations are to be served.

The goal statements a decision maker may develop should be expressed as a well-defined and consolidated list of school needs that the administration is willing and able to support. Some examples of the types of goal-statement lists are as follows:

1. One type would be a well-defined list of statements such as "all secondary students shall have one hour of computer math instruction per week." This list could include a wide range of goals regarding ratios of students to computers and time spent on computers, to name two examples. It could also include a list of materials for teacher instructional training.

2. Another type is a list that has a priority ranking assigned to each goal statement. For example, 1 = first preference, 2 = second preference, and 3 = last preference would be used to rank the following goal statements: developing computer hardware literacy skills for teachers *(1)*; develop a computer training program in math *(2)*; purchasing new computer equipment for the resource room *(3)*.

3. Goal statements can also have calculations that identify performance gaps from a set of standards. For example, my math students have an average score on the addition test of 56%. I need to increase the average score to 80%. (Note a performance gap of 24% and a set standard of 80%.)

4. Goal statements can also be expressed in numerical charts, tables, or graphs that represent magnitudes of need gaps.

ORGANIZING PARTICIPANTS

The organization of participant roles will vary depending on the complexity and resource needs of a proposed school computer program. Getting specific people involved during the planning phase and assigning them specific tasks is an important step in the planning process. Careful planning should be given to role development. Not only should assignments be clearly stated, but administrators, as decision-makers, must be sure each task assignment responds to the overall program plan.

The major emphasis in organizing participant roles is determining who should be part of planning and development and how to structure their involvement in various stages of the process. Professionals should make every effort to include as many subgroups as possible, because individuals, groups, and agencies are valuable resources in projecting and formulating key planning goals. Whether just a few participants get together to carry out a computer project or a large number work together through task groups, the need to establish some type of organizational structure is necessary.

Essentially, role and task assignments will provide a framework for directing activities and communicating information between work groups. The size of the organization and/or committee structure should be comprehensive, yet not unwieldy. Too often, large organizational structures require time and organizational maintenance that is often at the expense of innovation and responsiveness.

The organization phase of planning should begin by identifying those individuals, groups, and organizations that are significantly affected by any future computer implementation. Second, the school should also identify those people who want to work with the school. Some examples of these participants would include administrators, teachers, support staff, students, parents, school boards, local education agencies (LEAs), business community, college and university groups, local user groups, and even consultants.

The planner, by identifying a variety of participants, provides a rich source of information for identifying school needs, and secondly, provides participants with a strong sense of interest in and commitment to the success of the program. Often, by developing commitment among participants, a planner can reduce the effects of resistance to change. As a computer issue, resistance to change can be a serious deterrent to successful microcomputer programs.

Once participants are identified, effort should be directed toward developing working relationships between these diverse participants and your school. These relationships can be either informal or formal, depending on the school and how it relates to participant groups and the community. In developing these relationships, attention should be given to encouraging advocacy activities, developing channels of communication, and determining participant roles and responsibilities. These endeavors will facilitate development activities and focus participant attention on your development efforts.

Because the roles of interacting groups can be comprehensive and varied in the planning process, it is often very helpful to outline both planning activities and the levels of interaction between different participant groups. We can define this interaction as an intention to direct efforts and energies toward information exchange and feedback during planning activities. This information exchange can be defined through three levels of interaction (Bender and Church, 1985). These levels of interaction include: (1) primary; (2) secondary; and (3) tertiary interaction levels. With this three-level concept of information interaction, a program planner can direct timely information to specific planning activities.

The primary interaction level will encompass all those individuals who need direct and ongoing contact during the planning process. This interaction usually implies some degree of dependency between working groups. This dependency can be characterized either by a direct need for functional interaction between participants during the development process and/or the degree of information that is required between participating groups in order to accomplish project tasks. For example, the administration provides decision-making skills, initiative, leadership, and support for teaching staff. Conversely, the teaching staff provides input for administrators and technical staff concerning curricular suggestions and identifying student needs.

A secondary interaction level typically does not share the same continuity of contact between groups but does provide some direct service and information that supports the planning, design, and implementation of computer programs. Some types of information support may include planning policy, information on available resources, or technical assistance on the use of computer equipment to school personnel. An example of secondary group interaction might include colleges and universities that provide specific technical courses or workshops supporting special teacher needs. In addition, the LEA may be involved in secondary interaction through financial and material support. An example of this would be a situation in which someone designated by the LEA works with the school's computer liaison or coordinator to help facilitate effective use of available resources.

Tertiary interactions involve information and resource exchange by outside groups or agencies that can provide important input for decision making and general planning activities. These groups usually provide data, indirect support, and/or new ideas for supporting school implementation projects. For example, the views and input of parents fulfill this type of tertiary interaction. Parents, with consent from the school, can also act as a potential resource for raising funds for computer software that may not be available through routine channels.

Obviously, the emphasis of these procedures is on supporting all those functional activities necessary to preliminary organizational planning and development. To be useful in organizing participant relationships, one should view these levels of interaction as flexible working relationships. Some groups may become more active during different stages of computer implementation, resulting in a functional change from one interaction level to another as the program evolves. Also, school environments may prescribe very different interaction levels depending on the school's knowledge base, the leadership style of the administration, and the interrelationships with the community. Finally, one should consider that the links between levels of interaction may vary dramatically across different functional work groups.

In summary, by fostering participation, providing role and task assignments, and supporting planning activities through organized information links, the organizational process will strengthen commitment among diverse individuals and groups toward a favorable acceptance of program goals and objectives. Secondly, defining roles and tasks will help focus task activities and provide an open atmosphere for critical discussion of school needs. Finally, by encouraging broad participation, new ideas and implementation approaches can be supported through a rich source of experience and knowledge.

THE PLANNING ENVIRONMENT AND DECISION-MAKING

In the previous sections an organizational framework was developed that set the stage for planning computer use. This same framework will assist in exploring the decision-making phase of the planning process. By developing goals, setting constraints on the problem, identifying participants, and developing preliminary roles, the process of decision making becomes more systematized. With both a planning framework and an organizational vehicle, the administrator is in a more desirable position to optimize alternatives to resolve a problem or attain a goal.

One can describe the decision-making process in terms of four elements. These elements include the following: (1) tool selection; (2) development of planning standards; (3) identifying planning constraints; and (4) selecting the best solution approach.

The tool-selection phase of decision making provides the user with a set of planning tools for describing variables within an environment. For us, this includes the educational environment and its structural and situational variables. These tools provide a modeling approach that enables the planner to quantify these variables in order to represent the problem situation. Basically, tools process raw data and use this information to develop a knowledge base for problem solving. Although some models require the planner to have higher levels of mathematical expertise, many of the planning models used in the planning process require minimal levels of quantitative expertise. Giving the reader a thorough understanding of the design and use of these models in an implementation situation is beyond the scope of this book. Nevertheless, the reader is encouraged to further an understanding of the model-building process by studying some of the references listed at the end of this book.

Developing planning standards, as a second phase of the decision-making process, consists of goal statements that represent the focus of the planning problem. Planning standards structure the problem into specific need statements or objectives for decision makers. This framework will prioritize program goal statements. Thus, the decision-making process will be guided by a goal statement "map" that converges activities and attention on relevant planning activities.

Planning constraints, by definition, would imply those environmental factors that establish practical bounds for a specific set of solution approaches to the planning problem. The variety of planning constraints a decision maker must consider as part of the problem solving process is largely based on the educational environment. For example, planning constraints include such items as available funding for computer equipment or software; ability to obtain knowledge and/or the ability to improve the knowledge base; physical space limitations; or even the ability to control and maintain equipment.

Finally, the process of selecting the most favorable solutions allows the decision maker to review the results of the planning tool technique(s) by analyzing the data relationships found between key variables in the problem environment. With this information in hand, a decision maker can compare the existing environment with the planning standards or goal statements in order to determine actual need. Based on the planning constraints of the educational environment, the decision maker can determine what is feasible in terms of solutions to the problem environment. Finally, this phase of the decision-making process allows the planner to select the most favorable approach to solving the problem.

The problem with many decision-making environments is that data is often found in highly informal frameworks and is often not recorded or monitored. This is especially true when administrative and teaching staffs rely heavily on communicating information verbally. Similarly, for many schools, the major difficulty in planning for computer utilization is obtaining the right information at the right time. Successful planning and development of school microcomputer programs is based on a school's ability to collect data, process the data into useful information, and use the information to develop practical planning knowledge. As a result, this planning knowledge can be used effectively for formulating responsive educational programs.

SUMMARY

The educator planning the utilization of computer technology has many planning models available to use as guides for computer implementation. Each model represents a different style of planning approach. There is no one approach that will fit all planning needs. The choice of planning approaches available to the educator will depend on the complexity of the computer project, his/her administrative style, the dynamics of the implementation environment, and the formal and informal structure of the organization.

As part of the administrative planning process, it is important to develop appropriate information when making decisions. There are a number of planning tools available for collecting data, developing information, and turning the information into a knowledge base for computer planning.

Finally, there are a number of guidelines that can help facilitate the planning process. These guidelines help organize participants, develop roles and communications, assist in developing program goals, and provide a framework for making decisions based on information and knowledge bases. The planning process can help educators plan, develop, and facilitate responsive instructional programs utilizing computer technology. Chapter 3 will introduce the reader to microcomputer technology and supporting devices that can be utilized in school settings.

The following are sample review questions and some follow-up activities students may wish to pursue. These activities can be used to further develop the concepts and practical applications presented in this chapter.

REVIEW QUESTIONS

1. Why is planning for microcomputer instruction important? Why is it difficult?
2. What is the major contribution of the stages of growth to planning theory?
3. What are the characteristics of a systems planning model?
4. What type of sampling is being used in the following examples?

   a. A sample from two computer-using student groups, including both males and females, has each group in the sample as representative of the whole population.
   b. Assign a number to each computer in the district and, using a table of random numbers, select a sample of 10 for maintenance checks.
   c. Using a random number table, select a random place to start, then select every tenth student from a list.

5. What are the advantages of project planning in both small and large schools?
6. What level of measurement is implied in the following examples?

   a. Computer experience, in years
   b. Computer equipment, by type
   c. Software, by title
   d. Software, by function
   e. Printer output, by pages per minute

SUGGESTED FOLLOW-UP ACTIVITIES

1. Survey the current literature on the subject of planning for microcomputer use in education. Are there other planning approaches or frameworks?

2. Visit a local school using microcomputers. What planning processes does the school use?

3. Explain the importance of a knowledge base with respect to planning computer utilization in schools.

4. Construct a table for determining the expected value of student usage patterns in a computer lab (in hours per week for administrative scheduling purposes. Given are a 30-week data collection period and the following raw data of hours of use and number of occurrences respectively: (20hr/2wk), 14hr/1wk), (21hr/4wk), (17hr/3wk), (16hr/5wk), (18hr/3wk), (19hr/5wk), (23hr/4wk), (12hr/1wk), (15hr/2wk).

5. Locate a local computer-using school and identify the participants of the computer program. What levels of interaction can be identified between these working groups?

CHAPTER 3

*Understanding
Computer Fundamentals*

In 1977, Apple Computer introduced the Apple II personal computer. This small, inexpensive microcomputer was instrumental in ushering in a dynamic new information age. Only a decade after microcomputers were first introduced, they have become an integral part of many people's lives, helping them to perform many jobs in ways never before thought possible, expanding information horizons, and offering powerful tools for education. Over the past ten years, the capabilities of computers to process, store, and share information have steadily increased, while computer costs have decreased.

The classroom has been no stranger to the historical trends in the microcomputer industry. Since the late 1970s a number of computer manufacturers have entered and supported the school market. Microcomputers from Apple, Atari, Commodore, Franklin, IBM, Tandy Computers, and Texas Instruments, to name a few, are familiar sights in classrooms across the country. These early personal computers and their associated capabilities were quite remarkable for the 1970s. In fact, some early computers contained enough memory to hold a few pages of information, provided microcomputer electronics that could process thousands of instructions per second, and even supported limited color graphics capabilities. The evolution of educational computer technology is proceeding at a rapid pace. Today, for example, one can purchase microcomputer systems with enough internal memory to hold the contents of an entire book, powerful electronics that can process millions of instructions per second, and super high-resolution color graphics screens that can display up to 16 million colors on the computer screen.

Emerging hardware developments can have important implications for educators planning instructional microcomputer programs; however, new computing opportunities are often obscured by confusion over the plethora of available technologies. In recent years competition in the microcomputer market has become so fierce that the task of selecting a microcomputer for the school setting grows increasingly difficult. What kind of new computer hardware should a school or teacher consider purchasing? If our school purchases a new computer, can we still use the school's old printers and software? How can we take advantage of changing computer technology with such a limited school budget?

Often, the major difficulty in most school planning efforts is the confusion over the dynamics of computer technology, the associated technical jargon, and, most importantly, what capabilities or advantages the technology may hold for educators and students. The planning and development of effective school-based computer programs naturally require a basic understanding of microcomputer technology. Hence, at the outset it is important to have both conceptual and functional understandings of a microcomputer. This chapter's intent is to provide readers with a general introduction to some fundamental microcomputer concepts and terminology.

INSIDE THE MICROCOMPUTER: HOW DOES IT WORK?

The purpose of this section is to introduce the educator to some of the fundamental concepts and basic terminology that will be used throughout this book. One should realize, however, that this book provides a *general* overview of the technology and that some of the more specific books listed in the references at the end of this book should be consulted if more background information on any of the following subjects is required by the reader.

There are a variety of microcomputer systems in schools, and these systems come in various sizes and shapes; they may even require several separate pieces of equipment to be complete. Although microcomputers take on many different forms, all microcomputer systems share the same fundamental components. A closer look at the components of a microcomputer will show how they fit together to make a functional system.

THE SYSTEM UNIT

The operation of most microcomputer systems is very similar. Basically, the microcomputer is built around a *system unit,* which controls all the functions of a computer. The system unit is built on a printed circuit board located inside the microcomputer. The printed circuit board is a sheet of fiberglass or epoxy onto which electronic components are attached. These components exchange electronic signals via wires or etched traces of metal (see figures 3-1 and 3-2). This printed circuit board consists of thousands of electronic components that contain millions of microelectronic circuits. Together these electronic components and microelectronic circuits make up the system unit.

A typical microcomputer system unit consists of three main parts: (1) central processing unit (CPU); (2) read only memory (ROM) and random access memory (RAM); and (3) input and output (I/O ports). Figure 3-1 shows the three major parts of a system unit on the main circuit board of a computer. Although the operation of the system unit is generally the same for all computers, a manufacturer's expression of the basic circuitry design in the system unit are usually proprietary and often very different in physical design from that of manufacturers making similar computers. Different design philosophies make manufacturers' computers unique and often incompatible with one another.

The Central Processing Unit

The central processing unit (CPU) is composed of microelectronics (millions of microscopic electronic wires and components) that are neatly designed

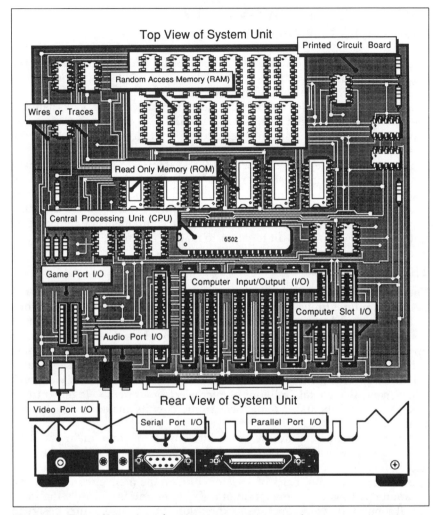

Figure 3-1. Top and rear view of a microcomputer system unit.

and cut into a tiny silicon chip. This tiny silicon chip is specifically designed to combine all the millions of microelectronic wires into many whole, functional, microelectronic circuits. These silicon chips, because of their vast organization of microelectronic circuits, are often called "integrated circuits" (ICs).

The job of the CPU is to control all of the functions of the computer. It is the "brains" of every microcomputer. Hence, this system unit component is the central control center of the microcomputer. To accomplish the job of controlling the computer, the CPU is composed of three internal microelectronic sections. The three sections of the CPU include: (1) control unit (CU); (2) arithmetic/logic unit (ALU); and (3) registers. Without these internal components, the CPU would not be able to control the computer.

The control unit (CU) serves as a "traffic controller" for all the computer's actions, the functions of which include the following: (1) controlling the access of computer memory; (2) constantly interpreting series of instructions that tell it how and when to perform its chores; and (3) directing and passing all data to and from the computer.

The second major part of the CPU is the arithmetic/logic unit (ALU). The ALU is controlled by the control unit; basically, the CU sends data to the ALU for performing mathematical operations. These operations involve all math activities such as addition, subtraction, multiplication, division, and logical expressions *(and/or/else)*. If the CPU didn't have an internal ALU, the computer would not know how to do any mathematical calculations!

The last part of the CPU is the *registers*. The reader can think of these areas in the CPU as temporary storage areas or "scratch pads" for manipulating data. Both the CU and ALU use the registers for manipulating data in the manner dictated by the software program currently running on the microcomputer. Similarly, these storage areas act as indicators or signals for the CU. The registers make the CU aware of various actions while the computer is running. The number of registers in a computer depends on the design of the CPU.

Every microcomputer's CPU contains these three functional parts. Together, these microelectronic parts control the various functions of the computer, including processing of instructions and data, directing information exchange, and monitoring internal and external functions. Because the CPU does all of these tasks, it is often referred to as a *microprocessor*.

Microcomputer Memory

The second component of the system unit is a computer's memory. The reader should not confuse the type of memory with that of a human being. Human memory can recall pictures, images, sounds, places, thoughts, smells, feelings, and emotions. A computer's memory only holds millions of ones and zeros, all of which represent information. In addition, a computer's memory only contains information that the manufacturer and the user put into the computer. While human memory is stored in complex nervous tissue, computer information is stored on silicon chips. Located on the system unit near the CPU are two kinds of computer memory chips. These two kinds of memory are called read only memory (ROM) and random access memory (RAM). Like the CPU, these chips, or integrated circuits, are made up of thousands of microelectronic circuits.

ROM is part of the computer's memory that contains vital operating information. This information includes basic computer operating instructions for the CPU or sometimes application programs like word processing software. The information in ROM is permanent; it doesn't vanish when you switch off the computer's power. ROM makes it possible for the microcomputer to operate again after the power has been turned off. Without these permanent instructions, the microcomputer wouldn't know what to do once its power is turned back on. This start-up information is encoded in the ROM chips by the computer's manufacturer.

RAM is part of the computer's memory that stores information temporarily while the user is working on the computer. RAM can contain information on both application software (i.e., educational software programs) and users' information (students' scores from educational game programs or students' spelling words for a spelling game). Because information in RAM is temporary, it is gone forever once the power is switched off. Thus, if a teacher or administrator wishes to keep the student's information, it must be transferred from the computer's RAM to a permanent storage device such as a diskette.

Both ROM and RAM are commonly associated with computer terminology such as "64K" or "512K." For example, 64K refers to the number of *kilobytes* of computer memory. The kilobyte (K) is a unit of measurement consisting of $1,024$ (2^{10}) bytes. In this usage, *kilo* (from the Greek, meaning "a thousand") stands for 1,024. Thus, 64K memory equals 65,536 bytes. If the amount of memory reaches increments of one million bytes, the terminology becomes *megabytes* (MB).

To get an idea of how much storage a computer with 64K memory really has, one should consider that a byte of information usually represents a single character, letter, or number in a computer's memory; as such, 64K would equal about 64,000 characters. However, the reader should be aware that the user usually doesn't have access to all of this memory. For example, just loading an application program of even moderate function (i.e., a word processing program) into RAM would use most of a 64K computer's memory. As a general rule, software program(s) that use large multiple files, store large complex data, or use graphics are usually very "RAM-hungry." Some examples of these types of programs include word processors with spelling checkers; integrated software packages containing a word processor, spreadsheet, and data base; drawing programs emphasizing computer graphics; and software programs using digitized graphics, sound, or voice as part of their functionality.

Computer Communications and Input/Output

All microcomputers communicate all their instructions internally through the system unit. The CPU communicates with the computer using the binary numbering system. Our decimal numbering system makes use of 10 fundamental digits. The binary numbering system, however, uses only two digits: 0 and 1. The computer's CPU performs all its internal operations using binary numbers; this is because it has available to it millions of micro-electronic circuits that can easily be electrically turned either *on* or *off* to represent the binary digits *1* and *0* respectively. The smallest amount of information that a computer can hold is called a *bit*, or binary digit (a bit being 1 or 0). These binary digits are often called digital data.

The computer then takes these bits and it groups, or strings, them together to form larger values called *bytes*. A byte usually consists of eight bits that represent a single unit of information. As an example, eight bits can be grouped together to form a byte, which represents a unit of information such as a letter, number, or character. Because a byte usually represents a single character, this unit of information becomes very handy as a unit of measure for the storage or memory capacity of a computer; hence, the byte is used as the basic unit of measure of a computer's memory (ROM and RAM).

The system unit's CPU processes the digital information in bits. The number of bits that can be processed at any one time by the CPU usually represents the size and power of the CPU. For example, older educational computers, like the Apple II + and Apple IIe, have CPUs that can handle only eight bits, or one byte, at a time. However, other educational computers, like the IBM PC and Apple Macintosh, can process information in 16- and 32-bit lengths. As such, these computers' CPUs can manipulate, or handle, two bytes and four bytes of data at a time respectively.

In order to use data, the computer must be able to move units of information from one part of the computer to another (i.e., CPU to RAM). This information travels in the form of bits through what is termed a bus (see Figure 3-2). The bus is a set of wires or traces on the printed circuit board of the system unit that carry bits from one part of the computer to another. One can think of a bus as a "highway" on which sets of bits travel from one place to another. Further, the wires or traces are "lanes" on the highway through which each bit of information travels. Hence, the system unit uses this bus to send and communicate information, or data, between the CPU, memory, and input/output ports.

A microcomputer's system unit has two types of buses: an *address bus* and a *data bus*. The CPU uses the address bus for accessing information in the computer's memory. The address bus (or highway) determines how much memory a computer can access. For example, the CPU of the Apple II + and Apple IIe, (called the 6502 microprocessor, has a 16-bit address bus for accessing computer memory. These types of microcomputers can typically use 16 address wires (or lanes on the highway); and since each of these wires (lanes) can be on or off, the 6502 CPU is only capable of addressing 65,536K of total memory at any given time—65,536K = 2^{16} (2 = on or off electrical state of bit; 16 = the 16 address wires[or lanes of the highway]).

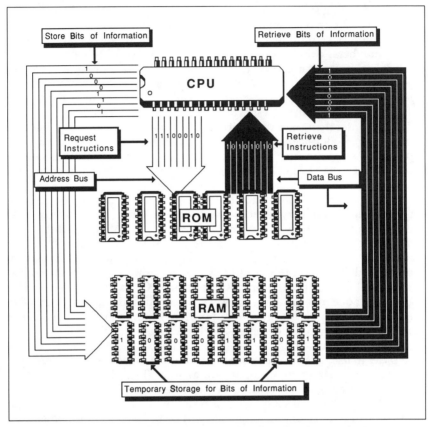

Figure 3-2. Address and data bus: the highway for internal and external microcomputer communications.

The CPU uses the data bus to transfer and manipulate data within the system unit. The data bus on the 6502 microprocessor is an eight-bit bus (eight-lane highway). The computer uses this bus to move important data and computer instructions between the many electronic components of the system unit.

The computer's input/output (I/O) is the third major part of a microcomputer's system unit. The job of the I/O is to exchange information with the outside world. This information exchange involves both putting information into the computer (input) and receiving information from the computer (output). A computer's I/O consists of hardware connectors on the system unit's printed circuit board. I/O hardware has two basic types of connectors. These I/O hardware connectors can either take the form of *slots* on the printed circuit board or *ports* on the back or side of the computer (see Figure 3-1).

Slots are built on the bus of the system unit. Slots are peripheral or device connectors that provide a physical link for the computer's system unit with the outside world. This physical link allows the user to add devices to the computer's system unit. Open computer architecture allows the user the ability to add additional functions to the computer. These functions are usually added by means of an internal card that can be plugged into one or more slots on the computer's system unit. These slots can hold many different types of cards that perform many different functions. Examples include cards that add computer RAM; cards for printers; cards for communications; graphics cards; computer-emulation cards; accelerator cards for the computer; and cards for voice synthesizers.

Ports also provide a physical link for the computer's system unit with the outside world. The major distinctions between a port and a slot include the port's physical connector shape and configuration, which are usually fixed and built into the computer's system unit (usually in the back of the computer). The port generally does not take on the shape of a slot and will not provide a means for plugging in cards. In addition, the port is usually limited to the particular types of function or configuration. For example, a video port is limited to video signals that are sent to a computer's monitor or screen. In addition, other I/O ports, such as the serial and parallel ports, provide a computer with much more flexibility in terms of I/O functions. For example, these ports can support printers, disk drives, a modem, and other appropriate peripheral devices. Also, I/O ports allow making connections between the computer and peripheral devices much easier than with internal slots.

Microcomputer I/O ports are usually configured in six general types: (1) serial; (2) parallel; (3) video; (4) audio; (5) game controller; and (6) musical instrument digital interface (MIDI).

• *Serial ports.* This type of I/O hardware connector is used for transmitting digital data sequentially, accomplished by sending each bit of the transmitted letter, number, or character one after the other, a bit at a time, over a single wire or channel. Serial communication is analogous to a single-lane road where each car (bit) must follow the other. The bits are sent at rigid time intervals by the CPU. The transmission speed is called the *baud rate* and is equivalent to the number of bits sent per second. Common baud rates are 300; 1,200; 9,600; 12,000; and 19,200.

After all the data bits have been transmitted for the character, a *parity bit* and one or more *stop bits* are sent to mark the end of the character. Parity bits are a form of error checking for the transmissions of data. This way, a computer can determine whether a character was sent correctly. Stop bits are rest times for the computer to allow the receiving device to assemble and process the incoming character. Serial connectors and cables are usually referred to as RS-232 serial interfaces (see figure 3-3). Serial ports are designed specifically for terminals and modems. However, it is not uncommon to find these ports being used for printers. The serial interface is the best choice for making connections between a computer and some external device that is located more than 10 to 15 feet from the computer. The serial interface can alleviate data-transmission problems that occur over long distances between computer equipment. Also, serial cables are relatively inexpensive. However, the price you pay for using cheaper lines of communications is speed; only about 30 characters per second (300 baud) can be sent over these lines.

- *Parallel ports.* This type of I/O hardware connector is used for transmitting information or data in sets of usually eight bits at a time, side by side, on a multiple wire or channel. The parallel-communications concept is analogous to a very short eight-lane highway supporting only one-way travel. At the start of the highway is a traffic officer to control access to the highway, and at the end of the highway are toll booth controllers. To avoid any traffic problems, only eight cars (bits) are allowed to cross at the same time. In addition, the cars (bits) must travel parallel with one another. Both the traffic officer and the toll booth controllers use signals to control traffic and to communicate with each other. The transmission of data starts when the traffic officer allows eight cars to enter the highway; when the cars reach the toll booths, the traffic officer signals the toll booth controllers. When the toll booth controllers have taken the tolls, they signal the traffic officer. This signal alerts the traffic officer that all eight of these cars are off the highway and the traffic officer is free to allow eight more cars onto the highway. And the cycle repeats until all the data bits have been sent.

  The parallel interface is often called a Centronics interface, after the company that developed it for its line of printers. The standard Centronics connector is a 36-pin *D* connector (see Figure 3-3). This interface was designed for high-speed printers. Typical printer speeds for simple parallel interfaces are over 100,000 characters per second (cps), as opposed to 30 cps on serial lines. However, these data-transmission rates are only possible when the distance between the computer and printer is very short (10–15 feet). Also, parallel connectors and cabling are usually more expensive than serial connectors and cables.

- *Video ports.* The video port on a microcomputer is used for providing information output from the computer's system unit. As noted previously, a computer represents all its information using the binary numbers 0 and 1. This information coding is also referred to as a digital signal (data generated by a computer's microprocessor). Hence, the computer's video signal output is also in a digital format. The video port can transfer the digital signal out of the computer to either a television, television monitor, or high-resolution color computer monitor. Each of these monitors is linked to the computer from the video port via a cable connector.

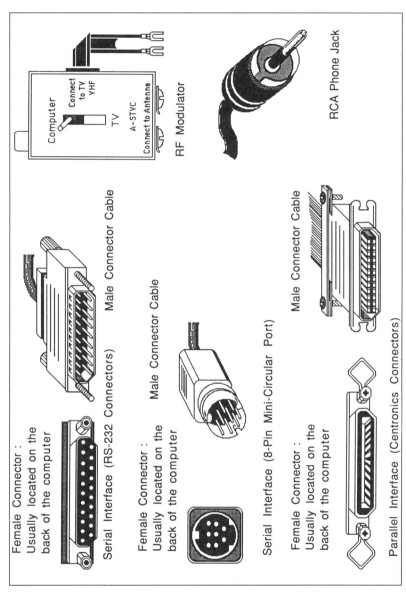

Figure 3-3. Common microcomputer input/output ports.

The home television was designed to receive only radio frequencies, that is, fundamentally analog signals such as live subjects photographed on camera or video, or subjects from slides, tapes, broadcasts, or cable networks. Hence, before a computer's digital signal can be displayed on a television, the digital output from the computer's central processing unit must be transformed into an analog signal the television can understand. This is done with a radio frequency (RF) modulator, which transforms the digital signal into an analog signal for presentation on a television screen (see figure 3-3).

In addition, some computers produce a colored video signal that is similar to television's analog signal. This type of video signal is often referred to as either a composite color video signal or National Television Standards Committee (NTSC) signal. Examples of computers using this video signal include the Apple II + and Apple IIe. This video signal allows the computer's digital signal to be transmitted directly through a single wire into either a computer or television monitor. Hence, a single, standard RCA phono jack can be used as a connector between the computer's video port and the monitor (see figure 3-3).

There are also microcomputers that use very high-resolution graphics for displaying information. These computer system's video ports use an RGB signal. Some examples include the Apple II GS, IBM PS/2 and Macintosh II personal computers. The major components of this video signal include three separate signals that are synchronized on three different wires representing the digital information. These three signals include a red, green, and blue video signal—hence the name RGB. These video signals require complex circuitry in the system unit in order to produce true RGB video output.

- *Audio ports.* The audio port in the computer's system unit provides external output for audio components. The audio port usually allows the user to play the audio from the computer's internal audio speaker into some other external audio device. These components include external speakers, amplifiers, or even a stereo system. The user can usually access the computer's audio ports via a standard RCA phono jack available at Radio Shack stores (see Figure 3-3).

- *Game ports.* The game port allows the user to connect input devices into the computer's system unit. Some of these devices include switches for the handicapped, light pens, joy sticks, paddles, graphics tablets, touchscreens, and children's keyboards, which are used to play games, run educational programs, and provide access to the computer. There are various types of game ports available on computers.

- *Musical instrument digital interface (MIDI).* The MIDI port allows the user to plug in various synthesizers and electronic musical instruments or devices. This port provides the ability to create whatever sound a human can hear, given the right kind of software and music-creating devices.

IMPLICATIONS FOR EDUCATION

The microcomputer's CPU is a very important consideration in determining what kind of computer is most applicable in an educational setting. The CPU is directly responsible for a computer's ability to access different sizes of computer memory. The ability to access memory, in turn, limits the graphics capability of the computer, the speed of software operation, and even the number of jobs the computer can handle simultaneously.

The ability of a CPU to access and handle memory is critical to the scope of instructional activities a computer is capable of doing in the classroom setting. For example, many of the older CPU computers can only directly access 64K of memory at any one time. This basic 64K memory ceiling directly limits the performance, scope, and broad function of instructional software programs.

As an example, many current educational software programs that are commercially available usually concentrate on only a few instructional concepts. This limited instructional functioning is largely due to the memory restrictions of the older computer CPUs. Limited memory restricts what functions a computer can do. Because of CPU memory limitations, many educational software programs that attempt to incorporate extensive graphics and use natural sounding human voice — or even human-speech recognition — as part of an instructional design, quickly run out of available memory. Hence, many of these advanced instructional applications can never be adequately developed on computers with limited CPU memory access. Although there are software tricks and hardware devices that support other means of accessing additional memory, they are often very slow, difficult to support and maintain, and can be incompatible with a school's educational software and hardware. In addition, they usually cannot attain the performance levels required when attempting to run very complex software programs.

The system unit's I/O also has implications for the special-needs student. Having the ability to put information into the computer in a variety of ways and to output or display this information in different forms can be very useful for both the special-needs student and teacher. Microcomputers that contain slots inside of the system unit provide a means of access to the outside world. As such, computers with slot and port I/O devices provide individuals with disabilities access opportunities to standard microcomputers. Such I/O devices allow such individuals to use alternative input methods such as keyboard adaptations (expanded keyboards or miniature keyboards), ability switches (single-touch or voice switches), speech synthesizers, enlarging screen systems, and braille printers.

MICROCOMPUTERS AND PERIPHERAL DEVICES

Throughout this book the reader has encountered the word "hardware" to describe various computer parts and devices. Hardware is defined as anything about the computer that a person can see or touch. With this concept in mind, one can define a peripheral device as a piece of computer hardware, such as a disk drive, printer, or keyboard, used in conjunction with a computer and usually under the control of the computer. Peripheral devices are usually physically separate from the computer, their only connection to the computer through slots or ports via wires or cables.

The computer is able to control the peripheral device by sending both instructions and information from the system unit to the computer's I/O slots and ports. This information is always represented in the form of digital data (0s and 1s). Finally, the instructions and information leave the computer's I/O port through wire or cable into the peripheral device. Hence, sending information from one piece of computer hardware to another is called I/O, or input/output, of information. The following sections will describe various peripheral devices that are commonly used in special and regular education settings.

MAGNETIC STORAGE TECHNOLOGY

Disk Drives and Diskettes

One of the most common peripheral storage devices found in the classroom is the disk drive. The disk drive is used for both retrieval (input) and storage (output) of information from a computer. Hence, a disk drive is an I/O peripheral device. The disk drive is analogous in function to a tape player and operates much like a conventional record player.

A disk drive, like a tape player, has the ability to store and retrieve information magnetically. A disk drive, like a record player, reads information from tracks on a round disc. However, instead of putting music and sounds on tape or grooves of a phonograph record, the disk drive can only read and write digital data (0s and 1s) onto a magnetic medium.

The magnetic medium used to store computer information is called a "floppy disk," or "diskette" (see Figure 3-4). Like phonograph records, diskettes need to be protected from damage. The disk is always covered in a plastic jacket to protect the inner surface from fingerprints, dust, smoke, liquids, and other pollutants. A spindle hole about the size of a quarter is punched into the disk's center. At the bottom of the protective jacket is an elongated elliptical opening that allows the disk drive to read and write magnetic data on the disk. Floppy diskettes come in a number of different sizes. However, most educational software applications use 5¼ inch and 3½ inch disks. These disks commonly hold from 160,000 to 1,400,000 bytes of information—160K and 1.4 MB respectively (roughly about 60–400 double-spaced pages of text).

Before one can record information on a blank diskette, the diskette must

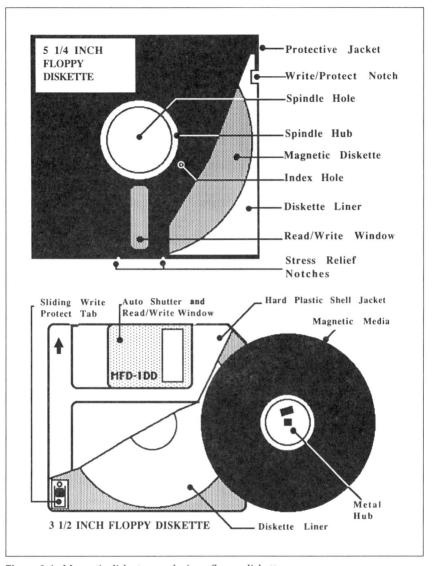

Figure 3-4. Magnetic disk storage devices: floppy diskettes.

first be *formatted*, that is, the blank magnetic surface of the diskette must be arranged into specially designated tracks (see Figure 3-5). These tracks must be created in order for the disk drive to record and retrieve information. The

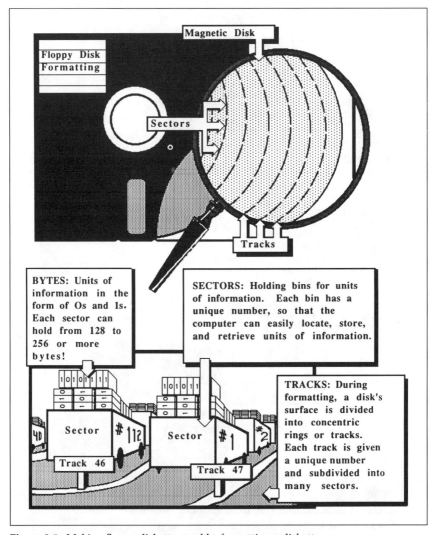

Figure 3-5. Making floppy diskettes usable: formatting a diskette.

formatting process also subdivides the tracks into *sectors*. Sectors are holding bins that store bytes of information, usually 128 to 256 or more bytes.
Each track and sector are also given unique numbers, much like mailbox
addresses. These numbers help identify specific locations on the diskette's
surface, so that the microcomputer can find the proper holding bin contain-

ing information requested by the user or software program (see Figure 3-5). Most floppy diskettes can be formatted and used with many different types of computers.

To transfer information from the system unit's RAM to the floppy disk, the disk drive is set spinning at a high rate of speed (most disk drives spin at 300 revolutions per minute [rpm]). Specially designed read/write heads in the disk drive move across the diskette, find the appropriate numbered track or sector, and instantly transfer the encoded information to and from the diskette.

The care and handling of classroom diskettes is a very important subject and needs to be discussed. Once a school purchases a new software program, or even if a teacher creates a student data disk for a popular instructional software program, observing a few guidelines of diskette care will, in the long run, preserve a teacher's work, protect the school's software investment, and keep student mishaps to a minimum. Figure 3-6 shows a list of diskette guidelines that are helpful for maintaining software in the classroom, computer lab, and office.

Hard Disk Drives

Another close relative in the magnetic disk storage family is the "hard disk." The hard disk is similar to a disk drive. However, the hard disk has three distinct features that make it a unique I/O peripheral device. First, hard-disk drives have all their magnetic disk media permanently encased in the unit; no floppy diskettes are used. The storage capacity of a hard-disk drive is another feature that makes these drives unique. Hard-disk drives can store millions of bytes of information. Typical storage capacities for hard disks range from 10 megabytes to 250 megabytes of data, roughly 3,200 to 90,000 double-spaced pages of information. Finally, one of the most important advantages of a hard disk is the speed at which the drive can store and retrieve information. Hard disks are able to save and retrieve programs and data much faster than floppy-disk drives.

The hard disk has two major groups of components: the microelectronics and the mechanical moving parts (see Figure 3-7).

The microelectronics send and receive digital information from the computer's system unit, usually through the I/O slots or ports. In addition, the microelectronics are responsible for properly arranging bytes of information on the magnetic disk media and also for helping locate the information stored on the disks' tracks and sectors.

The mechanical device of a hard-disk drive is rather simple, containing fewer moving parts than the average can opener. The basic mechanical elements of the hard disk include: (1) a stack of one or more disk platters (these are the *hard*-disk magnetic media that store information); (2) a spindle

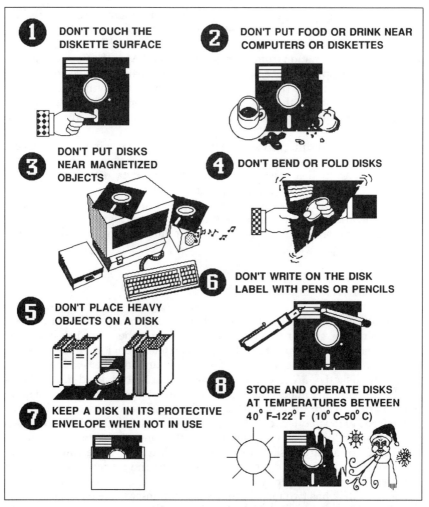

Figure 3-6. Classroom care and handling of floppy diskettes.

or shaft that rotates the platters; (3) a motor that turns the spindle; and (4) the read/write head(s) and motor (see Figure 3-7).

The disk platters, like floppy diskettes, are formatted with tracks and sectors, and hold bytes of information. However, unlike a floppy diskette, the platters are very hard, rigid, and always enclosed in an air-tight case to prevent pollutants from reaching the disk surface. The patters of a hard disk are usually thin but inflexible aluminum disks covered with a material that

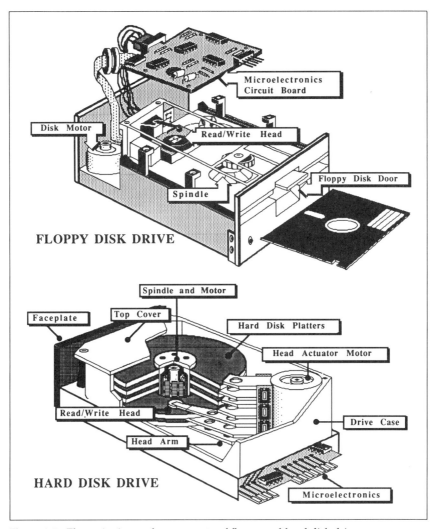

Figure 3-7. The major internal components of floppy and hard disk drives.

can readily be magnetized. This material is usually a ferric-oxide compound (basically, fine grains of rust!). Finally, most hard disks will have multiple disk platters, the number depending on the size of the hard disk.

The spindle and motor make the disk platters spin or rotate. Unlike floppy-disk drives, the hard disk platters *constantly* spin (at least while the power is on). The constant spinning makes information on the hard disk nearly instantly accessible (with floppy-disk drives, the user must wait a few seconds for the drive to light up and attain the right speed for accessing information). The hard-disk platters spin at nearly 3,600 rpm, faster than most sport-car engines. Floppy-diskette drives spin at about 300 rpm.

The read/write heads store and retrieve the information on the hard disk electronically. This is done by the hard disk's microelectronics. In most hard disks, one read/write head is associated with each side of a platter. Hence, each platter usually has two read/write heads. These read/write are connected to arms that allow the read/write heads to move over the platter. All of the read/write heads and their arms are linked together as a single moving unit. A special motor swings the arms across the platters. The read/write heads float about $\frac{1}{1},000$ of an inch above the platters (see Figure 3-8).

Because the read/write heads are so near the surface of the disk platters they are very susceptible to damage from sudden harsh movements, or even from dropping or shoving the hard disk just a quarter of an inch. Such movement bounces the read/write head on the surface of the disk platter, plowing little ferric-oxide furrows into the disk surface. This is often referred to as a "disk crash" or "head crash." These little accidents can ruin your day, important data, and the hard disk. In most school environments it is wise to keep hard disks away from any such hazards. In addition, because of the potential for accidents, those individuals wishing to use a hard disk should save copies of their information on separate storage devices. Two examples of such devices include tape and disk drives. This process of making duplicate copies of information is called data backup. Computer users should develop regular habits of backing up important data. Unfortunately, it is usually the one time the user does not back up information that accidents happen.

OPTICAL STORAGE TECHNOLOGY

Optical storage technology is the alternative to standard magnetic storage (the now-familiar floppy disks and hard disks). Optical storage technology will radically expand the kinds of things educators can do with the micro-computer over the next 10 years. The technology itself, which uses finely focused laser beams to store huge amounts of information, has the potential to bring volumes of encyclopedic information to the classroom computer on a single disk, including video, text, graphics, and sound.

Optical storage media have a number of inherent advantages over the traditional magnetic media. First, optical storage technology can hold considerably more data than a typical floppy or hard disk. Optical media can hold about 550 megabytes of usable data, which is equivalent to over 26 hard disks (20 MG) and over 1,500 floppy disks! Because optical storage media is read by a laser beam, the reading head mechanism can be farther away from the disk surface, making head crashes very unlikely. In addition, the disk

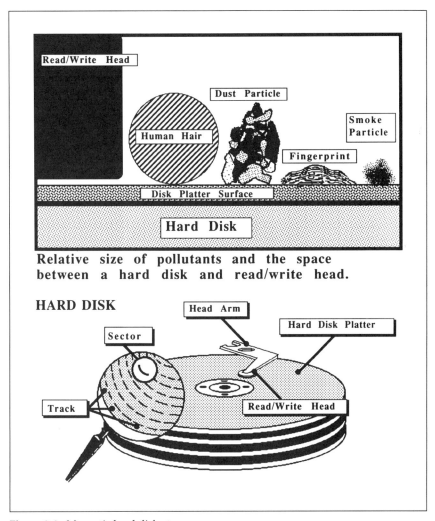

Figure 3-8. Magnetic hard disk storage.

surface of optical media is protected from physical damage, as from finger-prints, spilled liquids, magnetic fields, and scratches, by a transparent plastic coating. Finally, optical technology is a better distribution media than is magnetic media because optical disks can be stamped out, as cookies are with a cookie cutter, while magnetic media must be duplicated byte by byte electronically. Optical disks and the drives that use them come in three basic classes, each having a very distinct functional usage; these three classes are discussed in the following sections.

Compact Disk Read Only Memory

Over the next few years the most common type of optical medium will most likely be the read-only optical medium. These 5¼-inch silvery disks go by the name of "compact disk read only memory" (CD-ROM). This class of optical media is a descendent of the old popular 12-inch movie videodiscs of the 1970s, and more recently, of the audio compact disks being sold in music stores.

A CD-ROM is physically identical to the now-popular audio CD. Unlike the old analog tapes and phonograph records that preceded it, the audio CD uses digital information (0s and 1s). Basically, audio CD's consist of one hour of music in the form of billions of bits of digital data; these bits are physically pressed into the CD's surface (see Figure 3-9). CD-ROM disks are stamped out using the same process as for audio CDs; however, it doesn't matter whether the data is music or text information.

Unlike the many tracks on a floppy or hard disk, a CD carries a single spiral track that starts at the center of the disk and winds its way outward. Much like the grooves on a phonograph record, the turns in the spiral are so close together than over 15,500 of them can fit into one inch. The track is located on the flat surface of the disk, which is called *land*. This single track is divided into millions of sectors, and the sectors hold billions of tiny grooves. These tiny grooves, which are sunk into the surface of the land, are called *pits*. The pits represent digital data, or bits (0s and 1s).

A laser shoots a finely focused beam of light at the pits. The light beam, which is reflected off the pits, is read by the disk drive and converted into digital information, which the computer can then use. The laser is mounted on a reading head that moves radially out from the disk's center, allowing the laser to follow the track or spiral. The motor, which turns the disk, must gradually speed up as the reading head moves outward with the spiral. CDs that use this recording scheme require constant motor-speed adjustment over the disk spiral in order to access information. Unfortunately, this recording scheme can cause rather long search periods in finding some information. For example, computer applications that require continual data searches for large amounts of information may encounter access and/or speed problems due to constant speed adjustments in the laser's reading head. As a result, instant data access is often not possible. Conversely, most magnetic storage technologies, such as hard-disk drives, rotate the disk medium at a constant rate, allowing the same amount of information to be stored around each concentric track (tracks or circles one within the other) on the disk. As a result, the longer outer tracks of magnetic storage disks are not packed as densely with data, and a lot of storage capacity is wasted. This is

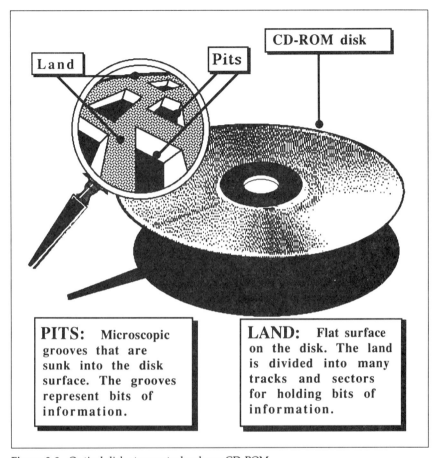

Figure 3-9. Optical disk storage technology: CD-ROM.

one major reason why CD technology can store more information than magnetic disk storage technology.

Write Once Read Mostly

Write once read mostly (WORM) technology is the second form of optical storage medium. Like CD-ROM, it stores digital information in the form of pits on the disk surface. Unlike the CD-ROM, the WORM drive is capable of creating, as well as reading, the pits. Because the creation of pits in the disk surface is irreversible, they cannot be altered, although they can be read as often as desired. These disks are therefore often called "write once, read many times," or WORM. The biggest advantages for the use of this type of optical storage medium is its physical durability and ability to record or write information to a disk, combined with its large storage capacity.

Unfortunately, WORM technology is considerably less standardized than the CD-ROM class of optical storage devices. For example, manufacturers are making WORM disks of different sizes; their protective plastic shells are of different shapes; their storage capacities vary widely (200 MB to over one billion bytes per disk); and, most importantly, these disks lack any file format standards for storing information. Presently, the American National Standards Institute is working on developing a consensus for a set of standards for this technology. This will greatly help WORM compatibility issues involving different CD devices and computers.

While WORM disks have both advantages and disadvantages, the WORM technology does not suffer from the same inherent access-speed problems as CD-ROM recording schemes. The WORM drive uses the same concentric tracks as the current magnetic storage media (hard and floppy disks). A laser beam is used to read and write information to and from tracks and sectors on the disk. This is important for CD instructional applications that require instant data access. After all, few users will use an application that requires them to consistently sit and wait in front of a blank screen for 10 to 15 seconds while the computer is busy accessing information.

Erasable Optical Storage

The third class of optical storage media is the erasable medium. This technology will probably not be available to the classroom on a cost-effective basis for a number of years. This storage medium will most likely be patterned off the current magnetic media storage formats. This format will include concentric tracks on a disk. The tracks will then be subdivided into blocks or sectors that hold billions of pits that represent digital information (bits). A laser will be used to read and write the bits to disk. The major advantages of this technology include: (1) an ability to both read and write data to the storage media; (2) this medium will be very portable and durable; (3) this medium can hold very large amounts of data on disk (200–600 megabytes); and (4) this medium provides easy distribution of the information.

Ultimately, because of these advantages, optical storage media will be the next evolutionary step in computer disk storage. Today, unfortunately, most CD-ROMs are priced too high for most classroom microcomputers. There are a number of CD-ROM applications on the market; the Educational Resources Information Center (ERIC), for instance, provides full references and summaries on all aspects of education regarding CDs. The price is about $2,000 for the three-disk set. Like ERIC, Grolier produces a CD-ROM disk set called *The Electronic Encyclopedia*, which is fully searchable by the user with just a few taps on the keyboard, allowing the user to find most information faster than with a regular encyclopedia in book form. However, one should not expect to see real growth of optical media until the mid-nineties. Until then, most schools will not likely find an overpowering reason to buy a CD-ROM or WORM drive by itself; when manufactures standardize the WORM market and when erasable optical 5¼-inch media and drives become available on a cost-effective basis, this technology may become a reality in the classroom.

PRINTER TECHNOLOGIES

Another peripheral device that is very handy in the classroom is the printer. The printer is a piece of hardware that accepts digital information from a computer's system unit. The printer receives this information from the system unit's I/O slots or ports, then displays this digital information on paper as text or graphics. In educational settings there are six common types of printing technologies: (1) impact dot matrix printer; (2) daisy wheel printers; (3) thermal-transfer printers; (4) ink-jet printers; (5) pen plotters; and (6) laser printers.

The values by which one measures the quality of a printer are often very misleading. Speed is often the first value to come to mind; it is measured in characters per second (cps). However, few people are interested in cps. One is usually more interested in the number of pages printed per minute. This value, unfortunately, can't be determined simply by cps. After all, what really constitutes a printed page?

The quality of print may also come to mind. Still, the print quality value doesn't lend itself to precise measurement either. Levels of print quality—draft quality, near-letter quality, or letter quality—all have their own standards and subjective criteria. In addition, many printers also contain special character sets and print features. These too will affect the control and quality of the printed page.

The cost factor also seems to be a common comparison measure for printers. Unfortunately, cost comparisons are very misleading. For example, many printers require the support of hardware, software, and special maintenance, all of which may affect cost over the short and long term. Similarly, how does one compare cost factors across different printer technologies? Laser printers, for example, usually require large amounts of RAM to function, and some even have their own CPU for directing printing functions. Both RAM and an intelligent CPU add to printer cost. These and many other printer characteristics and functions confuse cost comparisons among printer technologies.

As a result, this section will describe each printer technology and some of the unique features they offer. The selection of a printer really depends on users' printing applications. These specific printing applications then dictate a set of print guidelines or expectations required by the users. No one kind of printer is going to give users everything they want. Instead, users must identify specific needs and make a trade-off based on those features that may support or improve the printing task(s).

Impact Dot Matrix Printers

For educational applications, the impact dot matrix printer is probably the most common. The impact dot matrix printer uses *impact print* technology. This technology reproduces text and graphics by printing dots on paper. These dots are created by very small pins mounted on a print head (see Figure 3-10). These pins in the print head are fired electronically, impacting, or striking, the ribbon (hence the term "impact print technology"), which releases ink on the paper as the print head traverses the paper. Text and graphics are formed by arranging the pins to fire on an imaginary grid or matrix according to the letter or character being printed. For example, a dot matrix printer using a 5-by-7 matrix (five columns by seven rows) would print the letter *H* by firing pins in the print head only in the first column, middle row, and the fifth column (see Figure 3-10). These pins impact the ribbon and sweep back and forth across the line generating text or graphics. If one were to inspect the results of dot matrix printing, one would notice that there are very small gaps between the dots that make up a character. As a result, many manufacturers either add more pins to the print head or program the printer to go over the same printed line twice or more. On dot matrix printers with 18-pin or 24-pin heads, the gaps are reduced, and the letters appear more sharply defined. Dot matrix printers generally come in 8-, 9-, 18-, and 24-pin print-head configurations.

The major advantages of using this technology in the classroom include the following: (1) dot matrix printers can produce both text and graphics; (2) these printers can usually print in color using multicolored ribbons; (3) dot matrix print technology is very reliable; (4) impact dot matrix printer technology uses low-cost supplies; (5) dot matrix printers can usually operate in either draft- or near letter-quality mode.

The technology does have some shortcomings, however. The printed paper copy, often called "hard copy," is generally limited to paper. A teacher wishing to reproduce work-sheet transparencies would find the necessary feature to be generally unavailable on dot matrix printers. In addition, pins in the print head limit the potential definition of characters. Thus, the print quality is usually limited to only draft and near-letter quality. This may be an important factor when considering the use of dot matrix printers with important school correspondence, résumés, and evaluation reports.

Daisy Wheel Printers

Daisy wheel printers function very much like an IBM Selectric typewriter. However, daisy wheel characters are molded onto a plastic or metal wheel,

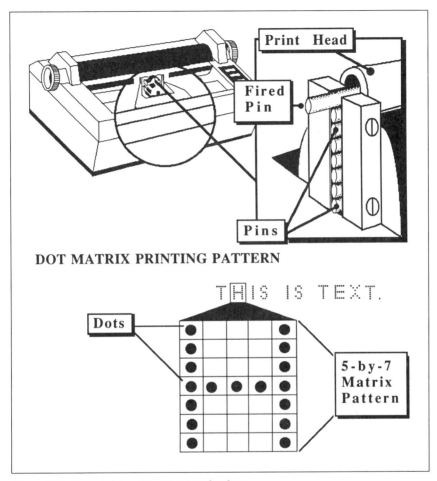

Figure 3-10. Impact dot matrix printer technology.

each character at the end of a separate spoke of a nultispoked wheel. The wheel looks very much like a daisy with many petals, but maintains the look of a wheel; hence the name "daisy wheel." The computer tells the daisy wheel printer to rotate the wheel until the appropriate molded character is in place. The molded character is then struck with a very small hammer located in the print head, which causes the character to strike an ink ribbon, placing the character's imprint onto the paper.

The major advantages of a daisy wheel printer include: (1) daisy wheels produce very high-quality text (letter quality); (2) these printers can change the typeface (style of character) of the wheel for different types of print jobs. The major disadvantages include: (1) daisy wheel printing is very noisy; (2) daisy wheel printing speed is very slow (12–90 cps); and (3) this printing technology is unable to print high-quality graphics.

Thermal-Transfer Printers

Thermal-transfer printers come in two types: serial (moving head) printers and fixed-head page printers. The serial printers, which are popular in school settings, cost less than $300. The fix-head page printers are primarily used for engineering and presentation graphics and cost between $4,000 and $10,000.

Thermal printers have three key elements in their construction: (1) a thermal print head; (2) a ribbon; and (3) paper. The thermal print head is composed of small electrical elements that selectively heat up when the printer applies electrical current. The thermal-transfer printer produces both text and graphics by passing the heated print head over a special ribbon. The thermal-transfer printing process uses a wax-coated ribbon between the thermal print head and paper. The ribbon is coated with a heat-sensitive wax film. The ribbon is heated from behind by the thermal print head, the wax-based ink coating melts, and the image is transferred to a piece of paper (see Figure 3-11).

Usually, one can't use just plain paper with these printers. For example, a smooth, low-rag bond paper is the best choice. If a school's office letterhead is on high-rag bond paper, the results will be often less than adequate. Hence, paper with a low-rag bond or polyester-base are the most appropriate. If the administrator or teacher wishes to use transparencies for staff meetings or classroom use, thermal-transfer printers can also print onto clear, polyester-based, acetate sheets.

The production of color text and graphics is one of the most practical uses for thermal-transfer printers in the classroom. Thermal-transfer printers use ribbons covered with bands of multicolored wax—usually cyan, magenta, and yellow, called the subtractive colors—to print color images. These colors can be combined to form the additive colors, which are red, green, blue, and black. When a graphic image requires more than these seven basic colors, a technique called *dithering* is used to print other color shades. The dithering process combines individual dots that are barely distinguishable to the eye and groups these dots into a matrix. Consequently, this group of tiny dots appears to the eye as a single color element. By grouping dots of varying colors in varying densities, many hues and shades of color can be produced.

Thermal-transfer printers produce color images through multiple passes of the subtractive colors on the page. In *serial* thermal-transfer printers, the thermal print head traverses the length of the print line with one color, then goes back to the beginning of the line to overprint with the next color, and so

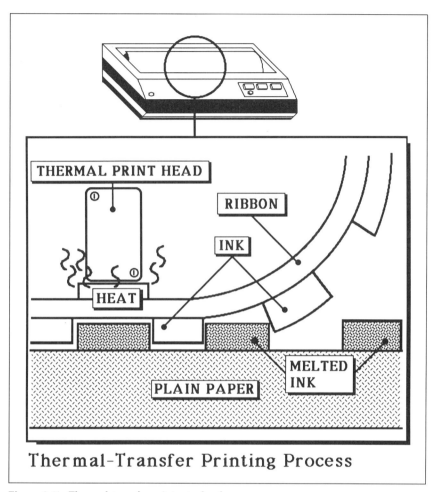

THERMAL PRINT HEAD

RIBBON

INK

HEAT

MELTED INK

PLAIN PAPER

Thermal-Transfer Printing Process

Figure 3-11. Thermal-transfer printer technology.

on, until the line is finished. The process continues until all the lines of the image are printed on the page. In *fixed-head* thermal-transfer printers, the thermal head prints the whole page in one color, then goes back to the top of the page to overprint in the next color, repeating this until all of the required colors have been printed on the page. Unfortunately, thermal-transfer ribbons wear out quickly (20 color pages per ribbon or 100 black-and-white pages per ribbon).

This printing technology has a number of advantages in the classroom. First, serial thermal-transfer printers offer the least expensive way to produce high-quality color print output. In addition, these printers offer high-resolution printing (200–300 dots per inch), producing fine letter-quality printing. Finally, the technology is very reliable during regular use. The major disadvantage to the school setting is the cost of supplies (the expensive ribbons and special paper with a smooth finish). Lastly, from a subjective viewpoint, some thermal-transfer–printer users object to the shiny paper output; some say it looks almost crayonlike.

Ink-Jet Printers

This printer technology, as the name implies, produces text and graphics by squirting very small high-precision droplets of ink directly onto the paper (droplets are about 0.06mm in size). These printers usually have print heads with multiple high-pressure ink nozzles or hoses (see Figure 3-12), which propel the individual ink droplets. Because of the extensive "plumbing" involved with making connections between ink nozzles, ink pumps, and ink reservoirs, ink-jet printers tend to be more expensive, ranging from $700 to $7,000. Unlike impact dot matrix printers, the ink-jet technology is *noncontact* technology, which basically means that the print head doesn't touch the paper during printing. There are three basic types of ink-jet printers: (1) continuous-jet; (2) drop-on-demand; and (3) phase-change.

The continuous-jet printer uses an older ink-jet technology that employs a continuous stream of ink droplets to the print head and nozzles. These printers use electricity to selectively bend (deflect) the continuous stream of ink toward or away from the page. The ink that is deflected from the white spaces of the page is diverted to an inkwell and usually reused.

Drop-on-demand ink-jet printers are much simpler in design. These printers form droplets of ink in the nozzles and eject them onto the page. The timing of each droplet ejection is controlled by the printer's microelectronics.

The relatively new ink-jet technology is the phase-change printer. This approach uses heat to liquefy solid ink pellets; the resulting droplets are then ejected from nozzles, each droplet cooled as it hits the paper. This process prevents the ink droplets from "bleeding" into the paper. The print quality is one of the best; the finished product resembles the print one would find on wedding invitations—raised, shiny, embossed print.

Most ink-jet printers can also print in color. Such printers usually have three or four separate ink nozzles for magenta, yellow, cyan, and sometimes black. The ink jet printers commonly use dithering for producing many different color shades and tones.

The major attraction for using ink-jet printer technology in the classroom is the color output. Also, the supplies for producing this type of printed output are of moderate cost. Some disadvantages in using this technology in school settings involve the cleaning process. As with anything that has to do with ink, cleaning the printer can be a nuisance and a very messy task. The

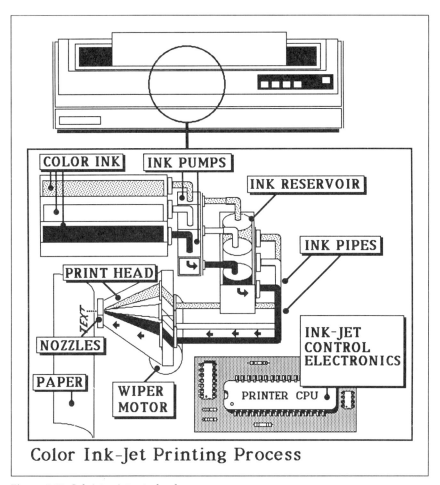

Color Ink-Jet Printing Process

Figure 3-12. Ink-jet printer technology.

print head must be kept free of dried ink to prevent clogs from developing in the nozzles. Some printers also require special paper to reduce bleeding of characters on the printed page (except in the case of phase-change ink printers). Lastly, these printers don't have the same reliability level as do other printer technologies.

Pen Plotter Printers

In educational settings, pen plotters have had limited use, being most popular in vocational and technical drafting applications. Plotters are one of the oldest printing methods for reproducing computer-generated images. This printer technology uses a mechanical system involving ink pens that actually write in order to produce text and graphics. Plotters are usually categorized by the size of the paper they accommodate for printing. A typical size is designated by one of five letters: *A* (8½-by-11-inch paper), *B* (11-by-17-inch paper), *C* (17-by-22-inch paper), *D* (24-by-36-inch paper), and *E* (36-by-48-inch paper). Most school environments use the *A* and *B* printer models. These types of plotters are small, portable, and relatively low-cost printing alternatives. However, the *E* type pen plotters tend to be large floor-type models that support engineering and related applications.

Most plotters fall into two basic groups, depending on whether the paper is moving or stationary during the printing process. The stationary plotters are referred to as "flatbed" designs. A flatbed plotter, as the name implies, contains a flat surface that holds the paper stationary while the plotter's mechanical pen, mounted on an arm or carriage bar, moves in one direction along the surface of the paper (much like a child's Etch-a-Sketch drawing board).

The second type of plotter uses a moving paper bed design for producing text and graphics. This technology moves the paper back and forth while the pen moves along an arm in one direction. The "drum" plotter is one type of moving bed system. This plotter wraps paper around a rotating drum. The drum moves the paper back and forth while a pen draws across the surface of the paper. Another variant of the moving paper bed technology uses a process that involves anchoring the paper with friction rollers on both ends. These rollers then move the paper back and forth while the pen draws on the paper surface.

Plotter technology offers a great deal of flexibility and practicality in educational settings. Pen plotters tend to be less complex than other printing technologies and are often less expensive. Also, plotters can print both text and graphics on various output media (paper, transparencies, vellum, or mylar). Finally, if high-quality graphics hard copy is needed, plotters can produce large documents with very precise detail and in many different colors. Caution regarding the use of plotters usually centers around their slow printing speed (3–20 minutes per page, depending on the complexity of the output). Similarly, because these printers use mechanical technology, their parts generally wear out more quickly and are less reliable as compared to other print technologies using fewer moving parts.

Laser Printers

State-of-the-art laser printers and their electro-optical cousins (light-emitting diode and liquid-crystal shutter printers) may radically change the future printing process of microcomputers. These technologies work much like the office photocopier, except that the input comes from the computer's system unit rather than a visible sheet of paper. The laser printer uses a light beam and a light-sensitive drum to produce text and graphics. As with dot matrix, ink jet, and thermal-transfer printers, the text and graphics are created by small dots. At the heart of laser print technology is a light-sensitive printing drum (see Figure 3-13). The drum is usually coated with a substance called selenium, which makes the drum sensitive or responsive to light. As the drum becomes light-sensitive, it develops electrical static charges in response to light.

Figure 3-13. Laser printer technology.

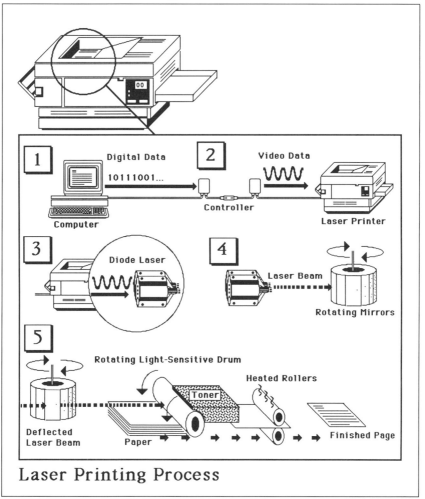

Laser Printing Process

The printing process starts when the computer sends a text or graphic image to the laser printer; after receiving this data, the printer turns the image into a representative pattern of light beams. The light beams are then focused by mirrors onto the surface of the light-sensitive drum. This process actually knocks off tiny electrical charges, leaving only highly charged static electrical fields on the drum. The electrical fields represent dots of the text or graphic image; as each row of dots is formed, a motor advances the drum by one row and the light source writes out the next line of the image. When finished, the drum surface contains the electrical equivalent of the entire image. As the drum rotates, it passes over a tank of toner (fine particles that are attracted to static or electrical charges). The highly charged static fields on the drum attract and hold the toner. As the drum rotates, filling the surface with toner, the drum comes into contact with a sheet of paper that has been electrically charged to a higher degree than the drum. The toner then "jumps" to the paper surface in the same way clothing sticks together from static cling after finishing a cycle in the dryer. A number of heated rollers than melt the toner to the paper to produce the finished page.

This printer technology can provide schools with many printing options and capabilities. Laser printers typically offer 300-dots-per-inch resolution. At this level, quality of the printed image to the naked eye looks comparable to professional phototypesetters. This resolution can enable a school to make high-quality graphic images of black-and-white photographs for yearbooks or newsletters. Most laser printers also offer a wide choice of type fonts and graphics options, enabling a classroom or school to combine text and graphics in virtually any way possible. Similarly, the speed of the laser printer is very fast (7 to 10 pages per minute once the image is received in RAM). Also, the printing process is very quiet as compared to the noise of dot matrix or daisy wheel technologies. Unfortunately, the price for this print quality, speed, and flexibility is high. Prices for laser printers can range from $2,000 to $10,000 and up, depending on the printer's features. For example, moving the printer's intelligence (the CPU) and image-storage capability (RAM) from the printer to the computer reduces the cost of laser printers. However, these laser printers are usually much slower and have very limited graphics capability. Conversely, more expensive laser printers with 600-dots-per-inch resolution usually require quadrupling the amount of memory in the printer. Similarly, these printers include software called page description languages, which provide full-page graphics printing and more flexible print features. These extra features result in higher prices. Finally, most current laser printers don't offer color printing. Laser printers offering color printing will probably start around $12,000 and won't be available for a few years.

Printer Spoolers, Buffers, and Interfacing. Because almost all of the printer technologies previously discussed are mechanical devices and computers are primarily electronic devices, printers operate far slower than computers.

This design factor is one reason why many microcomputers can't be used while printing documents. The computer sends information in small "chunks" to the printer, allowing the device the time to receive, process, and print the information. Hence, the computer is usually busy sending small chunks of information to the printer during the entire printing process.

Spoolers and *buffers* free the computer to do other tasks while the printer is busy printing documents. Spoolers and buffers can take the form of both hardware or software. Either way, spoolers and buffers must have sections of RAM dedicated for their specific use. Basically, spoolers and buffers receive information from the computer as fast as the computer can send it. The information is then stored in the spooler's or buffer's own space (which may include assigned computer RAM and/or the buffers own RAM) until the printer is ready to print. This frees the computer's RAM to do other tasks. The spooler or buffer then sends the data to the printer only as fast as the printer's mechanical system can accept them. Spoolers and buffers range in size from 8 to 256K of RAM and can cost from $100 to $1,000. Many printers come with built-in hardware buffers. Conversely, some spoolers are actually software programs that divide up the computer's own memory to use as a buffer for storing information to be printed. These software packages cost from $25 to $150.

Making connections between the computer and printer involve the identification of two major components: (1) right cable connectors or printer card and (2) identification of the type of computer I/O port the printer will use. Cables come in many different sizes and configurations. It usually isn't enough to just physically connect all the cables to the computer. The wires in the cable must match up with the pins or wires in the computer's I/O port. This allows proper communication between the computer and printer. Similarly, in order to communicate, some printers require a printer interface card to be plugged into a slot in the computer. This requires that the card be properly assigned to a specific slot and seated properly into the computer's I/O slot.

The second major consideration for connecting a printer to a computer involves identifying which type of computer I/O port to use. Microcomputers usually use a serial or parallel port for passing information to and from the printer. These ports are multiple-pin sockets that accept printer cable connectors. Serial printers use a serial port using an RS-232 cable (see Figure 3-3). Parallel printers connect through a parallel port using a Centronics or Dataproducts parallel cable (see Figure 3-3). Most computers provide the option of using either serial or parallel ports for communicating with printers.

COMPUTER DISPLAY SCREENS

One of the most obvious computer output devices is the computer's display screen. Display screens, or monitors, are peripheral devices that display information sent from the computer's system unit to the user. Hence, they are referred to as output devices. Although many low-cost computers can be easily connected to a television, the resolution and sharpness of the picture is usually not as good as a high-resolution computer monitor. If students use the computer on a regular basis, a high-resolution display monitor is usually essential. For example, classroom applications involving moderate to heavy word processing require that a monitor produce a bright, well-contrasted, sharp display. If the TV in question can't produce this kind of display, don't use it. Otherwise, students' eyes will suffer, especially under continuous classroom use. If a TV is to be used, it is necessary to convert the computer's digital video signal to an analog signal a TV can understand. This is done by connecting a radio frequency (RF) modulator between the computer and TV (see Figure 3-3). This device converts a computer's digital signal into an analog signal that a TV can understand.

The alternatives to TV screens are dedicated computer monitors and computer monitor-TV receivers. Most dedicated computer monitors don't contain TV tuners (the part of the TV that selects channels); thus they can't be used for watching TV. Similarly, dedicated monitors use a special type of video signal that can directly receive digital video signals from the computer. This signal is called a composite video signal. Hence, there is no need to have an RF modulator connected between the computer and monitor. Dedicated monitors are connected directly to the computer by a single cable. Another type of dedicated monitor is called an RGB monitor. This monitor receives three separate digital signals from the computer. These signals include red, green, and blue — hence the name RGB monitor. These monitors can also be connected directly to the computer through special RGB video ports on the computer. Monitor-receivers are special TV models that are equipped with a tuner plus a direct connection for a computer's digital video signal. This allows the monitor-receiver to be used for both computer display and TV viewing. However, these monitor-receivers are more expensive than dedicated monitors or TV.

The size of a monitor's screen is measured diagonally across the screen's surface. Typical screen sizes are 9, 12, and 13 inches. Any of these sizes are fine for most instructional applications. Some display screens show very narrow columns of text, only 40 characters wide. These types of monitors are fine for younger student populations. For example, many instructional software programs for young children utilize large, easy-to-read characters or limit textual information to only a few lines. However, when students are dealing with large amounts of textual information, as in word processing applications, the screen should be able to display at least 80 columns of characters and no less than 24 lines of text. This allows the student to manipulate textual information much more easily.

Both dedicated and monitor-receivers can display information in either monochrome (one color, usually green or white on a black background) or color. For maximum crispness and legibility, especially with word processing applications, monochrome, or single color, monitors are preferable. Green-only or amber-only monitors are the most common in educational settings, although the latter is more expensive because flicker-free amber images are more difficult to produce. Full-color monitors are popular for young student populations, the reason being that many early-childhood software programs use color schemes as part of the teaching process. Furthermore, many educational software programs now use graphic screens to present instructional information; so color monitors really enhance the presentation of these color-oriented programs. RGB monitors should be used for obtaining the best color display, largely because of their three separate video signals. Dedicated color monitors, which use the composite video signal, will lose some resolution when presenting graphics. Similarly, text characters will lose considerable crispness with composite monitors, tending to blur against the background.

COMPUTERIZED SPEECH

Speech synthesis can offer individuals with disabilities a variety of alternatives for interacting and participating in educational settings. Individuals with impaired speech, for example, may utilize speech synthesis as a means of learning or improving articulations skills. For nonspeaking individuals, speech synthesis can replace lost voice and provide an augmentative communication device for self-expression. In addition, visually impaired individuals, using speech synthesis as a voice output device, can have access to textual information they have difficulty reading or are unable to read on the computer monitor's screen. Speech output can also provide a natural medium for communicating content information to children with cognitive and/or language disabilities.

The three most common types of speech technology presently in use in classrooms include: (1) text-to-speech synthesis; (2) digitized speech; and (3) linear predictive coding. Each of these speech technologies has unique qualities and offers both distinctive advantages and limitations under certain classroom situations. The following paragraphs describe each technology and its capabilities.

Text-to-Speech Synthesis

Currently the most common form of computerized speech technology in education and rehabilitation settings are text-to-speech schemes. This speech technology doesn't store or contain speech units, such as words or sentences; instead, it defines and stores the sounds of the English language as a set of rules or procedures. This accounts for the minimal memory requirements to text-to-speech technology. The rules describing sounds are called phonemes. Typically, text-to-speech systems program hundreds of such pronunciation rules to describe the English language.

In order to produce text-to-speech synthesis, computers must contain either their own built-in hardware sound chips (Apple IIgs, Macintosh, Tandy 1000 computers) or include an add-on peripheral board (Apple II+, IIe, IIc series and MS-DOS computers). There are a number of third-party speech peripherals for Apple and MS-DOS computers. Examples include Echo/Cricket Synthesizers by Street Electronics, Ufonic Voice System by Educational Technology, and Votrax Personal Speech system by Votrax International. These text-to-speech synthesizers generate speech through the use of mathematical models that analyze a word and translate the word into the appropriate phonemes. After analyzing the word, the phonemes generate sound and pitch codes so that the speech synthesizer can pronounce the word.

Text-to-speech synthesis has two distinct advantages in classroom situations. First, because the technology only stores pronunciation rules, not actual voice recordings, it is extremely compact, requiring minimal computer memory. In addition, because text-to-speech schemes contain a comprehensive set of phoneme codes, it has the potential to speak virtually any word encountered. This makes the technology very flexible. As such, its flexibility is advantageous for use with talking word processors that must deal with any text entered by student users.

The major disadvantage of text-to-speech technology relates to its sound quality. Robotic sounding voice output is common with the use of this speech synthesis approach. Hence, the degree of an individual's disability combined with their auditory needs can put distinct limits on the applicability of this form of computerized speech.

Digitized Speech

Digitized speech technology is very different from text-to-speech approaches. This technology doesn't store or contain phoneme rules to speak the English language. Instead, it stores the actual words or sentences in the form of digitized sounds. As a result, this speech technique requires very large amounts of memory when storing words and phrases. A combination of computer hardware and software permits the user to speak into a microphone using normal speech. The computer then samples the speech and converts each word or phrase into digital data.

To produce digitized speech a computer system must include a peripheral device that is capable of digitizing and playing the speech. There are a number of third-party sound digitizers for microcomputers. Examples include MacRecorder by Farallon Computing, FutureSound by Applied Visions, SuperSonic Digitizer by MDIdeas, and SoundBuster by Yam Educational Software.

Digitized speech technology has the advantage of producing very realistic sounding speech. In classroom applications involving vocabulary and foreign language skills, in which the quality of speech reproduction is important, digitized speech offers the user clear and natural sounding speech articulation. In addition, when appropriate hardware and software combinations are utilized, digitized speech can provide a very flexible environment for mixing and recording prerecorded sound sequences.

Currently, the major reason for the limited use of digitized speech in classroom settings is the technology is extremely memory-intensive. For example, 30 seconds of digitized speech can require over 140K of disk space. Even with speech-compression schemes, the storage requirements are often beyond the present limits of many school-based microcomputer systems. As more powerful and less expensive computer hardware enters the school market, educators will likely see more use of digitized speech technology in instructional software applications.

Linear Predictive Coding

Linear predictive coding (LPC), which many professionals often refer to as custom-encoded speech, spans the gap between text-to-speech and digitized speech techniques. As such, this technology utilizes a combination of speech digitizing and mathematical modeling to reconstruct and produce speech. The resulting blend of technologies greatly reduces memory requirements for creating speech.

In order to produce LPC speech, a combination of specialized computer hardware is required. These hardware devices include a sound digitizer and a sound chip or add-on speech peripheral card. The digitizing hardware provides for the recording of normal speech and converts each word or phrase into digital sound data. In addition, LPC technology compresses each digital sound, greatly reducing storage requirements. In order to reproduce the speech, a specialized speech chip or synthesizer is required to reconstruct and translate the digital data into appropriate sounds.

Many software publishers take advantage of the minimal memory requirements of LPC and include custom-encoded words and phrases in their instructional software. LPC technology is commonly used in reading, language arts, and mathematics software.

The speech produced by LPC is of much better quality than text-to-speech methods. However, it is not as clear and natural sounding as digitized speech techniques. Still, students often find LPC speech more recognizable than text-to-speech approaches. Finally, LPC software programs are limited to speaking only those words that have been prerecorded and digitized for unique applications. Hence, this technology is not nearly as flexible as text-to-speech methods.

SUMMARY

When planning computer programs, educators need access to practical background information regarding the workings of computer technology. Through nontechnical explanations on such subjects as the computer system unit, CPU, microcomputer memory, and computer I/O communications, the educator can better understand the strengths and weaknesses of computer technology. Such discussions can eliminate much confusion over the technical jargon, dynamics, and potential of microcomputer technology in education. In addition, program planners may consider exploring information on the practical applications of microcomputers in classroom settings. Gaining information on current applications of computer technology is helpful for planning effective instructional programming. Similarly, teachers and administrators should also consider developing a knowledge of computer peripheral devices and how they really work within the context of a typical school microcomputer system. This knowledge can help school planners evaluate the capabilities and benefits of adding additional computer resources. Consequently, by developing an understanding of both the operational and practical applications of computer equipment, administrators, teachers, and support staff can more effectively plan for the implementation of computer-based instruction.

Chapter 4 will build on concepts presented thus far, exploring the workings of additional computer hardware that may support the special-needs classroom. Similarly, for educators, a number of practical methods and procedures will be presented for planning and managing the implementation of microcomputers in a variety of classroom settings.

What follows are sample review questions and some follow-up activities students may wish to pursue. These activities can be used to further develop the concepts and practical applications presented in this chapter.

REVIEW QUESTIONS

1. What is a microcomputer's system unit? Why is each part important to the function of the microcomputer?
2. What are the classroom advantages and disadvantages for using the following printers in the classroom: (1) dot matrix printer; (2) thermal-transfer printer; and (3) daisy wheel printer?
3. What are ROM and RAM? Why are they different? How are they expressed?
4. What is digital data? How is it stored in a computer's memory? Why is it different from human memory?
5. How does the system unit transfer information between different parts of the computer?

6. What is microcomputer input/output (I/O)? What are the major types of I/O ports?
7. What is a peripheral device?
8. What are the major differences between magnetic and optical storage media?
9. What is a floppy diskette?

SUGGESTED FOLLOW-UP ACTIVITIES

1. Visit or call a local school using microcomputers. Identify the school's procedures for handling diskettes and managing their software in either the computer lab or classroom. Are there any problems?

2. Visit or call a local school using microcomputers. List the major types of computers and peripheral devices being used. What types of instructional applications are they being used for? Are there any instructional problems or limitations due to the type of equipment being used? Is the school planning any future purchases of equipment? If so, why?

3. Obtain access to a microcomputer. List and identify the parts of the system unit and associated peripherals. Based on the list of features, describe the possible instructional capabilities of this microcomputer.

CHAPTER 4

Using Microcomputers in the Classroom

Chapter 3 described the internal workings of the microcomputer and covered peripheral storage devices and common printer technologies. With this knowledge one is ready to explore additional microcomputer components that can be beneficial to the classroom. The first section of this chapter will explore a number of alternative ways for students and teachers to interact with the computer. This introduction includes a variety of alternative computer input devices that provide various methods and tactile approaches for enhancing student-microcomputer interaction. In addition, this chapter will provide educators with a number of techniques for planning and implementing microcomputers in the classroom. Typical topics include guidelines and procedures for computer lighting and space allocations, appropriate furniture, microcomputer security, and computer scheduling techniques. These and other topics will provide the teacher with practical techniques for using microcomputers in the special-needs classroom.

ALTERNATIVE INPUT DEVICES: SUPPLEMENTING THE KEYBOARD

Many student populations, whether learning-disabled, mentally retarded, physically disabled, or sensory-impaired, have the potential to benefit from alternative input devices. Alternative input devices allow the user to enter information into the computer by means other than the traditional keyboard; they have three basic information input functions that provide: (1) a physical hardware link to the computer's system unit for information input; (2) a sensory input environment between the user and computer (tactile, voice, etc.); and (3) user control over computer operation. This section will cover the mainstream of alternative input devices, specifically mouse systems, touch-sensitive screens, tablets and pads, and adaptive keyboards and switches.

MOUSE TECHNOLOGY

Mouse technology is not new. The technology was really legitimized on the microcomputer when Apple Computer introduced an integrated mouse system with the Macintosh personal computer. Since then, many manufacturers have developed similar devices for their personal computers. A mouse is a small device that the user rolls around a flat surface next to the computer. The function of the mouse is to point at and pick text and objects on the computer screen. A pointer (small arrow shape on the screen) is used to simulate and follow the movement of the mouse. When the user moves the mouse, the pointer on the screen moves correspondingly. The user makes

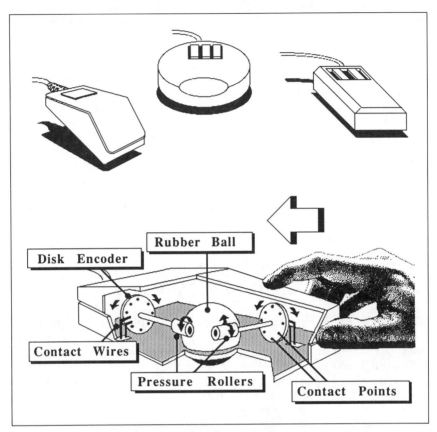

Figure 4-1. The operation of mechanical mouse technology.

selections by clicking one or more buttons located on the top surface of the mouse. Mouse systems usually connect to the computer's system unit through a serial port or an internal slot. As alternative input devices go, the mouse is one of the best computer hardware devices for pointing functions. For example, students can effortlessly pick and move graphic objects in a drawing program; or they can quickly select parts of sentence, whole paragraphs, or fragments, including spaces before and after a sentence in a document for word processing applications. However, a mouse is not the best type of alternative input device for freehand graphics drawing or writing; a stylus device or keyboard often proves less frustrating for students.

There are three basic technologies used in the construction of a mouse: (1) mechanical; (2) optical; and (3) opto-mechanical. Figures 4-1, 4-2, and 4-3 present the internal workings of each mouse technology.

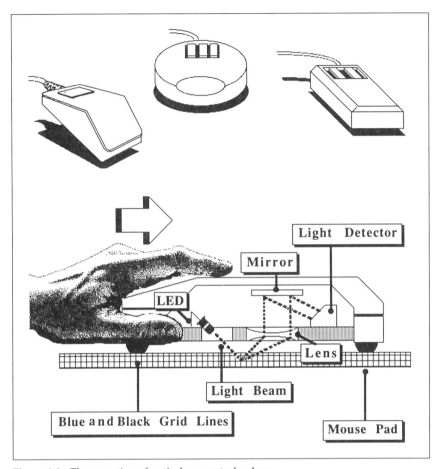

Figure 4-2. The operation of optical mouse technology.

Mechanical Mouse Technology

A *mechanical* mouse uses three mechanical parts in order to accomplish the task of pointing, hence the name. These parts include a rubber ball, pressure rollers, and an encoder disk (see Figure 4-1). The small rubber ball is seated in a slightly smaller hole on the bottom surface of the mouse and, as a result, a portion of the ball hangs out of the hole just touching the flat surface under the mouse. This ball is used to sense the pointing movement and direction of the mouse. For example, as one moves the mouse across the flat surface, the hard rubber ball naturally rolls in the same direction. Two pressure rollers,

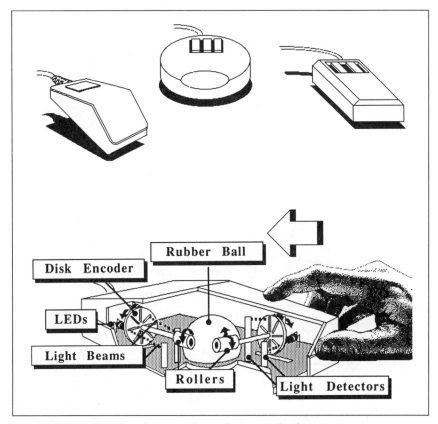

Figure 4-3. The operation of opto-mechanical mouse technology.

placed perpendicular to each other, turn as a result of movement from the ball. At the end of each roller is attached a flat disk called an encoder. These encoders rotate in conjunction with the movement of the attached rollers. The encoders have a number of contact points on their rims. The contact points touch wire contacts located near the encoder rims. This produces signals that the microcomputer translates into screen pointer movement.

Optical Mouse Technology

Optical mouse technology eliminates the mechanical parts of the previous mouse design. An optical mouse uses light, a lens, and mirrors to indicate pointing movement and direction (see Figure 4-2). Unlike the mechanical mouse, optical devices must operate on a special reflective pad surface. The surface of the reflective mouse pad contains very small grid lines that look very similar to graph paper. Grid lines in one direction are painted blue, and lines in the other direction are painted black. The bottom surface of the optical mouse contains two small light-emitting diodes called LEDs. These LEDs each emit a different kind of light—one LED produces red light that all blue grid lines absorb; and the other LED emits an infrared light that all black grid lines absorb. This light-absorption process allows the mouse to detect movement. Each break in the light source, produced by crossing blue and black grid lines, represents a specific distance that the mouse has traveled. The number of light breaks and colors give direction and distance information that the computer can use to determine the position of the screen's pointer.

Opto-Mechanical Mouse Technology

An *opto-mechanical* mouse is a combination of the mechanical and optical mouse technologies. The opto-mechanical mouse uses the same components as does the mechanical mouse, but it uses different encoder contacts for detecting mouse movement. Unlike the optical mouse, the opto-mechanical system doesn't use a reflective pad surface. However, the encoders on the opto-mechanical system do use LEDs for detecting motion. As Figure 4-3 depicts, LEDs on one side of the encoders emit light, and a light-sensitive device on the other side of the encoders detect the LED's light through evenly spaced slots on the encoders' surface. The light that is detected through the slots is translated into electronic signals that the computer can understand. These electronic signals represent the direction and motion of the screen's pointer.

Each of these three mouse technologies can be effective in classroom settings. However, the optical mouse tends to be more reliable due to the elimination of moving mechanical parts. Each mouse system requires a flat surface for proper operation. The classroom location for the mouse should be free of dust, chalk, and other pollutants, all of which have a nasty habit of clogging the surface of the ball and pressure rollers inside the mouse. After a few weeks of regular use, pollutants collect on the surface of the mouse's rollers, greatly impairing their performance. Hence, regular mouse-cleaning schedules are necessary in classroom settings. Cotton swabs lightly dipped in isopropyl rubbing alcohol work well for cleaning the surface of the mouse's rollers.

TOUCH-SCREEN TECHNOLOGY

Like the mouse, the function involved with a touch-screen is to point. But unlike the mouse, touch-screens use an intuitive and natural pointing device—the user's finger. The intuitive input process makes touch-screen technology a very natural and direct method for students to interact with the microcomputer. The pointing process usually requires a finger's touch on a particular part of the computer screen's surface. The touch-screen then uses its electronics to interpret the exact position of the finger's contact with the computer screen. The position is converted into *x-y* coordinates (horizontal and vertical positions of the contact point), which are sent to the computer software program using the touch-screen. The software program interprets the coordinates and converts them into movements for the screen's pointer or cursor. Similarly, these movements can be interpreted by the software to perform software commands, select menu options, or even follow commands for drawing graphics on the computer screen.

There are two touch-screen technologies presently being used in school settings: light-emitting diode (LED) touch-screen and capacitive touch-screen. Each of these screen technologies can either take the form of optional add-on peripheral devices, or they can be built into the computer's own screen or monitor. With the exception of monitors having built-in touch-screen capability, add-on touch-screens connect to a computer system unit through the game port, serial port, or internal expansion slot.

Light-Emitting Diode Touch-Screens

Light-emitting diode (LED) touch-screen technology basically involves a process by which the user's finger breaks a continuous stream of invisible infrared light beams (see Figure 4-4). The touch-screen consists of a square frame placed over the computer's monitor. Along the top and one side of the frame are rows of LEDs. These LEDs emit a continuous stream of invisible infrared light. Along the bottom and other side of the frame are light detectors that receive the invisible light beams. Both the LEDs and light detectors create a matrix of light beams. The matrix of light beams represent *x* (horizontal) and *y* (vertical) screen coordinates. When a user's finger points at the screen, it breaks the matrix of light beams. The touch-screen's electronics then obtain the *x-y* coordinates and send them to the computer. The computer then calculates the position of the finger contact on the screen.

Capacitive Touch-Screens

Capacitive touch-screen technology utilizes the user's finger to complete an electronic circuit located on the touch-screen's surface. The touch-screen usually has one or more transparent plastic coatings on its surface. These transparent coatings have the ability to conduct electricity, similar to copper wire in an electrical switch. When the user's finger applies pressure to the transparent coatings, the conductive coatings touch each other and connect or complete the circuit—just like two copper wires completing a circuit for

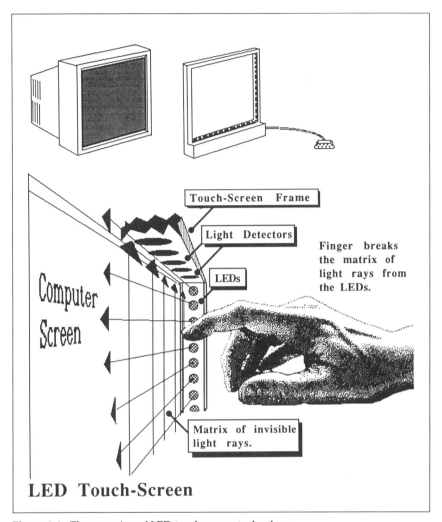

Figure 4-4. The operation of LED touch-screen technology.

an electrical switch. The transparent plastic sheets represent either x or y coordinates. The touch-screen sends the coordinates to the computer software program for processing.

A variation of the capacitive touch-screen technology uses a computer screen with a surface bearing a single transparent coating that has the ability to conduct electricity (see Figure 4-5). When a finger touches the conductive surface coating, current or electricity running through the screen's transparent coating is drained off through the user's finger. Special electronic sensors placed at the four corners of the screen detect the current drain and determine the position of the finger on the screen. The position is then sent to the computer software for processing.

Although touch-screens offer an intuitive method for students to access the computer, a few problems do arise with the use of this technology. When using touch-screen technology in classroom settings, consider such factors

Figure 4-5. The operation of capacitive touch-screen technology.

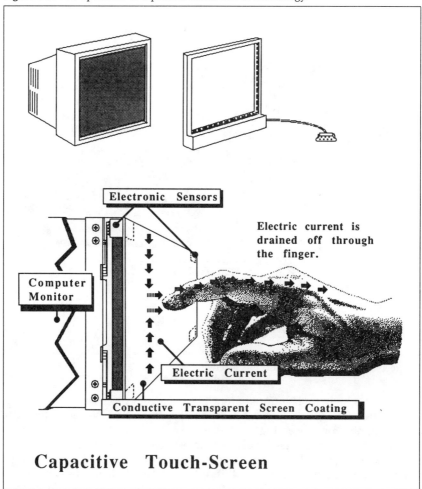

as student fingerprints, screen glare, and viewing angle. As with many classroom activities, leaving fingerprints is a common occurrence. When children use a touch-screen they leave fingerprints on the screen surface, which increases screen glare. Screen glare produces reflections and greatly affects the readability of the computer screen. Because many schools don't have computer screens with nonglare surfaces, the glare problem can become enhanced. As a result, classroom applications usually require a regular surface cleaning of the touch-screen.

Finally, improper viewing angles also cause problems. For example, a common viewing-angle problem called the *parallax phenomenon* results when a touch-screen frame is mounted on the rim of a computer monitor and a gap is produced between the touch-screen surface and the computer monitor surface. When a student looks at the touch-screen from an angle, most finger contacts with the screen overshoot the required contact point. The combination of wide viewing angles and the gap between the computer monitor and touch-screen produces a finger-contact point that is usually outside of the real contact point, accidentally producing incorrect or unintentional readings by the touch-screen. Some touch-screens eliminate the problem by mounting the transparent touch-screen surface directly on the face of the computer monitor. Despite these minor problems, touch-screen technology has much to offer as a computer input device for student populations.

GRAPHICS TABLET TECHNOLOGY

A very popular input device for classroom microcomputers is the graphics tablet. This peripheral device can be used in a variety of classroom applications. For example, students can use graphics tablets for operating game software, painting, drawing, keyboard input, and even writing. A majority of computer graphics tablets reproduce common paper-and-pencil functions by measuring pen movement through various methods involving microelectronics. Basically, the process translates any type of pen or stylus pointing (analog information) into the 0s and 1s (digital information) the computer can understand. Most graphics tablets consist of a flat drawing surface, analogous to a piece of paper, and a pointing device such as a stylus, analogous to a pencil or pen. In a majority of painting and drawing activities, the graphics tablet tends to be the most natural computer input device for students. In general, most graphics tablets offer greater drawing flexibility to students in painting or drawing applications that does mechanical mouse technology. The three most common types of technology used in graphics tablets are electro-magnetic, membrane, and acoustic systems.

Electro-Magnetic Graphics Tablet

Electro-magnetic graphics tablets contain three main parts: (1) a pen or stylus; (2) a flat tablet surface; (3) and control electronics (see Figure 4-6). The pen or stylus transmits a continuous stream of electronic signals out of its tip. The electronic signals produce an invisible magnetic field around the pen's point. The function of the flat tablet surface is to detect these magnetic signals emanating from the pen tip, in much the way antennas receive broadcast signals. Hidden under the surface of the tablet are hundreds of long, thin, metal strips that are laid out in horizontal (x coordinates) and vertical (y coordinates) directions, producing a grid pattern of intersecting metal strips—much like the intersecting lines on graph paper. This grid pattern acts as a receiving grid for the pen's magnetic field. Finally, the graphics tablet microelectronics control the electronic signals in the pen tip and convert the strongest magnetic fields received by the tablet surface into x and y coordinates. These coordinates are sent to computer software for determining the pen's exact location. The computer receives graphics tablet information from either the system unit's game port, serial port, or bus (see Chapter 3).

Figure 4-6. The operation of electro-magnetic graphics tablet technology.

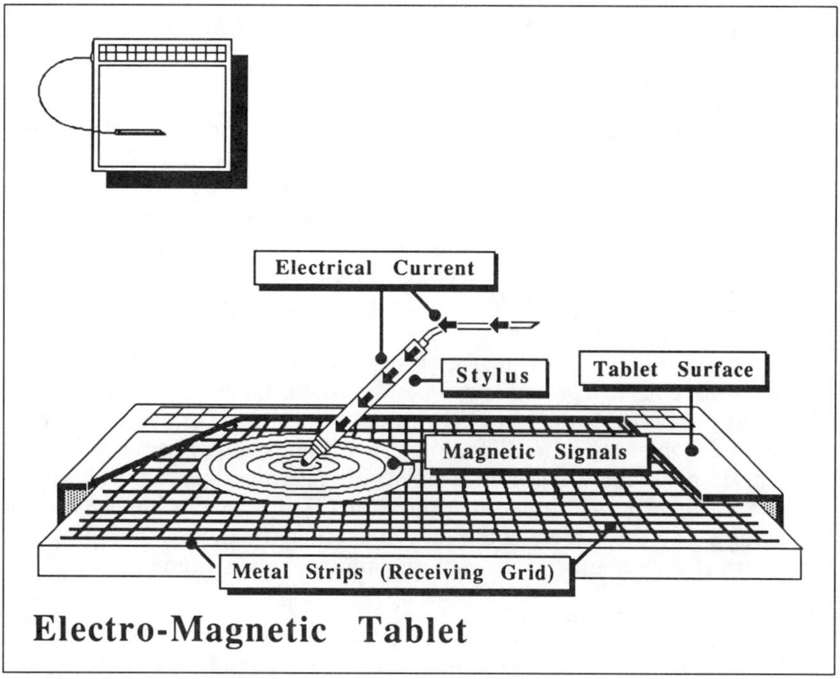

Electro-Magnetic Tablet

Membrane Graphics Tablet

Membrane graphics tablets consist of two electrically conductive surfaces separated by tiny spacers of non-conductive material (see Figure 4-7). These two surfaces correspond to x and y coordinate values. Each conductive surface has electrical current running through its surface. When the two surfaces come into contact from the pressure of a stylus, a small electrical current flows from the bottom surface to the top surface. The graphics tablet microelectronics measure and convert the values from the two surfaces into digital coordinates that are sent to the computer software. The computer receives graphics tablet information from either the system unit's game port, serial port, or bus.

Figure 4-7. The operation of membrane graphics tablet technology.

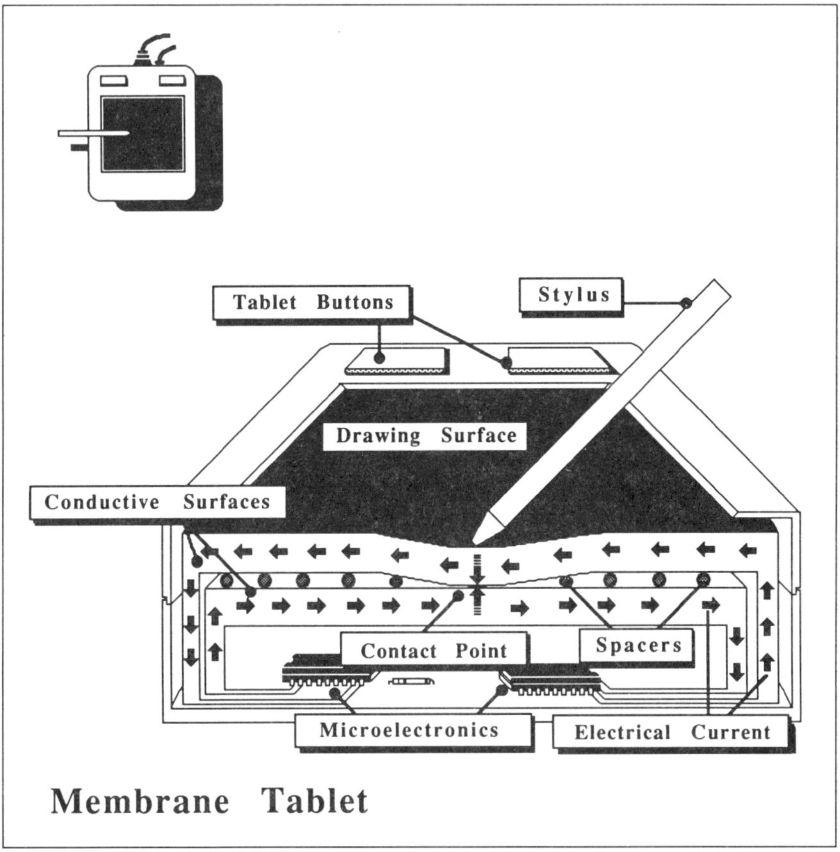

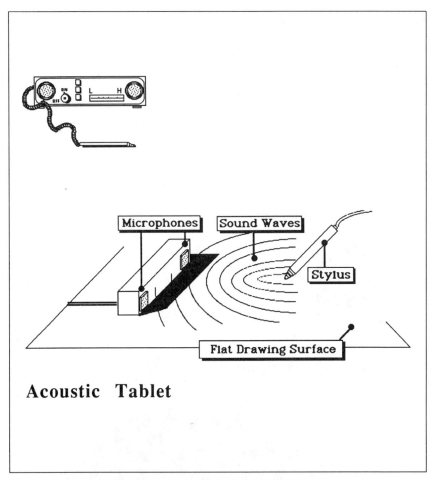

Figure 4-8. The operation of acoustic graphics tablet technology.

Acoustic Graphics Tablet

The *acoustic* graphics tablet technology does not require a tablet surface to operate. Instead, pen movement is determined by sound waves emanating from a transmitting pen or stylus. The acoustic system uses a special stylus that transmits very high-frequency sound waves from its tip (see Figure 4-8). Because the sound frequencies are so high, the human ear is unable to hear them. However, special microelectronics and microphones can receive the high-frequency sounds and can be attached to any work area, including a desk top or even the rim of the computer screen. The signal strength of the high-frequency sounds is measured at each microphone to indicate distance of the stylus. A process called triangulation is used to determine the exact location of the stylus. Basically, the triangulation process uses trigonometry principles to mark the stylus area with imaginary triangles for measuring distances and determining the exact stylus position. The acoustic system's microphones and microelectronics send stylus position data to the computer software through the system unit's game port, serial port, or bus (see Chapter 2).

Each of the preceding graphics tablet technologies can be used effectively in classroom settings. However, in developing effective classroom computer graphics applications, one must also purchase graphics software for operating and controlling the graphics tablet. Some graphics tablet manufacturers provide drawing software with the purchase of a tablet. In addition, many commercial software vendors also sell graphics software packages. Graphics tablet technology in combination with appropriate software can greatly enhance classroom applications requiring intensive computer graphics work such as freehand drawing or painting. Good graphics software should provide students with a complete set of easy-to-use drawing tools for creating boxes, lines, circles, polygons, color palettes, text, and special effects. However, a word of caution is necessary. Some graphics software packages use their own picture-file formats to save drawings to disk. Because of the wide variety of picture-file formats being used in schools, many graphics packages are incompatible with other software applications. In addition, most graphics software packages contain special programs, called drivers, that enable the software to communicate with different types of graphics tablets. Because of the wide variety of graphics tablets available on the market, most commercial software packages cannot always include every graphics tablet driver in their programs. As a result, graphics software can be incompatible with some manufacturers' graphics tablets. Therefore, before considering the purchase of either a graphics tablet or drawing software package, check with vendors on computer hardware and software compatibility issues.

ADAPTIVE KEYBOARD TECHNOLOGY

For many individuals, the process of interacting with a microcomputer normally involves the use of a traditional keyboard, mouse, or other similar pointing device. In addition, most of the microcomputers and commercial software applications they operate also expect the user to input information by typing on the keyboard. However, many disabled student populations don't have the physical or cognitive capabilities to effectively use many of these traditional methods of computer input. As a result, a wide variety of adaptive keyboard devices are now available for unique student populations, so that they can access microcomputer technology without the use of traditional computer keyboards. The implementation of adaptive keyboard technology into school environments can greatly enhance the learning opportunities for preschool, early elementary, learning-disabled, mentally retarded, sensory-impaired, and severely physically disabled student populations. Two kinds of adaptive keyboard technology presently support special-needs students: keyboard emulators and alternative keyboards.

Keyboard Emulators

Keyboard emulators provide the ability to connect and communicate with the computer using several different types of input devices other than the computer keyboard. These input devices may include expanded keyboards, and single or multiple switches. Figure 4-9 illustrates various functions of keyboard emulators. In addition, keyboard emulators send input device information to the computer without the need for specifically written software programs. Keyboard emulators electronically simulate the operation of microcomputer keyboard input. In fact, as far as the microcomputer knows, any information it receives has come from the regular keyboard. This information input process is often referred to as "transparent" operation. The major advantage to transparent operation is that disabled student populations can use a wide variety of special input devices and can run regular off-the-shelf software applications. This keyboard emulator feature eliminates the high cost of writing and supporting specialized software applications for the handicapped. Similarly, transparent operation provides a large source of useful mainstream business and educational software applications for disabled populations. Finally, most keyboard emulators provide a variety of input methods for assisting disabled populations with the task of entering information. For example, with a single-switch user, a scanning or encoding input method can be used for entering information into the computer. The user can input information using a scanning system, morse code, or other scheme depending on the emulator. These and other input methods all provide a means through which a single- or multiple-switch user can enter the variety of different characters found on the keyboard. These alternative input methods provide assistance to the mechanical processes, by which disabled users must enter information, via specialized input devices.

Traditional computer keyboards are essentially composed of a set of electrical switches. When these switches are turned on or off, they send electronic signals to the computer system unit. A switch is turned on by closing the switch and turned off by opening the switch. Each switch is actually represented by a key on the keyboard; therefore, every switch can be turned on or off by applying pressure to the appropriate key on the

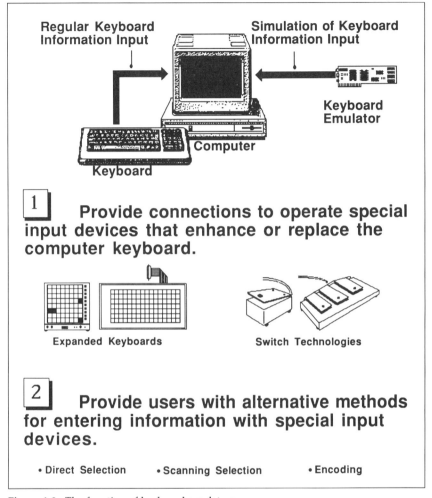

Figure 4-9. The function of keyboard emulators.

keyboard. When a key is pressed, it sends a specific electronic signal to the computer. The system unit then processes the electronic signal and determines which key was pressed.

Alternative Keyboards

An alternative keyboard is basically just another set of switches that replaces or supplements the traditional computer keyboard. Adaptive keyboard devices have keys that are specially designed for easy use by physically disabled individuals. Unlike keyboard emulators, alternative keyboards don't simulate the function of the keyboard; instead, they simply plug into the system unit and operate the microcomputer in the same manner as the standard keyboard. Figure 4-10 illustrates various functions of alternative keyboards. However, a key feature of alternative keyboards is the layout and design of the keys or switches on the keyboard surface. For example, some alternative keyboards have individual keys placed two or more inches apart on a flat surface, so that unintentional movements, caused by involuntary tremors or movement, don't cause an unnecessary switch closure. In addition, other adaptive keyboards replace finger movement with eye gaze. By look at characters on the keyboard, a physically handicapped user can send the same switch signals to the computer that would be sent by the regular computer keyboard. Reflected light is used to detect eye movement and determine key inputs. There are many different designs for alternative keyboards, but they all provide the basic function of facilitating keyboard input by physically disabled persons through specially designed switches or keys. This is usually accomplished by either enlarging the size of the keys; adjusting the pressure or sensitivity required to close a switch; providing different tactile and sensory means for operating switches; expanding the number of keys; or altering the physical location of the keys on the keyboard surface.

ADAPTIVE SWITCH TECHNOLOGY

This section describes adaptive switch technology, which allow severely handicapped users access to microcomputers and adapted electronic toys. These devices are being utilized in classroom settings for play, therapeutic training, speech and communications, and mobility and microcomputer interfacing. To begin, a switch is a hardware input device designed to be used in place of the computer's regular keyboard, and it provides individuals with motor-control problems the ability to operate a computer, communication device, or other electrical device (see Figure 4-11). Switch operation is straightforward. It either opens or closes an electrical circuit, controlling the flow of electricity to some electronic device—much like a light switch in a house that turns the lights on (closed circuit) or turns the lights off (open circuit). One of the most important features of adaptive switches is how each controls the opening or closing of the electrical circuit. It is the method of operation that makes a switch useful and adaptable to specific needs of severely handicapped individuals. There are a variety of adaptive switches available to classroom settings. Some include: (1) sound switches that open and close a circuit through verbal or other sound sources; (2) myoelectric switches that open and close a circuit by sensing electrical current produced

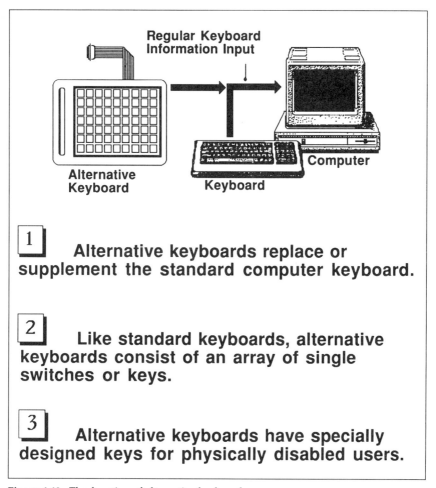

Figure 4-10. The function of alternative keyboards.

by muscles; (3) optical switches that open and close a circuit by detecting interruptions in light sources; and (4) contact switches that open and close a circuit by a slight force or pressure from muscle groups.

Adaptive switch technology usually requires one additional piece of equipment to operate in computer or battery-operated toy environments. This critical piece of equipment is called the switch interface. A switch interface provides the ability to physically connect single or multiple switches to control a microcomputer or some other electronic device.

A computer switch interface usually plugs into the microcomputer's input/

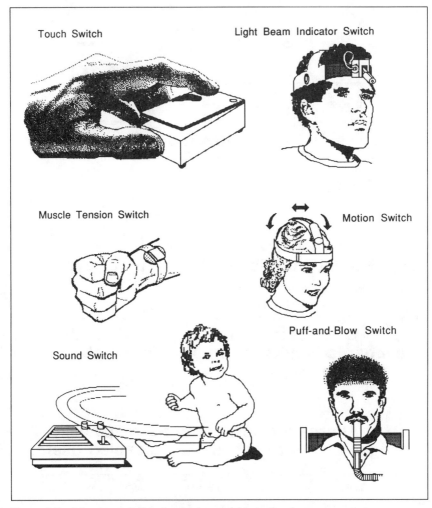

Figure 4-11. Adaptive switch technologies available to the classroom.

output port or through an appropriate keyboard emulator. In addition, a microcomputer switch interface can control a computer under nontransparent and/or transparent operation. A switch interface using "nontransparent" operation requires specifically written software drivers that allow the computer to recognize the switch interface and any connected switch. Therefore, switch interfaces using nontransparent operation won't work properly with instructional software not containing the appropriate software drivers.

However, switch interfaces using transparent operation do not require special software drivers. These switch interfaces electronically simulate the operation of microcomputer keyboard input; as far as the microcomputer knows, any information it receives has come from the regular keyboard or game port. As a result, transparent switch interfaces can work with many popular commercial software programs without the need for special software drivers.

Switch interfaces designed for battery-operated toys usually involve connections to size D, C, and AA batteries. Basically, this interface consists of a small nonconductive spacer disk that slides between two batteries or between one battery and the metal battery clip in a batter-operated toy. This interface simply breaks or interrupts (turns off) the electrical circuit in the toy. The nonconductive spacer disk allows the electrical circuit in the toy to remain open (turned off) until the switch is pressed, resulting in the electrical circuit closing (turning on). The switch will continue to operate the battery-operated toy until the switch is released.

COMPUTERS IN THE EDUCATIONAL SETTING: DESIGN CONSIDERATIONS

The primary purpose of this section is to provide administrators and teachers with the information necessary to make design decisions regarding the implementation of microcomputers in school settings. Developing useful information for such programs requires different approaches, resources, and procedures. The most important and difficult part of planning computer implementations is deciding what information is necessary and relevant to the design and development process. Many often confusing, sometimes conflicting, educational factors affect the development of microcomputer programs. The planner's task is to discover which factors affect a program and what is the significance of each influence. Once important factors have been identified, planners must then decide how they interact with one another and with the proposed goals of the program.

FACTORS THAT INFLUENCE COMPUTER IMPLEMENTATION

There are two major groups of factors that are relevant to the planning development, and implementation of school microcomputer programs. These are human and physical design factors. The human factors include all aspects that pertain to administrative, teaching, and support activities associated with school-based microcomputer programs. These factors might include, for example, available funds; the school's organizational structure; policies; instructional objectives; size of the student population and demographic characteristics; daily schedules and activities; communications; access; etc. The physical factors involved n school-based microcomputer programs are often more easily identifiable. They include such concerns as classroom space configuration and dimensions; operations; equipment/ furnishings; lighting and noise conditions; security; storage; etc.

Human and physical factors represent the kinds of issues that might be investigated in developing school microcomputer programs. A more extensive, but not exclusive, list of design factors is presented in Table 4-1.

The listing in Table 4-1 represents a possible way of reviewing, organizing, and categorizing design factors as part of computer-program–development efforts. It should be noted that it would require much staff time and many resources to analyze every human and physical design factor for a particular school computer program. Depending on the nature and scope of the microcomputer program, the school's implementation plan may concentrate on addressing a primary set of design factors or a set of critical design issues, such as classroom space use, security, or financial feasibility. However, in most school settings integrating microcomputer technology into the classroom must be comprehensive; it must, at least, address as many factors as possible from both the human and physical design factor groups. For planners to exclude any for the sake of time, for example, may actually hinder the flexibility, expansivity, and effectiveness of school microcomputer programs through inappropriate recommendations for implementation.

Depending on the school's objectives, specific factors will have prominent influence on the microcomputer program. They may be determined by such circumstances as time, funding, space limitations, operational or administrative problems, staff limitations, instructional goals, or public interests. Educators can gain important planning direction by identifying which factors have the most significant impact on proposed microcomputer projects. Many prominent design factors may not be obvious at the outset, but the planning process should provide the means for identifying them so that none are excluded from consideration. Obviously, staff time and funding sources constrain the scope of investigation into the impact of design factors. Without neglecting any important considerations, planners must estimate the time and resources needed to develop information for the school computer program. If it requires more than the administration is willing to support or more than the staff is willing to commit, then the scope of the microcomputer program must be scaled down. The planner's information needs and how the information will be used determine the scope of investigation.

The primary sources of information for making computer-implementation decisions come from the school setting. Direct observation of the elements and functions of the school setting and of how users interact in it provide a substantial portion of the background data for making design decisions. Other sources of information might include observation of similar school

Table 4-1. DESIGN FACTORS FOR COMPUTER IMPLEMENTATION

Human factors	*Physical factors*	
School activities/scheduling	Site location	
Classroom	Classroom	Resource room
School	Media center	School
District	Computer lab	District
Instruction	Site Conditions	
Instructional objectives/goals	Electrical	Communications
Methodology	Lighting	Locality
Learning approaches	Security	Sound
Instructional strategies	Space	
Curriculum	Types	
Content skills	Functional relationships	
Content sequence	Dimensions	
Basic skills and literacy	Equipment/furnishings	
Compliance programs	Computers	Desks
Values/personal skills	Printers	Tables
School organization	Software	Chairs
Hierarchy	Workstations	Bookshelves
Functional groups	Display areas	Bulletin boards
Positions	Support services	
Student characteristics	Access	Storage
Demographics	Uses	
Special needs	Functions	
Political forces	Circulation	
Staff attitudes/values	Environment	
Behavioral/perceptual	Comfort	Humidity
School interactions	Visual	Separate
Communication	Noise generation	thermostat
Student management	Noise zones	Floor/wall
School management	Fire control	finish
Support services	Plumbing	Ceiling finish
Intrinsic Qualities	Temperature	Electric power

Comfort	Efficiency	Control
Security	Safety	Safety
Coordinated	Privacy	Access
Productivity	Convenience	

Energy use/conservation

Durability/flexibility

Legal restrictions (building codes)

programs, research findings, consultants, colleges, and universities. The efficacy of information collection involves knowing what types of data are needed and selecting the appropriate means of eliciting, obtaining, and analyzing them. The following section describes some techniques that offer a variety of approaches for evaluating design factors in school settings.

TECHNIQUES AND TOOLS FOR COMPUTER IMPLEMENTATION

Every computer-implementation project should begin with background data research. This preliminary investigation of needs, relevant issues, and existing information is necessary for establishing program goals, organizing the computer implementation effort, and obtaining direction for further investigation. The collection and recording of data are probably the most time-consuming and tedious aspects of computer-program planning, design, and implementation. Anything that planners can do to reduce the amount of time and paperwork for these tasks without compromising the quality of information will make the effort more economical and efficient. Often, to reduce the time and effort required to collect data, planners use standardized forms. Such predesigned and preorganized sheets help to identify the type of information to be collected for computer implementation projects. For example, the data-collection sheet shown in Figure 4-12 provides planners with information on potential school sites for computer placement.

This data-collection technique provides the user with a quick form for evaluating a classroom as a potential school site for microcomputers. First, the sheet is completed with those human and physical design factors that have importance to the success of the program. These design factors represent the school's functional criteria for computer implementation. The identification and completion of functional criteria should be done by planners and staff involved with the utilization of the computer program. The data sheet uses a rating system to perform room evaluations. Using a weight (an assignment of a number to a single functional criterion based on its importance to other criteria). For example, in Figure 4-12 a weight of 1 is assigned to criteria that are considered important, and a weight of 3 is given to criteria considered very important. The data sheet measures or evaluates three different proposed classroom sites for a computer classroom based on the set of functional criteria. Each criterion is given a satisfaction rating from 1 to 5, 1 being very bad and 5 being very good. This rating is often called a "raw" score. The sheet produces a weighted rating for each criterion satisfied by the classroom site. The weighted rating is produced by multiplying the weight by the raw score. At the bottom of the sheet is a weighted total that indicates the score for each proposed classroom site. The comparison of the weighted total scores of the three classroom sites can then be used by planners for a selection of recommended school site.

Many times, especially in large school systems, it is very difficult to track computer resources, establish equipment standards, and identify resource needs for classrooms. As another example of a data-collection tool, Figure 4-13 provides a simple checklist that evaluates a classroom as a potential site for microcomputers and identifies resources. However, no quantitative rating is given. The data sheet simply provides planners with a checklist that

ROOM REQUIREMENTS SHEET

DESIGN FACTORS	WEIGHT	SCHOOL SITES					
		SITE A		SITE B		SITE C	
		RAW	WEIGHTED	RAW	WEIGHTED	RAW	WEIGHTED
1 ACCESS							
1. accommodations for handicapped students	3	3	9	4	12	2	6
2. major traffic flow should not go through instructional areas	2	5	10	3	6	3	6
2 SPACE							
1. size is adequate for the proposed computer lab	3	3	9	3	9	3	9
2. instructional area is adaptable to accommodate changing group sizes	2	5	10	4	8	4	8
3. adequate space for existing activities	1	5	5	5	5	4	4
3 ENVIRONMENT							
1. noise level adequate for instruction	3	2	6	3	9	4	12
2. site has separate controls for temperature and humidity	2	3	6	5	10	4	8
3. adequate fire protection	2	4	8	4	8	3	6
4. adequate power outlets	2	5	10	4	8	4	8
5. adequate lighting	2	4	8	4	8	5	10
6. adequate security	3	4	12	4	12	5	15
4 SITE DEVELOPMENT COSTS	2	3	6	5	10	4	8
5 STATUTORY CODES 1. fire and space codes	2	5	10	5	10	4	8
6 EXISTING SERVICES							
1. site suitable for conversion and/or expansion	2	4	8	4	8	3	6
2. maintenance	2	4	8	4	8	4	8
3. alter existing school services	2	5	10	5	10	4	8
WEIGHTED TOTALS			135		141		130

Figure 4-12. Example of work sheet for evaluating various school sites for potential as computer classroom locations.

identifies specific data on the physical characteristics and equipment needs of a room. Such lists can be helpful for identifying existing school resources, as equipment inventory control, and/or as a measurement tool for identifying future resource requirements.

ROOM DATA   **ROOM NUMBER:**   **DATE:**

A. PURPOSE OF AREA			3. SPRINKLERS		9. POWER STRIPS	
1. MAIN			F. SOUND		10. SURGE PROTECTORS	
2. SECONDARY			1. IN NOISY AREA		11. COMPUTER LOCKS	
			2. IN MODERATE AREA		12. CABLE BRIDGES	
			3. IN QUIET AREA		13. MODEM	
3. HOURS OF USE			G. FLOOR		14. T-SWITCHES	
4. PEAK USE			1. NONSLIP		15. ACOUSTICAL COVERS	
			2. CONDUCTIVE		16. NETWORKING	
B. CLASS USE	HRS.		3. RESILIENT		17. PERIPHERALS	
1. INSTRUCTION			H. WALLS		18. SUPPLIES	
2. RESOURCE RM			1. WASHABLE			
OTHER			2. STAIN-RESISTENT		L. LIGHTING	
			I. CEILING		1. INCANDESCENT	
			1. ACOUSTICAL		2. FLUORESCENT	
			2. SOUND DROP DB.		3. SUNSHINE	
			J. FURNITURE			

ROOM DATA	ROOM NUMBER:	DATE:
C. ACCESS	1. DESK	4. SUN CONTROL
1. EMERGENCY EXIT	2. TABLE	5. SUBDUED
2. OUTSIDE EXIT	3. CHAIRS	6. NIGHT LIGHTING
3. HANDICAPPED ENTR.	4. BOOKSHELVES	7. REFLECTION FACTORS
4. NEAR MAIN HALL	5. SECURITY CABINET	**M. ELECTRIC POWER**
5. NEAR SERVICE ENTR.	6. CLOCK	1. NUMBER OF OUTLETS
6.	7. DISPLAY AREA	2. VOLTAGE
	8. BULLETIN BOARD	3. CONTROL IN ROOM
D. CONTROL	9. COMPUTER DESK	4. EMERGENCY
1. DOOR LOCKS	10. PRINTER STAND	5. CHILDPROOF
2. NUMBER OF KEYS		6. WEATHERPROOF
3. #PEOPLE W/KEYS	**K. EQUIPMENT**	**N. STORAGE**
4. VISUAL SITE	1. *COMPUTERS	1. CABINETS
5. ISOLATED SITE	2. *DISK DRIVES	2. SIZE
6. LOCKING CABINETS	3. *HARD DISKS	3. STORAGE UNITS
7. #CABINET KEYS	4. *PRINTERS	**O. DIMENSIONS**
8. #PEOPLE W/KEYS	5. *COLOR MONITORS	1. LENGTH
E. FIRE PROTECTION	6. *MONO MONITORS	2. WIDTH
1. COMBUST. CONTENTS	7. *PARALLEL CABLES	**P. AIR**
2. CHEMICAL EXTING.	8. *SERIAL CABLES	1. SEP. THERMOSTAT

Figure 4-13. Example of checklist for identifying classroom resources and tracking computer equipment resources.

Finally, Figure 4-14 demonstrates a data-collection method that uses a survey technique for rating the effectiveness of an existing microcomputer-implementation project. A school administration wishes to evaluate the performance of the school's resource room as a computer classroom. In addition, administration is very interested in questioning the school staff utilizing the site. Hence, the following data-collection method is designed to support this administrative endeavor by measuring staff perceptions. The data-collection method asks administrators, teachers, and support staff to rate the school's resource room using a descriptive list of antonym-adjective word pairs. The descriptive antonym-adjective word pairs provide a scale or range for measuring peoples' perceptions of the resource room environment. Each antonym pair has a five-interval range that describes the particular school setting. The typical five-interval range is based on the following:

GOOD   BAD

| extremely | moderately | neither | moderately | extremely |
| good ____ | good ____ | good or bad ____ | bad ____ | bad ____ |

In order to complete the survey, each staff member in the sample identifies and checks one point on the five-interval range that represents his or her feelings about the descriptive antonym pair, continuing the process until completing all 14 antonym pairs. When all of the questionnaires are tabulated, a composite profile of a mean (average) score of the three groups' responses is charted on the scale sheet. This procedure is called a semantic differential testing method. This form of data collection enables planners to quantitatively and graphically describe user perceptions and preferences, identifying general tendencies for each group in the sample.

Standardized data forms are most commonly used in microcomputer programs to identify hardware, software, and to tabulate routine information on class scheduling, supplies usage, etc. Data forms not only provide a convenient and consistent means of compiling brief descriptive or numerical data, but they also offer additional advantages. Standardized forms may also help organize computer-program data in a consistent format so that they are easy to identify and retrieve. Program planners may also use data sheets as a repository for compiling data as they accumulate. In other situations, data forms may be used to inventory existing program conditions, evaluate program activities, or help in identifying new program objectives.

Most standardized forms should consist of four essential parts: (1) a method for easily entering data (checkmark; fill-in-the-blank; tally; cross-out); (2) a method to identify the subject about which data are to be collected; (3) a means of organizing and identifying variables to be measured; and (4) a labeling scheme for identifying specific features of the study subject (equipment type, room number, etc.).

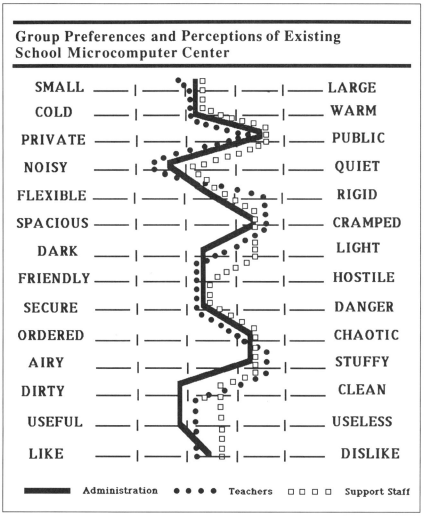

Figure 4-14. Example of data collection technique for measuring staff perceptions of a school microcomputer facility.

THE MICROCOMPUTER CLASSROOM

With many schools recognizing the benefits of computer technology and the increasing trend in the number of computer purchases, it is not unusual to see microcomputers competing for space with tables, desks, and chairs in many classrooms across the country. With proper planning, microcomputers in classrooms offer unprecedented opportunities for innovative instruction. As computerized instruction decisions have increased in importance, planning and design activities have become more prevalent as a means for determining computer-program scope and function as well as assisting in determining feasibility. These applications now include data research and analysis for many stages of the planning and development process, and these methods extend to the evaluation of computer-program effectiveness. At the same time, the scope of information that must be communicated and investigated is expanding. Nowhere is it more evident than in the attention to student instructional needs and program effectiveness. Requirements for computerized instruction extend beyond a listing of school hardware and software. They include the instructional, functional, social, psychological, and behavioral needs of those individuals who learn in, teach, administer, and otherwise use a school computer program. Understanding and accommodating user needs necessitates the adoption and development of research techniques that enable planners to analyze human and physical design factors effectively and efficiently and to incorporate them into program design requirements. This section will focus on several planning and design considerations for classroom computerized instruction. Although there are many different classroom designs and space configurations, many of these guidelines are applicable to most school settings.

Classroom Layout

There are several design characteristics that should be considered in the selection of a computer classroom. With regard to the physical layout of the classroom, the most obvious design characteristic is room dimensions — width and length. The room should have most, if not all, walls free of windows, partitions, dividers, or irregular support-beam surfaces. These items restrict and often reduce the available wall space required for the placement of computer desks or workstations. Generally, rectangular classrooms provide more effective use of wall space for the placement of computer equipment than square classrooms. Irregularly shaped rooms tend to cause more difficulty than necessary when arranging computer equipment. Figure 4-15 offers a few examples for placement of microcomputers in classrooms. Notice that both the rectangular and square classrooms have nearly the same space (375 sq. ft. vs 380 sq. ft., respectively). However, the wall lengths of the rectangular classrooms provide for the placement of more machines and, more importantly, for better movement and flow patterns in the rooms.

Similarly, microcomputer wall-layout patterns tend to give students a directed and unobstructed view of activities involving the teacher, blackboard, and slide or overhead projector. This layout pattern is very conducive for large-group instructional activities. Conversely, the microcomputer cluster layout breaks a classroom into small work areas for individualized and small-group instruction. Depending on the size and purpose of the classroom, both layout patterns may be utilized.

Microcomputer classrooms should have no windows, or as few as possible. Aside from problems with available wall space, windows have two major disadvantages to computer sites. First, sunlight through windows causes a considerable amount of glare on computer screens. Glare under any conditions causes problems for a computer room; however, glare from direct sunlight and reflected light can cause eye strain, discomfort, fatigue, and other viewing problems (Mourant, Lakshmanan, and Chantadisai, 1981). For schools having computer rooms with unavoidable glare problems, there are a number of special screen covers available for monitors. These covers have anti-reflective optical coatings that absorb 99 percent of glare, increase text contrast, and reduce blurry characters. Also, low-gloss wall-paint finishes, window shades or blinds can reduce glare. Nevertheless, when making computer room selections, it is best to avoid such situations.

Finally, most schools would agree that computer technology is a big investment. As such, in the rush to embrace the computer revolution, planning should not lapse when it comes to security. Malicious mischief and electronic thefts are a growing concern as computers continue to advance and proliferate. At the moment, the best vehicle at a school's disposal in protecting computers is good security. Highly visible computer rooms attract attention and therefore can encourage unauthorized access and maximize a site's vulnerability.

Classroom Electrical Power

Because a computer room must support a variety of electrical equipment, the computer classroom must include enough power outlets for all of the microcomputers and associated peripheral devices. Typically, a computer desk or workstation will average two or three power plugs (for the monitor, computer, and printer). As a result, a room with two or three workstations will quickly use up the available outlets. As a general design guideline, plan on using a minimum of two electrical outlets per workstation. Also, the outlets should be spaced at appropriate intervals along the wall in order to accommodate a classroom with several workstations. Some schools try to circumvent this problem with the use of extension cords and power outlet strips. However, this scheme causes inevitable problems like tangled wires, overloaded circuits, confusing connections, or even worse, lost data due to a pulled plug by a fidgety student. If this situation can't be remedied, cable bridges (flat rubber floor strips that allow cables to slip easily into channels with pre-slit bottoms, out of sight) make it safer for teachers and students to

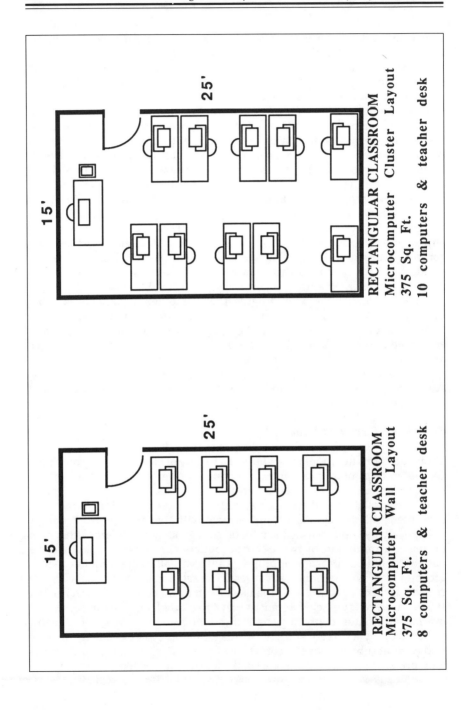

15'

25'

RECTANGULAR CLASSROOM
Microcomputer Wall Layout
375 Sq. Ft.
8 computers & teacher desk

15'

25'

RECTANGULAR CLASSROOM
Microcomputer Cluster Layout
375 Sq. Ft.
10 computers & teacher desk

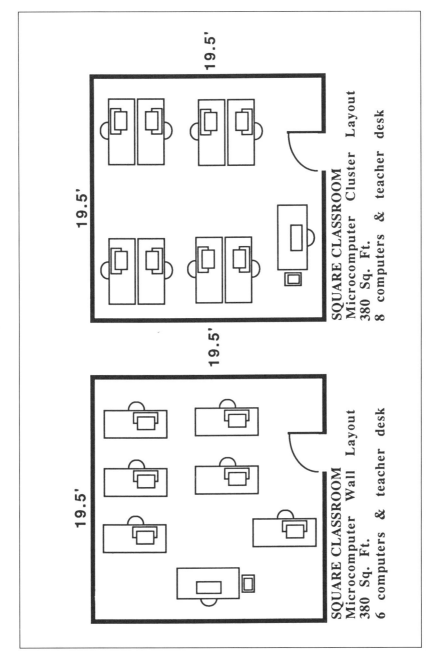

Figure 4-15. Examples of microcomputer equipment placement in classrooms.

walk over cables running through traffic areas. In addition, each outlet used for computer equipment should be protected from sources of frequent, unpredictable electric power problems. The following is a list of six typical electric power problems that can affect classroom computer equipment. Some problems are more frequent than others. However, on the average, a classroom can unknowingly experience anywhere from 10 to 20 power problems per month.

1. *Blackouts.* A blackout is a total loss of commercial utility AC electric power.
   a. It is beyond the control of a commercial power utility.
   b. Blackouts cause computer equipment damage and/or loss of computer data.
2. *Brownouts.* These occurrences are planned electric power reductions by commercial utilities due to excessive electric power demands.
   a. Brownouts cause AC voltage to fall under minimum operating limits.
   b. Brownouts cause computer equipment failure.
3. *Electrical frequency deviations.* Frequency deviations are severe changes in the cycle of AC voltage.
   a. Frequency deviations typically result from large electrical equipment loads.
   b. Frequency deviations cause improper functioning in the computer by affecting the operation of the computer's crystal clock and logic circuits.
4. *Electrical noise and static interference.* Electrical noise and static interference is transient transmission pollution and interference in electrical signals.
   a. Typical causes include:
      • TV transmission or radio frequency interference (RFI).
      • heavy electrical equipment and lighting usage.
      • poor equipment grounding.
   b. When affected, computer equipment acts erratic and can damage microelectronic components.
5. *Voltage spikes.* Voltage spikes are momentary high-frequency spikes in AC voltage wave forms.
   a. Spikes are caused by improper grounding of electrical equipment or motors in office equipment.
   b. Spikes cause erroneous signals to computers, resulting in computer memory loss, program damage, data losses, and damage to microelectronic components.
6. *Voltage surges.* This electrical anomaly causes high-level increases in AC voltage.
   a. Typical causes include:
      • large loads (e.g., air conditioners, elevators, power machinery) being suddenly disconnected.

- large loads being turned on.
b. Surges cause computer equipment to fail, cause damage to drive motors, and produce memory loss.

Most of these electrical power problems can be eliminated by purchasing surge protectors, voltage regulators, or the more expensive uninterruptible power supplies (UPS). Surge protectors and voltage regulators usually protect against voltage spikes, surges, and electrical noise. However, most UPS systems protect against blackouts, brownouts, RFI, and voltage spikes. As a general rule, a school's computer classroom should be on a separate power circuit. This prevents other school equipment with heavy power loads from causing power fluctuations, which have the potential to damage computer equipment and data. Finally, consider the installation of separate switches for controlling electric power and lighting. These wiring installations make it easy to control lighting and equipment from a centralized location.

In addition to electrical power wiring, a computer classroom should have proper telecommunications capability. This feature can be added simply by having a separate telephone line installed in the classroom. This feature provides the physical link for communications with other computer sites over standard telephone lines. Avoid the installation of regular phone extension numbers at the computer site. These lines cause many problems during telecommunications activities and can interfere with and disrupt normal office telephone service.

Classroom Environmental Design

The effectiveness of instructional activities in the computer classroom often depends on the planning and design recommendations and criteria established for addressing operational, psychological, and behavioral needs of the user population. Effective design of the classroom environment basically requires translating functional criteria of the computer facility into the instructional goals and requirements of the school. This involves planning and developing classroom design options that take better advantage of proposed or new computer facilities. Planning activities should help in identifying, analyzing, and providing criteria for those classroom conditions that affect health and safety of students and staff. Planning activities should also help physical performance of instructional tasks and other support activities. Finally, they should help in developing strategies and criteria for those human aspects of a classroom that affect motivation, learning, perception, attitudes toward individual, group, and intergroup interaction, control, psychological well-being, etc.

Classroom Air and Temperature

Providing an effective environment for computer equipment can greatly minimize the cost of maintenance and unanticipated interruptions in operations, and can increase equipment reliability. Individually controlled thermostats for heat and air conditioning in computer classrooms greatly aid these environments by regulating the temperature and humidity at a constant level. Microelectronic components are very susceptible to changes in temperature. As an analogy, consider the neighborhood sidewalk during summer and winter. Temperature fluctuations during these periods cause the sidewalk to expand and contract, often resulting in cracks in the sidewalk. Similarly, very frequent temperature extremes or fluctuations in the classroom environment cause computer chips to contract and expand, which causes them to unseat themselves in the computer system unit, often resulting in equipment malfunction. In addition, humidity and condensation can cause exposed metal surfaces to rust. All computer classrooms should have a means to regulate the environment. Typical operating temperatures should be between 55°F to 95°F (10°C–35°C), with an optimal operating temperature of 75°F. The relative humidity should be 5 to 80 percent (noncondensing). Older computer systems may have somewhat different operating levels.

Proper temperature control also provides a comfortable work environment for users. Computer equipment under normal operating conditions gives off large amounts of heat. This natural heat-transfer process can become problematic, especially when computer equipment is enclosed in classrooms without windows. Effective temperature regulation can reduce heat buildup problems in the classroom.

The air quality in the computer classroom is also very important to the effectiveness of the classroom. Dust, chalk, cigarette smoke, and other abrasive, microscopic, airborne particles can cause computer software and hardware malfunction and failure. For example, disk drives are very susceptible to abrasive airborne pollutants. These particles can damage or destroy read/write heads. To protect equipment and the air quality of the environment, consider the following guidelines: (1) computer sites should have air filters on all air vents; (2) computer rooms should be nonsmoking areas; (3) computer classrooms should not use chalkboards (use felt-tip or ink-pen boards); (4) dust covers for computers should be included for keyboards and printers; (5) software not used should be stored in proper envelopes; and (6) cleaning kits that contain screen wipes, compressed gas for removing dust and lint from inaccessible areas, and cleaning solvent and/or cleaning "disks" that remove dirt from disk drive heads should be used.

Classroom Noise and Lighting

When planning computer environments, one should consider the potential impact of environmental noise conditions on the function and effectiveness of the instructional setting. In most school settings, computer classrooms have the biggest noise problems (aside from outside noise) from printers.

Obviously, printer equipment usually fits into the overall functional scheme of the computer classroom. However, depending on the types of printing and frequency of printing at a computer site, noise levels can be very disturbing in instructional environments. Operating noise is measured in decibels (db). For example, consider the fact that many dot matrix and daisy wheel printers have very high sound levels. Depending on draft or letter-quality modes of operation, each can produce noise levels between 60 db and 85 db. Should the reader not be impressed with these noise readings, consider the fact that the average rock concert has noise levels between 95 db and 110 db.

Variables such as printer type, number, and/or function will affect noise levels in the classroom. There are a number of methods available to schools for reducing printer noise. If, for example, printing functions are central to the operations of a specific classroom, a school may consider the purchase of quieter types of printers, such as laser printers, or, if funds are limited, the purchase of acoustical sound covers for printers, which muffle up to 85 percent of printer noise, should be considered. In addition, with proper wiring a computer classroom can send printing tasks to a separate room for printing. Planners can also consider ceiling and wall acoustical tiles, which absorb noise.

Removing glare and combating eye fatigue should be added to the list of overall design objectives. Historically, when energy was cheap, in-ceiling lighting was used to provide uniform light levels on work surfaces. However, recent increases in the costs of energy have made in-ceiling lighting more expensive. Currently, ambient (indirect)/task lighting is fast replacing over-head lighting fixtures, largely because ambient lighting systems are easier to control in work areas, less expensive, and they reduce glare (IBM, 1984; Kaufman and Hayes, 1981). For example, direct overhead lighting mounted in the ceiling is static once it's in place. As a result, overhead lighting is difficult to control, and some classroom design flexibility is lost because computer furniture must be positioned around overhead lighting. With regard to cost factors, ambient lighting only uses about 1.5 watts per square foot, compared to 3 or 4 watts per square foot for ceiling fixtures. In addition, task lighting is very flexible and helps eliminate high contrast between computer task areas and noncomputer work areas.

Lighting considerations in the computer task area will vary depending on the type of instructional application. There is no one specific lighting level that is most effective for all applications (Stammerjohn, Smith, and Cohen, 1981). If the instructional activity involves both computer and pen-and-paper tasks, the lighting level should be medium or high. In activities that exclusively involve viewing the computer screen, such as word processing, computer-aided instruction, or educational games, the lighting level can be reduced to moderate or lower levels. This reduces glare problems and increases contrast on the screen for easy student viewing.

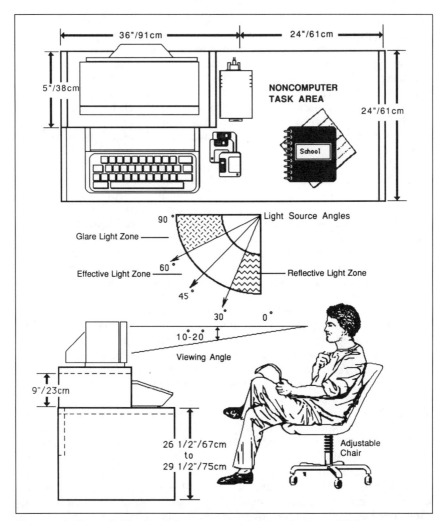

Figure 4-16. Top and side views of computer workstation design and lighting.

The lighting angles involved with overhead lighting fixtures in relation to the positioning of the computer monitor can have an impact on lighting problems associated with glare and reflection. Figure 4-16 illustrates three general lighting zones associated with an overhead lighting source and the angle at which the computer screen receives light. For example, when a computer screen is positioned to receive overhead light at an angle between 0–30 degrees, users will usually experience light reflection problems on both

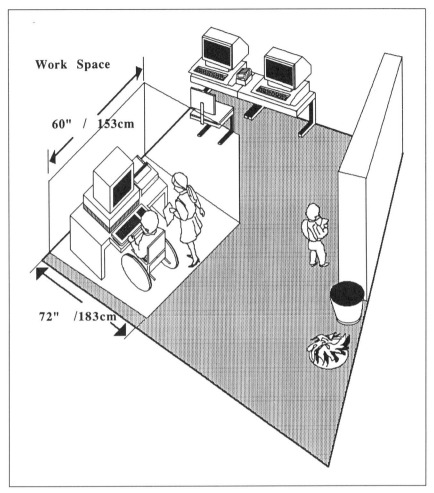

Figure 4-17. The computer work-space concept allows teachers to plan effective work areas for students.

the screen and work surface. This lighting zone is referred to as a reflective lighting zone. The most effective lighting angle for users is between 30 to 60 degrees. This zone is called the effective light zone. This zone provides adequate lighting for work surfaces and screen viewing. Finally, lighting angles greater than 60 degrees cause lighting problems associated with screen glare. As with reflective lighting zones, glare lighting zones should be avoided when possible.

COMPUTER WORK SPACE

The student computer work space has important design implications when considering physical performance of instructional tasks and other activities. Its design implications are also important for supporting those human aspects that affect student motivation, learning, perception, control or sharing of territory, and psychological elements. A preliminary design consideration should be a clear definition of what a student computer work space is. To begin, think of a computer work space as an environment marked with imaginary boundaries, in which one must support the placement and storage of computer equipment and peripherals; provide easy access to computer equipment; support comfortable seating and work areas for users; and integrate these component elements so as to optimize user performance in the planned work-space area. It is the interplay between the work environment and human behavior that occurs within this work space.

Figure 4-17 illustrates the work-space concept. This work-space area (60" × 72" or 153cm × 183cm) is capable of handling most typical school configurations. This example takes into consideration the space required for a workstation or computer desk; placement of computer equipment; access to the workstation by handicapped users and their support equipment; sufficient space for teachers and others to interact in the work space; and adequate space for maximizing work effectiveness. Planners should consider the following criteria when designing work-space zones for minimum and maximum areas in computer classrooms:

Design Criteria for Computer Work Spaces

1. Dimensions of computer workstation in work space
2. Number of computer components in the work space
3. Number of peripheral devices supported by the work space
4. Types of activity in the work space
5. Number of students utilizing the work space concurrently
6. Provisions for access by users with disabilities
7. Provisions for accessing equipment and cables
8. Provisions for access to adequate lighting and electric power
9. Adequate space for free movement in work space and between work spaces and general room traffic

Finally, the work-space concept is very effective for determining room capacities and room-layout patterns for microcomputers. For example, suppose school planners have determined that adequate computer work-space zones should contain dimensions of 60" width × 60" depth. In addition, the school plans to implement six new microcomputer systems into one classroom space. These work-space standards or specifications address not only individual student work spaces, but also provide planners with a measurement tool for visualizing classroom layouts. Based on the work-space zone dimensions, planners can obtain diagrams for each proposed classroom and map out on paper all six computer work-space zones while taking into consideration traffic flow in the room, space use, location of electrical outlets, furniture placement, etc. Such modeling techniques are very helpful in the room-layout and design process and for the evaluation of each proposed classroom plan.

Computer Workstation and Furniture

Thoughtful design considerations for planning a computer classroom should, in addition to adhering to the design criteria already discussed, attempt to explore the selection of computer furniture that supports the instructional setting. Integrating appropriate computer workstations and furniture with intended instructional uses of a computer facility can greatly enhance the physical performance of instructional tasks; it can also support other human aspects in the classroom that affect motivation, learning, perception, attitudes, control and sharing of territory, and psychological well-being. Properly designed workstations can provide convenience and comfort and have been proven to increase learning and productivity (Mandal, 1982).

The following workstation guidelines, which include dimensions for determining work-space zone requirements, should be used as minimal guidelines when designing computer workstations. It should be noted that a school's specialized needs may influence these guidelines. For example, access by disabled users, physical characteristics of users, size or shape of equipment, and the number of computer components and peripherals may affect final design recommendations.

In general, the computer workstation should provide enough space to accommodate several basic computer-system components, including the main computer unit, keyboard, disk drives, computer monitor, and printer. In addition, the computer workstation should provide adequate desktop surface for pen-and-paper tasks. Finally, the workstation must also provide adequate chair and leg space without interference from cables, storage drawers, workstation legs, paper-catch baskets, boxes of paper, etc.

Figure 4-16 provides general dimension guidelines that are based on a single microcomputer workstation design. Overall outside dimensions should be 60" length × 24" width or 152cm length × 61cm width. These recommendations will provide sufficient space for supporting a computer, keyboard, monitor, and disk drives. The workstation should also be capable of supporting a monitor shelf, openings for printer paper, and access to computer cables. In addition, a good workstation should be flexible to future instructional needs by offering expansion and support for accessories such as supply drawers, work surface extensions, and printer stands.

Another key design feature of workstations is the provision for an adequate desktop surface for noncomputer tasks such as pen-and-paper activities. At a minimum, workstations should provide a 24" × 24" or 61cm × 61cm area for these noncomputer activities. This task area provides users with space that maximizes effectiveness and minimizes fatigue. Depending on the instructional circumstances, the noncomputer task area can provide space to accommodate an additional student at the workstation. If a printer is required at the workstation, a printer shelf may be added above the noncomputer task area. However, avoid placing printers or other large peripherals in desktop work areas.

Dimensions for workstation table top height should be between 26½" and 29½" or 67cm and 75cm for the recommended keyboard typing height. Some workstations provide height-adjustable keyboard shelves that provide tilting surfaces for supporting the wrist and adjusting the viewing distance from the monitor. The work surface should feature rounded-edge vinyl molding that prevents chipping, peeling, clothing snags, and headaches. Furthermore, the work surface should be finished in low-gloss, light-colored veneer or laminate. This type of desk-top produces a low-contrast desk-top surface for reading and pen-and-paper activities. Consequently, low-contrast work surfaces reduces the eye strain caused by instructional activities requiring frequent viewing of both the computer screen and worksheet, books, or other written material.

The workstation should also provide an easily adjusted monitor shelf that lets the user choose height and angle for viewing comfort and glare relief (AT&T, 1984; Human Factors Society, 1986). The monitor shelf should also provide enough depth for the user to adjust the proper viewing distance to the computer screen. The monitor shelf should be positioned so that the computer screen's center is 10 to 20 degrees below the user's horizontal eye level. This reduces neck strain and discomfort during instructional activities involving frequent viewing between the computer screen and activities in noncomputer tasks areas.

Fitting the seat to the workstation is not an easy task, especially with the wide variety of student sizes and age groups utilizing most school computer classrooms. The best choice for seating is an adjustable piece of furniture that can accommodate a variety of configurations. Human factor research has shown that adjustable chairs are more comfortable in work environments and are preferred by user (Mandal, 1982).

MICROCOMPUTER SECURITY

As microcomputer applications expand and consume larger portions of school budgets, the security of classroom hardware becomes a key implementation issue. Establishing a comprehensive and yet rational school microcomputer security plan can be a perplexing task, partly because tightened security can restrict easy access and increase the administrative burden, and, in addition, it is often difficult to determine exactly what equipment and resources to protect.

There are a number of security risks, both intentional and unintentional, that can threaten computer equipment. In recent years, the most publicized threat has been computer hackers, persons or groups of individuals who try to penetrate computer systems or decode private encryption scheme. Others plant software "viruses" or "Trojan horses" in computers for the sole purpose of altering or destroying system and data files; and others swap or borrow equipment for personal use. In addition, some computer threats come from innocent users. These threats may include accidental disk formatting, file overwrites, or equipment damage through ignorance or incompetence. Another large source of security problems for computers is internal maliciousness and revenge committed by inside employees. Finally, outright theft in offices and classrooms is and will always be a security problem for out-in-the-open microcomputers.

The process of protecting computer hardware involves analyzing four basic security levels: (1) computer facility protection; (2) microcomputer equipment protection; (3) microcomputer access protection; and (4) data and information protection.

At the most basic security level, classrooms containing computer equipment should have locks installed on all doors. In addition, the number of keys and the management of those keys should be monitored and controlled. Other protection measures for the computer classroom include locating the facility in a centralized area of the building and, avoiding entrances and windows that have direct access to outside public areas. Consider removing any signs that identify a computer facility in a bold or alluring fashion; such advertising often attracts unwanted attention.

Locks are a low-cost solution for securing computer equipment and peripheral devices to workstations or desks. These security devices require minimal installation and are inexpensive, usually costing from $25 to $150. Typical locking schemes include aircraft-strength steel cables and cable-connector plates with super-strong self-adhesive; locks with sensitive motion-detection circuitry that produce a high, piercing, siren noise when moved; and locking steel security enclosures that protect the entire computer system unit. Locking the computer to the workstation, furniture, or other permanent fixture can provide a good measure of protection from theft.

The third level of computer security involves preventing unauthorized access to the microcomputer. Such unauthorized use can lead to the swapping of internal boards, tampering, and theft of computer components. Protection systems for this level of security should require at least the following: a keyboard and/or on/off-switch lock that can prevent others from using the computer; and back plates, cover screws, or enclosures that also lock the computer chassis and prevent under-the-hood access to the computer.

Security measures for the computer room and computer can often be implemented with minimal time and cost. However, protecting data and information requires a much greater level of sophistication than mechanical locks or bolts. There are a number of hardware and software devices that provide access controls to important and confidential data. Add-on security boards can provide a means of protecting data confidentiality and integrity. These peripheral devices usually restrict information access, prevent unauthorized use, and even provide some encryption techniques to make data unintelligible to unauthorized eyes. Hardware, although a more complex security device, provides better protection than software security schemes. For example, encryption software is vulnerable to expert hackers, who can modify the code and destroy files. Hardware provides more protection against knowledgeable hackers. Similarly, many hardware devices are built to become inoperative or lock up the computer if violated.

In the near future, the next level of security will address the issues of multitasking and multiuser environments. These environments are based on computer networks with many users sharing vast amounts of information. As computers proliferate and begin to connect with each other, the security and privacy issues will grow more complex. Granted an individual or group with enough time, money, and energy can find a way of defeating the best multilevel security system, a balanced set of security measures can greatly minimize most threats to the computer environment. When planning a security system, consider what the major hazards are for the computer facility, and then decide what computer resources need to be protected.

SUMMARY

Computer hardware can offer many advantages to the regular- and special-education classroom. The critical element in the success of the sue of computer technology, however, is the educator. When planning to make computer-based instruction more effective in the classroom, educators must be knowledgeable about the function and capabilities of the technology. It is the administrative and teaching staff who must use this knowledge to integrate the technology with the learning needs of students. Hence, any computer-implementation process should consider the wide variety of hardware and alternative input devices available to the special-needs classroom. Discussions and explanations of how the various technologies work and their functions and capabilities in the classroom setting greatly benefit both the teacher and administrator. Educators may find use for these devices in academic, vocational, personal, and recreational environments.

In addition, there are a number of design factors that influence the effectiveness of school computer programs. These implementation issues concern the impact of human and physical factors on the design of school microcomputer programs. Planners should identify critical design factors and determine what effect they may have on educational computer programs. Identifying and planning for design factors can greatly aid educators in making smooth program implementations.

Chapter 5 introduces the reader to software tools that are responsible for much of the microcomputer hardware functioning described in Chapters 3 and 4.

Listed below are sample review questions and some follow-up activities students may wish to pursue. These activities can be used to further develop the concepts and practical applications presented in this chapter.

REVIEW QUESTIONS

1. What are the benefits of alternative input devices for individuals with disabilities?
2. What is the difference between alternative keyboards and keyboard emulators?
3. What does the term "transparent" operation mean? What are the benefits to handicapped populations?
4. What are some advantages of using touch-screen technology? What are some of the technology's limitations in the classroom setting?
5. What are the advantages and disadvantages of using mouse technology in the classroom?
6. Why are software drivers important to peripheral devices? Can they cause problems?
7. Why is the collection of data important to the planning phase of microcomputer programs?
8. Why are human and physical design factors important to schools that are planning microcomputer implementations?
9. What is the work space concept and why is it important to planners?
10. What are the four levels of computer security?
11. Explain the purpose of an adaptive input device. In addition, describe the potential benefits for its use with handicapped populations.

SUGGESTED FOLLOW-UP ACTIVITIES

1. Contact a local school that uses computers and list their computer security needs. Identify any solutions or measures taken by the school to reduce the security threat.

2. Contact a local school that uses computers and identify important design factors that were taken into consideration in the planning of its computer program.
3. Develop a data-collection sheet for the purpose of hardware or software inventory control (classroom, resource room, etc.). Use the data sheet, and discuss its effectiveness or ineffectiveness for the stated purpose.

CHAPTER 5

Using Software in the Classroom

Educators will address many issues when planning and implementing microcomputer technology in special and regular education settings. The planning process is comprehensive and often requires consideration of many educational and technical factors in order to develop adequate information about the possibilities inherent to computer-based instruction. Previous chapters discuss planning issues concerning the use of technology in education programs, as well as provide the reader with functional information on the workings of microcomputer equipment. In continuation of the computer planning process, Chapter 5 will address software issues that become important factors when considering the integration of computer technology into classrooms.

Like the evolution of computer hardware, the concepts, expressions, and functions of instructional software are changing and will continue to evolve. Currently, instructional software design and development are in their infancy. In fact, software development is still struggling with the complexities of design and sound pedagogy. Some groups recommend software design guidelines that support a systematic approach to development (Alessi and Trollip, 1985; Orwig, 1983; and Steinberg, 1984). Still others have been successful implementing software through personal experience and intuition. The confusion over software development practices is largely due to the fact that learning and research theories don't always provide clear and obvious instructional design principles. Moreover, some traditional instructional design schemes simply aren't appropriate in computer environments. As a result, many instructional software-development efforts are based on unsubstantiated design principles and are often the result of much experimentation — with some success but often much longer histories of failure. In addition, a more pervasive problem is the lack of field testing for educational software prior to commercial distribution (Johnson, 1984). Often, software programs rely on response/reinforcement paradigms and almost exclusively use a behavioristic model for instructional implementation; these paradigms and model present a question to the student; obtain an answer from the student; evaluate the answer; give very simplistic feedback to the student; and proceed to another question.

However, there is optimism that this situation will change. Software is beginning to take advantage of new computers, graphics, and sound (Lathrop and Goodson, 1983). Similarly, many early, poor quality instructional programs are beginning to be replaced with a larger variety of quality instructional programs (Bitter, 1984; Eisele, 1985; Torgesen, 1984, and Truett, 1984). Instructional software will continue to evolve as schools gain access to more powerful computers capable of supporting more effective programming methods and instructional design practices.

THE EVOLUTION OF
INSTRUCTIONAL SOFTWARE TOOLS

Currently, selecting instructional software for the classroom is a highly iterative implementation process. For example, a teacher may begin the process by identifying important instructional needs. The teacher then develops some initial ideas for using microcomputer software. A software selection process is then initiated with offerings from the private and/or commercial sector. The software, depending on its effectiveness, may be utilized in classrooms; or teachers may come up with better ideas, try them, and with successive attempts find a piece of software that can approximate something that works. This process is largely the result of eclecticism in software development, design, and implementation approaches.

The reader should understand that there exists few proven or established principles for defining what constitutes computer-assisted instruction (CAI) and, in addition, what elements of CAI are most effective for different student populations. In fact, very little of the instructional software currently in school systems will be acceptable to educators in five to ten years, largely because the instructional design methodology, development practices, and implementation techniques will become outmoded or unfashionable. As a consequence, rather than approaching the explanation of CAI as a series of established principles or techniques, this section will attempt to cover the evolution of various instructional software schemes. This approach will provide the reader with basic information on current instructional design implementations and present research on the effectiveness of instructional software. It is the responsibility of the reader to decide what, if any, software elements have some relevancy or value for their specific classroom instruction.

DRILL SOFTWARE

Many instructional objectives in traditional classroom settings have concentrated on student learning that requires drill and practice for skill mastery. The standard method of drill and practice usually involves student work sheets. Unfortunately, incorrect exercises or procedures can be reinforced through the use of work sheets and can be difficult to unlearn. Similarly, traditional drill methods provide little or no feedback for student users. With these limitations in mind, many instructional software designs are evolving in an attempt to improve on this teaching technique.

Drill software programs support the acquisition of skill through the use of drill and practice paradigms that allow students to practice a previously introduced skill for proficiency. Like traditional drill methods, drill software allows students to develop automaticity of a component skill through practice. In addition, these practice activities usually require students to produce the skill within an acceptable time frame. However, a distinguishing feature of drill software is its ability to incorporate an individual's own content matter into the program and practice specific content. This feature provides students with increased opportunities to practice specific problematic lesson material.

Figure 5-1 shows an example of a drill and practice program. In addition to offering extra repetition for students having difficulty, drill and practice programs can include a variety of feedback responses for students for both correct and incorrect answers. For example, immediate feedback is often necessary for individuals performing at a low mastery level with material, and informational feedback is most effective for students after incorrect responses (Cohen, 1985). Drill and practice software can be programmed to provide both instant feedback after incorrect answers and delayed feedback to facilitate retention of information during instruction (Rankin and Trepper, 1978). Under these conditions, drill software can give students feedback

Figure 5-1. Drill program: *Sound Ideas: Vowels.* (Screen reproduced by permission of Houghton Mifflin.)

using short reinforcement phrases after correct answers or offer students the opportunity to respond again after an incorrect response.

In addition to feedback mechanisms, drill and practice computer instruction can also provide diagnoses of students' difficulties. These diagnoses can report on the frequency of errors and identify those instructional elements typically causing the student difficulty. By utilizing drill software in a diagnostic mode, teachers can quickly isolate problematic material for remediation purposes. A diagnostic listing can assist the teacher in generating appropriate student material for use with drill software. This allows teachers the ability to present problem elements more frequently to students; and the time spent on drilling mastered facts can be reduced.

The potential advantages that drill and practice CAI offer have helped facilitate the transition of conventional drill and practice techniques to microcomputer environments. Historically, drill and practice programs were one of the first computer implementations to evolve for instructional purposes, and this scheme continues to be a primary mode of presentation for instructional software.

There are many good instructional justifications for using drill and practice software. But these programs, by their nature, are usually limited to classroom situations in which the instructional goal is reinforcement, practice, or testing for mastery of prerequisite skills. There are many examples of commercial drill and practice CAI in classrooms across the country touting many different design schemes. Undoubtedly, educators should question their effectiveness.

Special educators often cite the most prevalent deficiency with drill and practice programs as their gamelike design. For example, many educators argue against the use of violent game designs in presenting instructional material. Cacha (1983) warns that "latent content" of some educational software teaches children to use aggressive tactics. In addition, many gamelike programs require "keyboard speed" in their designs. Without teacher control of speed settings, these programs can be self-defeating for many student users. For example, the intensity of some gamelike drill programs localizes attention on fast keyboard or joystick responses, and often results in the child's concentrating on the process rather than on instructional content. Similarly, the lack of teacher control over speed features can also frustrate special-education students with poor motor abilities or slow reaction times.

With regard to content-presentation features, some drill and practice designs can become overbearing. For example, by utilizing feedback mechanisms that continually play loud sounds and display animated screen devices, these designs may actually elicit unintentional student reinforcement, disrupt nearby activities, or, after repeated exposure, reduce the motivational tendencies of the feedback design.

The research on computer drill and practice activities suggests this software-implementation approach can be as effective as conventional drill and practice instruction. Some research suggests drill and practice programs can provide very effective supplemental instructional activities for student remediation (Alessi and Trollip, 1985). In fact, it has been suggested that increasing opportunities to practice individual skills may be the most effective method of CAI with mildly handicapped students (Torgesen, 1984).

In addition, drill and practice CAI may reduce the time necessary to learn new material as compared with conventional drill and practice activities Bracey, 1982; Grabe, 1986; Kulik, Kulik, and Cohen, 1980; Hasselbring and Cavanaugh, 1986; Jensen, 1982; Overton, 1981; Roblyer, 1986; Thomas, 1979). A practical implication of this research suggests that a potential advantage in the use of drill and practice software in the classroom over more traditional drill methods is the ability to automatize skills while saving instructional time and learning roughly equivalent material. The error-diagnosis abilities of drill and practice software combined with the ability to identify and present only those elements causing the student difficulty may be a key factor in research observations concerning time savings. For teachers the instructional time saved using drill and practice CAI can offer opportunities to spend more time with individual students, introduce new concepts or expand others, and provide students with intensified drill and practice activities for attaining instructional goals.

The effectiveness of feedback in drill and practice CAI appears to show that immediate feedback seems to be most effective for students having difficulty achieving mastery of skills and for tasks involving discrimination learning (Budoff and Hutton, 1982; Carter, 1984; Cohen, 1985). This research tends to support the belief that early error diagnosis may provide effective feedback mechanisms for students functioning below skill mastery. In addition, some research suggests that drill software's ability to provide delayed feedback may facilitate retention of information during CAI activities (Rankin and Trepper, 1978).

Characteristics of Drill Software

- A previously introduced skill can be practiced.

- Skill mastery can be tested.

- Individualized lesson content is provided.

- Procedural feedback is provided.

- Content feedback is provided.

- There is computer control over instructional delivery.

In summary, drill and practice software programs allow the student to practice a skill for proficiency; such programs include accurate reproduction of the skill, as well as producing the skill at an acceptable rate of speed. This software approach is not intended to teach new skills. As such, teachers may consider using drill and practice CAI as a supplement to classroom instruction, thereby providing students with increased opportunities to practice component skills. Further, teachers should consider using drill software for practicing single-component skills. Incorporating multiple extraneous skills into instruction can hinder drill activities. By utilizing single-component skills during instruction, students can concentrate on practicing the individual skills for proficiency and automaticity.

TUTORIAL SOFTWARE

In traditional classroom situations, when new skills are introduced, new information is usually presented by the teacher, practiced by students, and, in some situations, additional information is given in textbooks. Unfortunately, not all students understand a new concept during initial instruction. In addition, the teacher may not know how well new content material has been communicated to students.

CAI is also finding applicability in learning situations involving the introduction of new information or concepts. Instructional software supporting the teaching of new skills is commonly referred to as tutorial software. Like more traditional tutorial lessons, tutorial software is designed to teach students new information. Computer tutorials teach new skills by introducing new rules, prompting the student to recognize and identify rules or procedures, and prompting the student to produce the procedure or skill. However, unlike drill and practice software schemes, which emphasize skill acquisition through repetitive practice, tutorial software schemes concentrate on rule learning. This is the key feature of tutorial software programs.

Figure 5-2 provides an example of a tutorial software program. As an alternative to traditional teaching methods, microcomputer tutorials have some potential advantages in the classroom. First, tutorial software can provide error diagnosis of student responses during instruction. This can provide teachers with the ability to overcome the limitations of more traditional techniques by identifying incorrect student responses during the course of instruction. This is very difficult to accomplish consistently using more conventional teaching methods.

In addition to error identification, tutorial CAI may provide alternate explanations of new material at the point of student misunderstanding. Tutorial software can also provide specific information feedback at the point of misunderstanding or provide reinforcement to students for recognizing rules. Consequently, by providing appropriate information feedback to

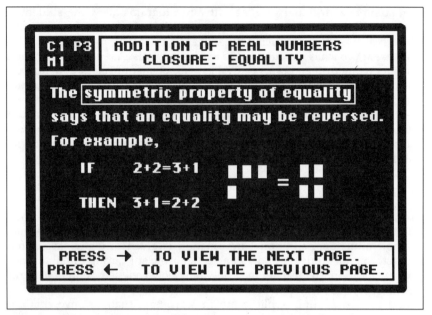

Figure 5-2. Tutorial program: *Algebra II*. (Screen reproduced by permission of Britannica Software.)

students at critical points during instruction, computer tutorials can reduce student misunderstanding. Similarly, by supplying students with alternative lesson presentations after correct responses, tutorials can accelerate rule learning by providing additional information. The ability of a lesson to deviate or alternate presentations is called *branching;* it provides students with different instructional modes to correct understanding or provide alternate explanations of material. This feature has the potential to accommodate students who have a wide variety of individualized learning styles.

Although lesson branching is a potential strength of tutorial software, it can also be one of its major weaknesses. For example, because tutorial software designs must pre-plan and program all content in advance, all possible student responses and branching schemes are fixed. The material in most cases can't be altered by the teacher to reflect specialized content needs. Limitations in software design often restrict the ability of tutorial software to incorporate comprehensive branching schemes. In many instances branching techniques provide only simplistic information assistance in correcting a student error. In fact, feedback assistance may only include reinforcing feedback. This feedback simply facilitates repetition of a response or motivates the user to continue. The primary function of feedback in tutorial software instruction should be to provide information rather than reinforce or motivate a response.

In terms of content presentation, many current tutorial software programs rely almost exclusively on text-presentation schemes rather than more sophisticated and interactive animation, graphics, voice, and video presentation methods. For special-education students requiring multisensory teaching approaches, one-dimensional text designs can limit content understanding and learning effectiveness.

The research on tutorial software is sparse and the effectiveness of tutorial software to date is largely undetermined. However, some promising applications are being developed using intelligent tutorials that can interpret student responses and redirect instruction (Sleeman and Brown, 1982). The PLATO tutorial system, developed by Control Data Corporation, is the best known tutorial subject of a research study. This research concentrated on studying the effectiveness of computerized tutorials in language arts and mathematics instruction. Results indicated that only tutorials involving fractions effected any significant improvement in student learning (Slattow, 1977).

Research concerning the effectiveness of tutorial software suggests that communicating new information to students is closely linked with the concept of "rule learning." The effectiveness with which one teaches new concepts is largely dependent on the ability to precisely define and sequence new rules using sound instructional pedagogy. This is especially critical when programming tutorials in computer environments. For example, teaching the mathematical operation of addition to students involves introducing a finite set of procedures or rules for producing the skill. As such, the definition and sequence of mathematical rules are more readily apparent and transferable to procedure-oriented computer environments. Conversely, tutorials involving language arts skills, although still programmable, may require much more instructional design effort in order to effectively define and quantify English rules for computerized environments. The complexity of rules and procedures associated with teaching new concepts may demand presentation media that are beyond the current design limitations of many current classroom computers. As such, the transferability and effectiveness of computerized instructional techniques over more traditional teaching methods may be limited by current technology.

Studies conducted on the value of tutorial information feedback versus reinforcing feedback seem to indicate very different learning outcomes. Briefly, information feedback gives specific information on student responses, such as corrective explanations for wrong answers. Conversely, reinforcing feedback simply notifies students of their response. Studies on computer feedback tend to agree that informative feedback is more effective than reinforcing feedback (Bardwell, 1981; Gilman, 1969; Lasoff, 1981; Robin, 1978; and Roper, 1977). The research also suggests that learning new rules or concepts usually requires more extensive information feedback because such learning requires concentration on higher levels of cognition. The Gilman (1969), Roper (1977), and Struges (1972) studies indicate that students receiving the most detailed or informative feedback learn the most. In addition, delayed information feedback during high-level cognitive instruction, such as in tutorial lessons, seems to be the most effective method of scheduling student feedback (Kulhavy and Anderson, 1972; Kulhavy, 1977; Rankin and Trepper, 1978; Tennyson, Christenson, and Park, 1985). Computer-based instruction that concentrates on presenting clear and detailed information may effect equal or greater retention levels in students over more traditional methods (Kulik, Kulik, and Cohen, 1980).

Characteristics of Tutorial Software

- New concepts are introduced.

- Student understanding during instruction is evaluated.

- At the point of misunderstanding, feedback is provided.

- Branching to supplement instruction is provided.

- There is computer control over instructional delivery.

In summary, microcomputer tutorials teach new skills. This process usually includes introduction of rules or concepts; providing opportunities to recognize rules; prompting responses for identifying concepts; providing information feedback; and giving opportunities to produce the new skill. Teachers may consider using tutorial CAI as a supplement to classroom instruction, namely reinforcing, identifying, or correcting misconceptions about content material from initial lessons. A second use may entail teaching new skills. However, due to the complexity of communicating new concepts to students, many tutorials rely almost exclusively on textual media for presentation. As such, teachers should closely monitor reading levels of these programs in order to appropriately match content material with students.

SIMULATION SOFTWARE

Instructional situations that model real-world events are often difficult to produce in classroom settings. For example, real-world situations may include driving a car, running a grocery store, or conducting dangerous chemical experiments. However, in regular classroom situations few teachers have the time or energy to focus on planning and controlling all simulation variables and still be able to have instructional time to interact with students, observe student processes, and communicate appropriate simulation relationships. In fact, many real-world situations are simply impossible to recreate and teach about using traditional classroom methods.

Microcomputer simulations offer a unique vehicle for simulating many difficult real-world events in classroom settings. An advantage to using computer simulations over more traditional methods is the ability to replicate and control replications of real-world events that are difficult or impossible to teach about in classrooms. Computer environments offer teachers control over time constraints when running simulation processes and can provide savings in school resources utilization. Probably the most important advantage to computer simulations is the ability to model very complex real-world situations. In these situations, students can interactively manipulate and manage many simulation variables and instantly watch the results of the modeling process.

Unlike drill and tutorial software schemes, which emphasize information acquisition and rule learning, simulation software focuses on demonstrating the interactions between variables describing real-world events. This is usually accomplished through any or all of the following four learning activities: (1) demonstration, which is designed to provide students with observational knowledge about the functions of events; (2) instruction, which provides students with rule sets about the nature of events; (3) modeling, which provides students with opportunities to apply various methods and strategies to the rule sets of events; and (4) simulation, which provides students with simulated events that require utilizing rule sets and various methods in problem-solving environments. Simulation software design may incorporate all four learning activities or may just elaborate on one or more activities.

In addition, simulations often give students much broader control over learning, modeling, and simulation activities. Conversely, in both drill and tutorial software programs, the computer controls the presentation, delivery, and feedback of instruction. The increased student control of simulations usually requires more interaction than required with drill and tutorial software. For instance, because simulations usually require frequent decisions regarding many different variables, students often work together, utilizing higher levels of feedback and peer interaction in order to solve problems. Figure 5-3 provides an example of a simulation program.

Some research indicates that computer simulations may have the potential to develop cooperative learning and foster peer interaction (Foster, 1984). For special-education students, simulations can provide a tool for understanding abstract concepts, develop active rather than passive roles, and increase socialization skills (Hasselbring and Cavanaugh, 1986). In addition, others suggest that using computer simulations as a supplement to regular classroom instruction can have a positive long-term impact on student understanding (DeClercq and Gennaro, 1986).

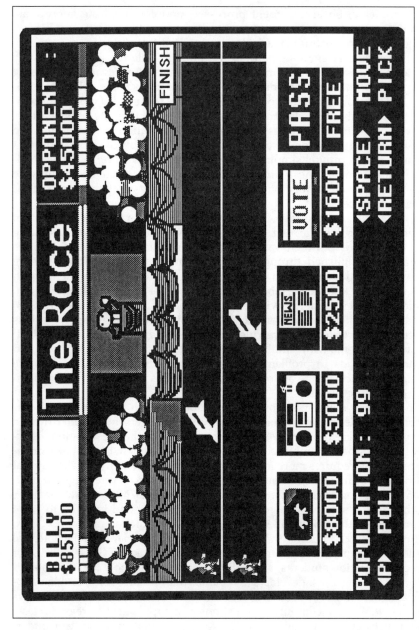

Figure 5-3. Simulation program: *Campaign Math.* (Screen reproduced by permission of MindPlay.)

With regard to quality of information feedback during instruction, computer simulations using purposeful corrective feedback can improve student understanding significantly more than can simulations using nonremedial feedback approaches (Zietsman and Hewson, 1986).

Indeed, microcomputer simulations can offer greater student control over program activities and processes. However, unstructured problem-solving practices may not always lead to understanding simulation outcomes. Some research suggests that science experiments using computer simulations can result in unstructured and haphazard scientific variable manipulation (Stevens, 1985). In a similar study involving science computer simulations, it was found that students with very little knowledge of the subject area learned very little from the simulation. However, when students used the simulation again after studying the material, they were much more effective in their reasoning and performance (Finley, 1986).

Because simulations often deal with large numbers of variables, students may not be able to systematically deal with the multitude of variable combinations. In addition, the problem is often compounded by the unstructured learning approach common to many simulations. This is especially true for many children with learning disabilities who require highly structured learning activities. Teachers can reduce the problems associated with using simulations and increase the prospect of learning by utilizing four classroom techniques. These include: (1) introduction; (2) observation; (3) intervention; and (4) summation.

Introduction activities allow the teacher to familiarize students with the real-world environment being simulated. This provides students with a general understanding of the dynamics and breadth of variables involved in the simulation. In addition, introductory instruction serves to focus student attention on key simulation variables. Observation permits the teacher to monitor student interactions and progress with the simulation. This activity is important for identifying any student problems associated with content matter, and for identifying procedural problems related to operating the simulation. Intervention techniques permit the teacher to intervene in the simulation. For example, during the course of the simulation the teacher may wish to provide assistance to students having difficulty with variable interactions, redirect student attention to relevant variable combinations, or simply add information or share information with students. Finally, summation activities can be conducted at the conclusion of the simulation. This activity provides both the teacher and students with the opportunity to discuss and share learning experiences. Summation activities may include discussions of student problems-solving approaches, both successes and failures, as well as reiterating important variable combinations and their impact on simulation outcomes.

Computer simulation software is continuing to evolve, and new implementation schemes abound. The rapid pace of new design and development techniques often lead to radically different simulation formats and presentations. For example, some social-studies simulations use gamelike environments involving a few basic real-world variables relevant to the simulation; but although appealing to student users, these simulations may suffer from lack of realism. In another example, the operation of a nuclear reactor is simulated utilizing a large number of variables, making student variable-management and decision-making much more complex.

Characteristics of Simulation Software

- An understanding of processes inherent in the situation being modeled is communicated.

- Real environments are approximated.

- Generalized skills in simulated environments are applied.

- The student has operational control of the simulation.

- Usually more classroom time is required for completion than with other types of software.

In summary, simulation software attempts to model real-world events by allowing students the freedom to manipulate event variables and to model various problem situations. The student-computer relationship is highly interactive and may facilitate student cooperation and logical-thinking skills. Teachers may consider using simulation CAI in individualized or group settings to supplement regular classroom instruction, or using the software approach for introducing content. However, because of the wide variety of learning objectives and content-specific information presented in simulation designs, teachers may experience some difficulty when integrating simulations into the curriculum.

PROBLEM-SOLVING SOFTWARE

There is much debate in educational circles about the learning precedents related to a shift in focus from traditional instruction and the products of learning to the processes of learning. The controversial issue of directed learning methods versus discovery learning methods has already caused educators to rethink many goals and objectives of classroom instruction. Although research of discovery learning methods do not substantiate any past claims of greater achievement, current investigations are proposing that computers can finally offer the unique learning environments required for discovery learning, and may result in greater achievement gains than previously thought possible. The interest in microcomputer instruction has served to renew and even accelerate interest in a variety of new instructional approaches. Here too, the debate over various computer-based instructional approaches is no less controversial. Still, there is much support that there can be greater achievement gains utilizing computer-based discovery learning approaches than from more traditional computer-based instruction (Papert, 1980).

Historically, in terms of instructional delivery and student interaction, drill and tutorial software programs have evolved with an emphasis on computer-controlled delivery; that is, these software implementation designs manage most aspects of instructional content, format, presentation, and feedback, offering very structured learning environments. To some extent, the evolution of simulation software has shifted the delivery of computer-controlled instruction toward more flexible student-controlled learning environments by integrating instruction with learner interaction.

The emergence of problem-solving software is now facilitating a movement away from structured learning situations toward substantially unstructured learning environments. One of the consequences of an increased focus on discovery learning is there are no specific step-by-step procedures that, if followed correctly, will produce a desired instructional outcome. Another important issue related to problem-solving software is whether or not problem-solving skills utilizing computer-based methods will transfer to higher-level skills and skills in related content areas.

One of the difficulties in discussing problem solving is that there is little agreement about what defines problem solving and what skills are necessary to the learning activity. Still, across every content area there is usually a continuum of skills or knowledge required for effective learning. Bloom (1956) used a taxonomy to divide this continuum into (1) knowledge; (2) comprehension; (3) application; (4) analysis; (5) synthesis; and (6) evaluation. Often, educators refer to the first three as lower-order skills and the latter three as higher-order skills. For example, mathematics instruction using lower-order skills, such as learning whole numbers and practicing basic operations, develops lower-level skills. On the other hand, using the higher-order mathematics skills, such as applying various math models to real-world situations, supports analytic and higher-level thinking skills. It would seem that effective problem-solving procedures require a mix of both lower-order and higher-order skills. Figure 5-4 provides an example of a problem-solving software program.

As a result, problem-solving software may often contain many elements of the continuum of learning. For example, some problem-solving software may require recall skills, identifying relationships or patterns, variable experimentation, or even synthesizing existing rules into new relationships. Because of the wide variety of lower-order and higher-order skills involved in problem solving, this software approach tends to be less curriculum-specific than drill and tutorial programs, and often requires much creativity on the

JOHN, which monster did you create?

Figure 5-4. Problem-solving program: *The Incredible Laboratory.* (Screen reproduced by permission of Sunburst Communications.)

part of teachers for integration into classroom instruction. For teachers concerned with the skill-level requirements for using these programs, the discovery learning approach of problem-solving software may lead to many different content, format, and presentation schemes. As a consequence, some problem-solving packages may require extensive reading and note-taking skills; other may only require students to recognize and manipulate a few variables (words, graphics, numbers, etc.); or some programs may require a combination of analytic and joystick skills in gamelike situations.

The impact of microcomputer instruction on lower-order skills has been documented to a greater extent than instruction with higher-order skills has been. Some research results have suggested that computers can enhance learning for students at lower-skill levels, for example information acquisition or rule learning, but computer influence diminishes when students attempt to interact with computers using higher-order skills (Dreyfus and Dreyfus, 1984; Kulik, Bangert, and Williams, 1983). In a review of research on computer effectiveness in developing higher-level skills, Jamison, Suppes and Wells (1974) found that remedial students made more gains with computer-based instruction than did students attempting higher-level skill development. Some studies have shown that problem-solving situations can have positive effects on the development of cognitive skills and academic achievement (Clements, 1985; Gorman and Bourne, 1983). However, others report little, if any, significant achievement gains through the use of computer-based problem solving over more traditional computer instruction (Bass and Perkins, 1984 and Pea and Kurland, 1984).

In regard to the impact of student learning through computer-controlled software versus student-controlled programs, studies by Lahey (1978) and Wilcox (1978) did not find any evidence supporting superior performance by either method of instructional delivery. However, others have found significant difference in favor of learner-controlled computer environments (Campanazzi, 1978).

Characteristics of Problem-Solving Software

- Generalized skills from many areas of the continuum of learning, including lower- and higher-order skills, are applied.

- This software is less curriculum-specific.

- Content, format, and presentation schemes vary widely.

- Students use the discovery learning approach.

To date, the evolution of problem-solving software may be characterized by approaches utilizing less-structured learning environments in such a way that the delivery of instruction has shifted from computer-controlled to learner-controlled methods. In addition, student interaction centers on discovery learning activities, which may encourage more analytic thinking skills. Because problem-solving software can incorporate a wide variety of both lower-order and higher-order skills, integrating these programs into a specific curriculum requires more time and creativity from teachers.

GAME SOFTWARE

Educational games have always been an integral part of the teaching process. They are commonly used for practicing creative, artistic, visual, and auditory skills, and are even used in classrooms for teaching instructional objectives. With the introduction and success of both home and commercial computer video-arcade games, interest has again centered on the experimental use of microcomputer gaming techniques in learning environments.

Typically, most commercial video games have few, if any, practical instructional objectives. However, these games may have some beneficial intrinsic qualities with some transferability to instructional situations. For example, games can encourage task-engaging behaviors, provide task challenge and motivation, and elicit goal-directed activities. As such, microcomputer gam-

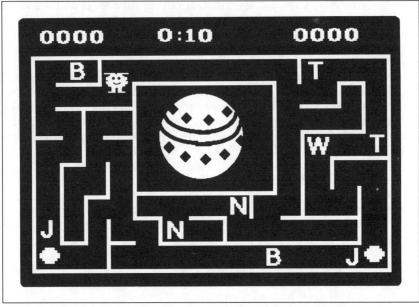

Figure 5-5. Game software: *Alphabet Zoo.* (Screen reproduced by permission of Spinnaker.)

ing may have the potential for these qualities when used in certain learning situations. Figure 5-5 provides an example of a game program.

In educational settings, games can be defined by their instructional approach and can be used for introducing concepts, teaching concepts, or as a drill and practice technique for previously introduced instructional material (Bright, Harvey, and Wheeler, 1985). In addition, games can be classified by the lower-order and higher-order cognitive skills being taught. Dennis, Muiznieks, and Stewart (1979) have characterized these game situations as free-form, rigid-form, and open-form designs. Free-form designs are based on simulating events, people, or other real-world scenarios, and usually require students to use analytic thinking skills. Examples of free-form game software include simulations of TV game shows, athletic events, or situations that require role playing of historic events. Rigid-form games use drill and practice methods, concentrating on developing students' lower-order skills such as information acquisition or rule learning.

In a review of current instructional software selections, many commercial drill and practice software programs use rigid game designs as part of their instructional presentation technique, providing students with practice lessons designed for skill acquisition. In addition, some open-form games use modeling or simulation techniques, encouraging the development of higher-order problem solving skills such as problem analysis and solution synthesis. However, open-form game software programs usually don't simulate real-world situations. Instead, these game designs manifest themselves in many now-popular adventure and fantasy game programs.

Examination of the literature regarding the motivational aspects inherent in game activities is abundant (Anderson, 1983; Bowman, 1983; Chaffin, 1983; Chaffin, Maxwell, and Thompson, 1982; Malone, 1983; and Pepin and Leroux, 1984). The general findings indicate positive motivational attitudes toward computer games. Similarly, computer game situations (at least at the motivational level) seem to be appropriate for individuals experiencing few successful instructional situations (Driskell and Dwyer, 1984).

In addition to the motivational qualities of video games, some research indicates that the interactive characteristics of gaming situations can be important to the transfer of student learning (Greenfield, 1984). There is also significant research that indicates early childhood games may enhance development of memory patterns, sequence tasks, and may serve as a tool for problem solving (Karoff, 1983 and Bowman, 1983). Ziajka (1983) contends that computer games may stimulate social interactions, encouraging young children to share learning experiences. Similarly, computer games may be beneficial in preschool settings when introduced through play activities (Boegehold, 1984).

However, the impact of gaming techniques on lower-order and higher-order skills has been mixed. Kraus (1981) successfully used computer gaming to teach addition facts; however, the same technique was unsuccessful in teaching spelling words. Bright, Harvey, and Wheeler (1980a) found that gaming situations were effective for the review of instructional material, and a long-term study indicates that games can help retain content skills. Conversely, Bright, Harvey, and Wheeler (1980b), in a study of the effects of increased student interaction, found that increasing student verbalization during game situations had little effect on student achievement.

Another manifestation of contemporary game software programs is the potential effect of video-game violence on student users. Levin (1982) suggests that violent fantasies in educational software may have negative effects by producing a "machine-like mentality" in its users. Similarly, others observe that combining high interaction with high violence can have a negative effect upon children, since these games offer models of violence and opportunities for practicing aggressive behaviors (Bandura, 1978; Stein, 1981).

Characteristics of Educational Game Software

- Logical thinking and self-exploration skills are encouraged.

- Goal-directed activities are elicited.

• This software is challenging and motivating.

• Task-engaging behaviors are encouraged.

• This software shares characteristics with all software domains.

In summary, game software can model real-world events by using simulation or role-playing techniques, thereby emphasizing development of analytic problem-solving skills. In other design approaches, gaming software may use drill and practice approaches for developing skill mastery, encouraging the development of lower-order skills. Finally, some gaming techniques foster discovery learning and highly interactive user participation, which may facilitate the development of higher-order skills such an analytic and logical thinking, and promote student cooperation skills. Teachers may consider using game software in individualized or group settings to supplement regular classroom instruction, provide exploratory learning activities, or as a device for motivating students.

INSTRUCTIONAL SOFTWARE TOOLS: CLASSROOM REALITIES

When reflecting on the instructional software programs covered in this chapter, it should be noted that each approach has evolved with unique instructional delivery techniques, and each design supports specific learning objectives, including both lower- and higher-order learning skills. When one combines these instructional realities with the fact that many thousands of educational software programs are now available to schools, it is no surprise that educators often have difficulty implementing microcomputer instruction in schools. As a teacher, one knows that the selection of teaching techniques is usually based on matching appropriate instructional objectives specific to student needs. Hence, decisions regarding the use of computer software must also center on identifying student strengths and weaknesses, defining the learning objective, and selecting a software environment that best facilitates the learning experience.

For instance, if a reading teacher wishes to teach some lower-order reading skills, such as having students recognize the alphabet, then drill and practice software may be an alternative to CAI. Or if higher-order analytic problem-solving skills are the learning objective, an example of which might be applying math skills to everyday life as with budgeting money, teachers may consider using simulations or problem-solving software. Clearly, in making effective software-implementation decisions, one must consider learning objectives and a software environment that complements the instructional activity.

To this end, Figure 5-6 provides the reader with perspectives on each of the current instructional software approaches, including (1) descriptions of each

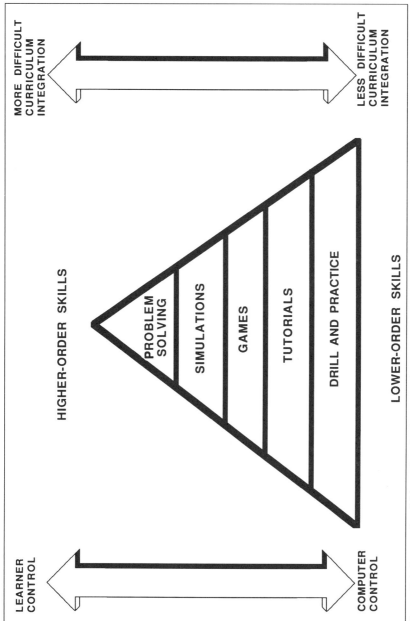

Figure 5-6. Instructional hierarchy of software tools.

software design and its typical instructional delivery system; (2) descriptions of the primary learning objectives inherent to each design; and (3) general indicators for teacher of the difficulty of planning, using, and integrating these programs into a school curriculum.

As Figure 5-6 illustrates, the emphasis of the model is on the current body of instructional software approaches: drill, tutorial, game, simulation, and problem-solving. Lower-order skills are inherent to those software applications at the base of the triangle hierarchy, and higher-order skills to those software designs at the top. The scale along the left side of the triangle describes each software design and its typical instructional delivery system. For example, the bottom of the scale represents a computer-delivered approach, characterized by computer control over lesson pacing, content, presentation, feedback, and prompted user interaction and response. The top of the scale represents a highly interactive and user-controlled software environment, characterized by discovery learning approaches. To the immediate right of this scale is one that reflects the primary learning objectives inherent to each software design. For example, the bottom of the scale represents lower-order skills, such as fact acquisition and rule learning. Conversely, the top of the scale represents higher-order skills, which may include analytic thinking skills and ultimately metacognition. The reader should note that these are generalities and some software programs may fit in several levels of the hierarchy. Finally, the scale of curriculum integration (the farthest scale to the right) provides a general understanding of the lesson planning, teaching, direction, feedback, and, possibly, training required to implement the software approach into school curricula.

One should consider microcomputer instruction as a general-purpose instructional tool, and, as such, can be used to accomplish different instructional objectives. Ultimately, the teacher must decide the "right" way and the "wrong" way to use this tool. Much of the power of a computer as an educational tool lies in the teacher's ability and creativity to enhance an idea, support it with knowledge of the technology, and implement the technology in a stimulating and motivating learning environment.

TEACHER TOOLS FOR DEVELOPING INSTRUCTIONAL SOFTWARE

Integrating instructional software into the curriculum often requires much experimentation and is generally characterized by an iterative implementation process. A typical classroom scenario has the teacher identifying student needs, accompanied by seemingly endless searches through educational catalogs, magazines, and/or journals for appropriate software, and culminating in some type of software selection process, which is often based on commercial marketing appeal rather than sound instructional design. Once purchased, the software is used in the classroom, evaluated, and very often found to have either marginal capabilities, limited content flexibility, or is simply inappropriate. As a result, the teacher provides alternative ideas, repeats the software-selection process, and possibly, with successive attempts, can select software that meets with the original instructional needs. Moreover, among classrooms with large student populations and heterogeneous needs, it may take too long for teachers to carry out this type of selection process and, unfortunately, can result in limited classroom opportunities for microcomputer utilization. Furthermore, even when teachers locate effective instructional software, these software tools generally provide lessons with very specific content and offer teachers little flexibility for individualizing content. In addition, the time and energy required to make software selections may not justify the results, especially when the software supports very singular and limited learning activities.

In response to these software shortcomings, a variety of teacher tools are evolving to address the problems of software accessibility, suitability, curriculum integration, and content flexibility. Instructional-software development tools attempt to provide a vehicle for nonprogrammers to create stand-alone instructional software lessons. In addition, these development tools, often termed *authoring* tools, use a variety of implementation approaches for allowing the user to generate instructional software (Jensen, 1982). The following sections will describe three current types of authoring tools that are designed to aid teachers in developing flexible instructional software.

EDITABLE INSTRUCTIONAL SOFTWARE TOOLS

To a large extent, the authoring approach of editable instructional software tools really doesn't create "new" stand-alone instructional software programs. Rather, it simply provides teachers with the ability to modify a few instructional elements of a finished software program. As such, teachers can enter new content, edit old content, or simply adjust selected presentation features such as sound or number of lesson questions. In fact, many current commercial drill and practice, game, simulation, tutorial, and problem-solving software packages incorporate these features. For example, utilizing a drill and practice spelling program, teachers can enter new lists of weekly spelling words or edit inappropriate word lists out of the software program; this offers teachers the flexibility for individualizing students lessons. Also, by adjusting presentation features such as speed controls, teachers can modify response times to accommodate students with physical impairments.

To accomplish these modification tasks, editable software programs contain an instructional program "shell" that provides the actual instruction and an additional small "edit" program that teachers use to edit lesson material. These edit programs usually present a series of user-friendly prompts and/or menus. By responding to question prompts, teachers can create, edit, and delete lesson content, or change selected presentation features.

The major advantage of using editable software programs in classroom settings is that they can alleviate some problems associated with fixed software content. By providing easy-to-use edit menus, teacher can quickly modify lesson content and some program presentation features without the need for programming skills.

However, editable software programs still have very structured lesson environments and usually don't offer the teacher much flexibility for changing lessons. For example, teachers usually can't change a screen display; they cannot modify a drill program to work as a simulation, rearrange a cluttered screen design, or substitute different lesson question formats, such as fill-in-the-blank for multiple-choice schemes.

AUTHORING SYSTEMS TOOLS

Under some classroom situations, editable instructional software tools can't always provide teachers with enough instructional flexibility for meeting all student needs. However, an alternative development tool can be used for creating more flexible instructional software. Teachers may consider using an *authoring system* approach. Authoring systems are more comprehensive and sophisticated than editable instructional software tools (see Figure 5-7). Unlike the finished instructional software and small edit programs found in most editable software tools, authoring systems usually don't originate as predesigned, ready-to-run, instructional software programs. Instead, authoring systems allow teachers to plan, design, and develop instructional software programs using frame-based or menuing schemes, as will be further discussed. For the moment, the reader should simply understand that these methods allow teachers to create software lessons "from scratch" without actually doing any computer programming. This is the key feature of authoring systems.

When creating lessons, authoring systems usually allow teachers to organize, integrate, and sequence most lesson features. Consequently, teachers are responsible for making many more instructional decisions regarding lesson design. This provides teachers with much greater flexibility and control over lesson development than is provided by editable instructional software tools. Teachers can make decisions regarding many software lesson features, including, for example, lesson content, instructions, questions, remedial feedback, student reinforcement, or even branching schemes for individualizing student learning. Still, the reader should note that the ability to author these various lesson features will vary dramatically in different

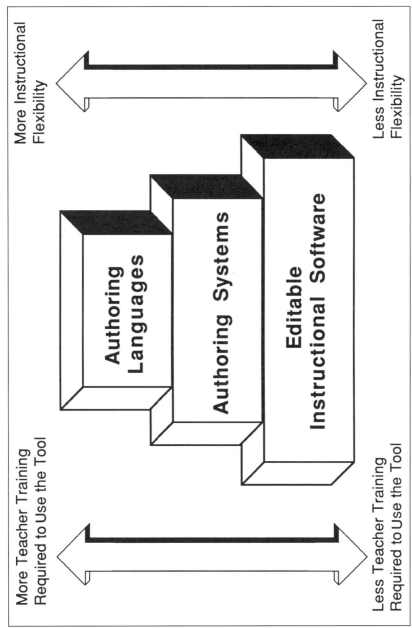

Figure 5-7. Characteristics of instructional software development tools.

authoring systems. The procedures that teachers must use to author lesson features are also diverse.

For example, some authoring systems present a series of predesigned menus and prompts to ask teachers for instructional content material, instructions, questions, answers, feedback, and so forth. The menu-and-prompting format provides teachers with a structured technique for designing and creating lessons. Authoring systems that incorporate menu schemes greatly facilitate use.

Another authoring system approach uses frame-based techniques for creating lessons. These methods often present blank screens on which the teacher can create instructional text fields, write lesson frames, draw graphic segments, or even create graphic animation frames. As the instructional designer, the teacher is responsible for organizing the lesson by sequencing the presentation of each frame. Although this technique requires more teacher effort than for menuing systems, it can increase lesson-design flexibility by providing the instructional designer with more control over screen design and lesson-presentation sequencing.

Generally, all authoring systems have the difficult task of trying to balance lesson-design flexibility with an easy-to-use system. Too often, attempting to provide ease of use while still supporting very high levels of authoring flexibility can prove to be a paradox—these two efforts actually cancel each other out. For instance, the lesson breadth and flexibility of menu-driven authoring systems are largely based on the quality and quantity of predesigned menu questions. As more questions are added to the authoring system, lesson flexibility increases; but as question prompts are added, teachers become overwhelmed with the information requirements and ease of use decreases. Similarly, authoring systems that use unstructured frame-based techniques often have comprehensive and flexible lesson-design environments. However, generating lessons often requires much analysis of student needs, identifying specific instructional strategies, mapping out appropriate branching techniques for individual learning styles, and matching all the other various instructional needs with effective computer design techniques. Unfortunately, few classroom teachers have the planning time and/or computer competencies required to maximize the capabilities of authoring systems during regular school hours. Consequently, teachers must seriously consider the added time required to learn and use authoring systems. Question how much time and effort are needed and how much utilizing authoring systems really contributes to classroom CAI. Teachers may wish to consider the following criteria when making decisions regarding the use of authoring systems:

1. Does computer instruction provide an appropriate alternative to more traditional methods?

2. Can an instructional software program meet the instructional needs of the learning activity?
3. Can editable instructional software programs meet the instructional needs of the learning activity?
4. Can a planned series of editable instructional software programs meet the instructional and student needs of the learning activity?
5. Can authoring systems meet the instructional needs of the learning activity?
6. Is there willingness to learn an authoring system?
7. Is there adequate teacher time and resources to explore, research, learn, and use an authoring system?
8. Is a menu authoring system or a less structured frame-based authoring system more suitable for teacher lesson development?
9. Does the authoring system provide adequate lesson-design features for meeting the instructional needs of the intended lesson?
10. Can the system provide appropriate tools for modeling-required teaching strategies?

AUTHORING LANGUAGE TOOLS

Teachers may find that editable software and authoring system tools can't always facilitate the creation of adequate instructional environments that are sometimes required by special-needs students. Under these circumstances, teachers may consider using an authoring language. These software development tools are much more powerful and flexible than editable software or authoring systems. Like most computer languages, authoring languages contain a set of commands enabling educators to design and build their own educational software. However, the major thrust behind the development of authoring languages is the belief that if one can make computer programming languages less abstract and easier to use, authors will be encouraged to write and develop their own software. Typically, authoring languages accomplish this task by reducing the number of commands required to build software programs. In this way, the author can use one command to accomplish a programming task rather than the whole set of commands that can be required by general-purpose programming languages. Similarly, these commands have become less computer-like and more English-like (Bender and Church, 1984). This type of programming vocabulary may reduce problems associated with integrating different software elements such as student input, text screen design, graphics and animation, sound creation, and lesson logic sequencing.

The major advantage of authoring languages is the vast authoring flexibility inherent to software lesson design. Teachers have control over many lesson decisions, such as autonomy over instructional design, content, presentation features, program-management features, and even student response modes. Basically, teachers build lessons from scratch involving few constraints other than the rules and syntax requirements intrinsic to the authoring language. While authoring systems are usually easier to learn than general-purpose programming languages and require fewer hours than in more traditional programming, they do require users to master computer languages and develop instructional design skills.

Although many authoring languages are easy to learn and use, they still require much planning and design effort in order to properly implement software development. In addition to mastering a programming language, teachers must also complement this training with effective instructional design skills in order to implement teaching lessons. Hence, it takes very dedicated and highly motivated teachers to use this tool on a regular basis for developing educational software. In studies regarding authoring-language utilization, it is shown that before undertaking lesson development potential users should closely match the authoring system's capabilities with the specific instructional situation (Gillingham, Murphy, Cresci, Klevenow, Sims-Tucker, Slade, and Wizer, 1986; Pattison, 1985). Furthermore, teachers are encouraged to scrutinize instructional objectives, evaluate instructional strategies, and carefully implement computer design techniques (Dick and Carey, 1985). Accordingly, few teachers regularly use these instructional software development tools in the classroom. Authoring languages require many skills from the teacher—computer programming skills, instructional design skills, and knowledge of computer-based instruction techniques.

To summarize software development tools, Figure 5-7 presents teachers with general characteristics regarding the utilization of instructional tools. These characteristics include ease of tool use, training requirements for use, and overall flexibility of the tool developing software. Educators, when planning microcomputer instruction, may consider these characteristics before implementing such development tools. This enables the educator to evaluate the time, resources, and effort required to effectively use these tools in classroom settings.

SOFTWARE PRODUCTIVITY TOOLS

For many educators it would seem there is never enough time to address all the learning needs native to the classroom, particularly in special-needs settings where intensive individualized instruction is the norm. This teaching process regularly demands many hours for planning, organizing, and creating specialized instructional material. At best, teachers are often required to balance precious little time between planning and instruction—and frequently only among the most pressing classroom needs. Software productivity tools have the potential to aid teachers in utilizing the time required to plan, design, and generate classroom materials. For example, these tools can assist teachers in designing and developing classroom tests, quizzes, school forms, art, or bulletin board materials. In addition, productivity tools can supplement educational evaluation tasks by providing testing diagnoses and analyses of student learning not easily available through traditional testing methods. These tools can also act as instructional vehicles for supporting classroom learning activities. For example, graphics programs can aid teachers in developing charts and maps. These are only a few of the many examples of microcomputer productivity tools available to classroom teachers. To adequately describe the variety of productivity tools presently on the commercial market is beyond the scope of this chapter. However, this section will discuss a few of the major productivity tools presently being utilized as instructional tools in classroom environments.

To begin, the reader should understand that unlike instructional software and authoring tools, productivity software tools do not provide CAI. These software systems lack most of the elements necessary for true interactive computer instruction. For example, software productivity programs usually lack an appropriate instructional design for delivering specific content material; lack instructional feedback mechanisms or remedial prompts; offer few techniques for creating individualized instruction; and provide little or no control for scheduling lesson presentation. Hence, when using these tools as a supplement to instructional activities, one should consider frequent interaction, feedback, and guidance between students and teachers.

WORD PROCESSING TOOLS

These productivity tools are often used in classroom settings that involve comprehension and writing activities. The primary purpose of word processors is to support the writing process by providing users with a tool that can electronically record and manipulate concepts and ideas. In support of this goal, word processing programs feature numerous methods for entering, deleting, editing, merging, and saving written material. The text-editing capabilities of word processing programs are very advantageous for students needing to revise the edit written material (Bean, 1983; Daiute, 1982, 1983; Hennings, 1981, 1983; Schwartz, 1984; Whithey, 1983). Similarly, these editing features may encourage students to do more revising during writing (Stromberg and Kurth, 1984; Womble, 1984). Word processing programs offer many modalities for communicating ideas and concepts, including written text, pictures, synthesized human speech, and a combination of these and others. Different writing modalities provide students with a variety of visual, auditory, and tactile assistance modes, offering a range of instruments for expressing concepts and ideas. When selecting a classroom word processing tool, teachers should find a writing modality that supplements students' learning strengths. Similarly, the writing tool should provide a balanced set of flexible editing features that meet the students' writing needs while not overwhelming the student with complex features and overly sophisticated procedures for utilizing the writing tool.

Some word processors offer writing modalities that support text entry in combination with synthesized human speech. These writing programs provide general text-editing functions, and, in addition, provide student users with some auditory feedback of written material. For example, students can request that the writing program speak letters, words, sentences, paragraphs, or even whole documents. Although synthesized speech is often not as natural sounding as a real human voice and many not always reproduce accurate pronunciations, it does provide auditory links and feedback to written material and can have potential as a compensatory instructional device. Some researchers have suggested that adolescents with learning disabilities find speech synthesizers as intelligible as a human tutor (Icabone and Hannaford, 1986).

Other writing programs provide students with the ability to develop ideas and concepts through the use of written text and pictures. Using this writing modality, students can write stories that include a mixture of text and graphics. This writing environment is very interactive and can be motivating for some student users. Similar writing programs, although limited in text-editing features and control of subject content, allow students to enter stories using regular text-entry methods. However, the software program animates the story with picture graphics based on the story's subject.

In addition, other writing programs support the ability to display differently sized screen text characters, giving visually impaired students access to text word processing. Furthermore, word processing tools that provide a choice of text-editing features and text screen modes, such as 20- 40-, and 80-column screen displays, can offer a cost-effective writing tool for both students and teachers. For instance, as students develop writing skills and master basic processes and features, they can move up to more complex features inherent to 80-column screen modes. Similarly, less introductory teaching is required because students use the same writing tool; as such, students can utilize the same word processing features mastered at lower levels as they advance to more complex word processing features. Figure 5-8 is an example of a word processing program that incorporates pull-down menus and icons and provides the ability to include graphics in the text.

Despite the variety of writing modalities and editing features inherent to word processing programs, these productivity tools provide relatively little feedback on the use of program features or even on writing mechanics. For example, few current word processing programs can adequately direct the student thinking process or provide students with idea-and-concept–development strategies. Indeed, word processing environments have many features that support writing and editing flexibility. However, word processing

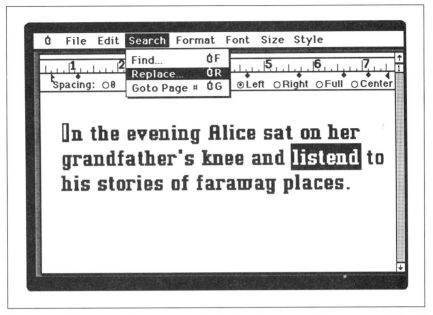

Figure 5-8. Word processing program: *MultiScribe.* (Screen reproduced by permission of StyleWare, Inc.)

is usually characterized by open-ended writing activities. Although these situations may encourage students to learn, unstructured learning activities can leave some students, especially those having difficulty organizing their ideas, with few effective tools for developing coherent concepts. Hence, when implementing word processing tools in classroom settings, teachers may wish to consider some instructional issues associated with student use of these tools.

First, because these productivity tools usually offer students only limited feedback on the use of word processing features, instruction must be provided on the processes inherent to the use of basic word processing features. MacArthur and Schneiderman (1986) suggest that many text-editing features are difficult to learn for special-needs students. For example, opening and closing files, understanding cursor movement commands, or recognizing the difference between text entry and edit modes may be difficult for some children to learn. Because mechanical issues tend to draw students away from focusing on composing their ideas, teachers may wish to respond to this issue by providing initial instruction on procedures for using word processing tools and then supplement word processing activities with appropriate procedural directions and encouragement during writing activities.

When contemplating the need for additional content feedback in word processors, teachers may consider the use of spelling and grammar features. Many word processing programs provide built-in electronic dictionaries, which can provide students with content feedback on some aspects of writing mechanics. For example, many electronic dictionaries can find errors in spelling, punctuation, capitalization, and can even analyze sentence, paragraph and document structure by providing the writer with statistics on word counts, reading level, or word repetitions.

Teachers may also consider developing other student skills that can facilitate student use of word processing tools. Depending on student's visual and motor abilities, teachers may wish to encourage the development of keyboarding skills. Such instruction may increase student familiarity with keyboard layout and cultivate fluency and rhythm in its use. Researchers examining microcomputer typing tutorials have found that, depending on the quality of the tutorial software, computer touch-typing can improve keyboard speed and accuracy (Schmidt and Stewart, 1983). For elementary school populations, touch-typing methods seem to be superior to hunt-and-peck methods (Stewart and Jones, 1983; Kisner, 1984). In addition, touch-typing during word processing can offer benefits when transcribing written material to the computer (Gentner and Norman, 1984). Unfortunately, once incorrect typing methods become habit, it is very difficult with many students to correct such problems (Stewart and Jones, 1983; Beverstock, 1984).

Finally and most importantly, because of the open-ended nature of word processing tools and their limited information-feedback abilities, teachers should consider developing appropriate instructional feedback mechanisms for students. Effective communication during the writing process should include timely and purposeful teacher feedback on and direction of student writing efforts. However, overemphasis on corrective feedback can hinder student writing. Still, teacher guidance is critical for effective classroom use. Wheeler (1985) suggests that the teacher role must be emphasized during the writing process if students are to improve. The literature also seems to indicate that information feedback helps to encourage student revisions (Fisher, 1983; McLeod, 1983; Metzger, 1983). Consequently, both student and teacher interaction during writing activities may encourage revision activities and improve student attitude toward writing activities.

The major advantage of using word processing tools in classroom settings is that they can provide a set of flexible writing and editing tools for developing ideas and concepts. By offering a variety of different writing modalities supplemented with easy-to-use text entry and edit menus, word processing tools can provide both teachers and students with powerful writing tools. However, word processing programs, by their nature, are very open-ended user tools and don't offer much feedback to the user. Hence, teachers must usually provide instruction in the use of these productivity tools, as well as furnish appropriate monitoring and feedback during student writing activities.

ADDITIONAL PRODUCTIVITY SOFTWARE TOOLS

Word processing tools can offer teachers and students unique microcomputer environments for facilitating communication and expressing ideas. Nevertheless, because communication often takes on forms other than written, a number of related software tools are evolving to enhance the capabilities of basic word processing tools. Some productivity programs are integrating, in addition to word processing features, a variety of software tools that can create, edit, and manipulate graphs, charts, and pictures. The combination of these tools has led to the emergence of *desktop publishing* software.

Desktop publishing tools, in conjunction with computer hardware such as laser printers, allow users to create professional-quality documents. For example, users can generate documents using traditional word processing programs and then import the writing into desktop publishing programs that allow users to change text styles, sizes, and page layout. In addition, using a range of graphic editing tools, users can blend and retouch photographic images and combine them with artwork created with other drawing programs. Finally, desktop publishing programs allow all the imported text, data, and graphics to be moved around the screen for page composition and layout tasks.

Currently, the authors are successfully utilizing Apple Computer's Macintosh microcomputer with a variety of productivity tools such as word processing, graphic design, and desktop publishing programs with learning-disabled students to create school newspapers and yearbooks. The Macintosh computer's highly integrated user interface is being used to facilitate the transfer of student computer skills developed in one software program to other computer tasks. For example, the computer's user interface supports very consistent menu commands across different software programs; also, the interface supports the ability for different software productivity tools to independently exchange text, data, graphics, and sound information. In classroom settings, these features have eliminated the need for students to learn large, comprehensive software packages, thus allowing teachers to utilize smaller, more manageable software programs while still retaining the ability to combine ideas and information across different software productivity packages. The Macintosh interface benefits the teacher by reducing the instructional time required to introduce new software programs. Furthermore, the consistent user interface benefits students because familiar commands and menu processes, standard across various software programs, encourage students by reinforcement to apply previously introduced computer skills.

Another productivity tool that can be used in classrooms is the *spreadsheet* program. These software tools allow users to enter, edit, and manipulate numbers. Most spreadsheets provide computer-screen work sheets that give the user the flexibility to enter and organize numbers. In addition, users can create formulas that perform calculations on any set of numbers. An advantage of a spreadsheet is that once numbers are entered, it can recalculate a work sheet very quickly, and the user need only change key numbers or formulas to see the results. This feature allows the user to alter key variables and perform sophisticated "what if" analysis on a set of figures. Similarly, many spreadsheets allow users to express numeric data as graphic information in the form of graphs or charts.

When classroom applications require collecting, organizing, saving, or sorting large amounts of textual, numerical, or graphical information, the most flexible productivity tool to use would be a data-base management program. These productivity tools provide quick and convenient access to large sources of information. For example, *HyperCard* from Apple Computer has changed the face of data-base software tools for many users. This program has opened up a unique new visual information environment for teachers and students. The program allows users to create and store many different types of information media, including words, documents, numbers, charts, pictures, photographs, sounds, music, recorded human voices, video images, and animation—information about almost any subject required. In addition, any piece of information can be linked together through the data base with very little or no required programming skills. The possibilities for instruction are endless. For example, if a student wishes to conduct a search on an American president, say John F. Kennedy, the student could access written text on his social and economic reforms, retrieve actual video and audio from his original speeches, or access charts and maps from international crises such as the Cuban Missile Crisis. The multimedia possibilities of this productivity tool have changed the nature of data-base management programs. As a result, the present scope and function of data-base programs will change dramatically over the next few years.

If classroom instructional activities require communications between separate computers, telecommunication programs that allow computers to share text, graphics, and other information over telephone lines are available. These productivity tools can allow schools to establish information links with other schools and organizations across the country and around the world. Typically, telecommunications are done over "bulletin board" systems. These electronic message boards are used to post information about events, research, computer-user groups, computer hardware and software, or just as a means to communicate with other individuals.

In many cases, it is desirable to have access to a number of productivity tools in a single software program. Integrated software packages provide the user with the flexibility and convenience of using multiple productivity tools within the confines of a single software package. In addition, integrated software programs provide the ability to easily exchange textual, numerical, graphical, and other information between different productivity tools. Basically, these programs combine a number of productivity tools into one software program for addressing many tasks. For example, an integrated software package may provide teachers with both a word processing tool for writing student reports or evaluations and a data-base management tool for recording and storing student names, test scores, individual instructional objectives, or other relevant information. By using both tools in association, teachers can manipulate and integrate both test score data and written material using a single software package.

Historically, integrated software packages have offered microcomputer users some of the flexibility and convenience found in larger mainframe computer environments that allow users to operate many large software programs in unison. Although most current school microcomputers cannot run multiple software programs simultaneously, integrated software programs do allow users to change software tools quickly for different tasks; and, in addition, they support easy transfer of information between different software tools. While integrated software packages will continue to be important for smaller, less powerful microcomputer systems, new advancements in microcomputer and software technology are providing users with more responsive and flexible task environments.

Many newer microcomputers are now supporting the ability to run separate software programs simultaneously, called *multitasking* computer environments, and hence allow teachers to perform a variety of tasks simultaneously. For example, future classroom multitasking computer environments will allow educators to run specialized evaluation and diagnostic software tools that can monitor student performance during actual CAI activities. While this evaluation is occurring, the teacher can run data-base management tools that capture and match student performance data with stored information in effective instructional designs, and the database tool can then feed back alternative instructional strategies to the CAI software. Smarter productivity tools and the ability to control multiple tasks will eventually make software and computers easier to use. Most importantly for teachers, all these instructional tasks will be able to be utilized and managed instantly during daily classroom instruction!

CAI software and the wide variety of support and productivity tools offer many opportunities for supporting the teacher and enriching the learning environment. Still, the critical element for successfully implementing educational computer technology continues to be the teacher. It is the teacher who understands the learning needs of students and who must take an active role in deciding what works and what doesn't work in the classroom. As with all learning devices, teachers must evaluate and enhance the technology in order to provide an effective balance between the potential benefits of microcomputers and the practical realities of classroom instruction. To this end, the following section will focus on issues related to evaluating instructional software.

EVALUATING INSTRUCTIONAL SOFTWARE

With the plethora of new instructional software programs entering the education market, it becomes harder for school systems to adequately review and evaluate the instructional promise of evolving software programs. In many cases, schools have few formal mechanisms for reviewing software and providing practical information to classroom teachers. Too often, magazines and journals are the only source of software reviews for teachers. Although sometimes helpful, few of these reviews can adequately detail information for application to the specific needs of individual children, or consistently provide responsive information on the special curricular needs of schools. Hence, it is not surprising to see the difficulty teachers experience when trying to integrate software into classroom settings. Nevertheless, what success CAI has enjoyed in schools to date is largely the result of efforts by very energetic and creative teachers. Unfortunately, the review and evaluation process does require much time and resource utilization; few teachers have the time to complete extensive software searches and still be able to accomplish planning and teaching activities. Consequently, when implementing microcomputer-based instruction, an essential preliminary planning function should include the development of a responsive school link to information resources.

ADMINISTRATIVE ROLES: DEVELOPING AND SUPPORTING INFORMATION LINKS

The need for information on a variety of subjects is always important when planning and developing school microcomputer programs. However, the demand for information seems to be acute when schools endeavor to implement instructional software in classroom settings. The process of information acquisition often involves reviews and evaluations from many sources. Therefore, schools usually must have information links to a variety of resources. Schools may consider several sources: local education agencies, private schools, independent school districts, colleges, community colleges, universities, and state education agencies. Many of these sources organize reviews or provide networks that coordinate and disseminate reviews related to educational software. Obviously, funding, time, and the availability of other resources limit the size and breadth of activities relegated to developing school information links. However, leadership and support must come from administrative sources. By providing direction and facilitating access to information on instructional software, administrators greatly reduce the work required of staff when searching through vast sources of instructional material.

In developing information links that facilitate effective information exchange, administrators may wish to consider the following roles: (1) develop and support a flexible and accessible information network; (2) acquaint teachers with the information network, its accessibility, and the links to available information sources; (3) direct teacher attention to curriculum-specific projects, research, and other hands-on information; (4) affirm and support staff release time needed to access information resources; (5) announce and document information for dissemination; and (6) provide the information network with an open channel for timely teacher feedback. These administrative actions help build and maintain a framework that is responsive to teachers who need to be able to locate and access information resources quickly and easily.

TEACHER ROLES: USING INFORMATION LINKS TO SUPPORT INSTRUCTION

In conjunction with the administrative efforts toward developing appropriate school communication and information links, teachers can provide direction for developing and refining a set of practical evaluation procedures for screening appropriate information from the school's information sources. For example, it would be unrealistic to suggest teachers be responsible for reviewing and tracking all current information on software applications. The pace of new educational software releases would make this task very difficult, if not impossible. However, scrutinizing information on instructional software must involve developing effective evaluation methods that embody suitable instructional criteria from which to measure instructional software.

For educators developing their own software through the use of authoring languages, authoring systems, or general-purpose programming languages, the literature does provide some documented processes for doing formative evaluations on instructional materials (Cohen, 1983; Jay, 1983; Roblyer, 1981). In addition, some studies document software design and student use as a result of using this method (Shaw-Nickerson and Kisker, 1984). These evaluation techniques can help instructional designers measure the processes by which instructional materials are developed. The criteria suggested for formative evaluations, and, in addition, examples of software programs that utilize these design techniques, provide educators with general guidelines on developing instructional software.

There are also various methods available to educators for evaluating existing commercial educational software. Methods and techniques frequently used for this type of review are often termed summative evaluations and usually measure the results of instructional software programs (Baker and Schutz, 1971; Kandaswamy, 1980). In addition, there are other evaluation and screening techniques that require little experimental investigation (Futrell and Geisert, 1984; Steinberg, 1983). In fact, some evaluation methods can measure software ease of use, interest levels, and student interaction and behavior. Typically, these evaluation methods involve rating scales, surveys, or general observations.

Finally, when utilizing these methods, administrators and teachers should consider the time, energy, and resources required to implement these evaluation tools. Software evaluations as a process should provide a careful balance between the informational needs of teachers and the preparation and management necessary for undertaking such analyses.

SOFTWARE EVALUATION METHODS AND TECHNIQUES

Typically, information-screening techniques for reviewing instructional software involve some type of standard evaluation form. These forms, whether utilizing *yes/no*, multiple-choice, or checklist formats, generally contain information on a variety of software characteristics, for example (1) a review of the program's instructional content, which usually covers quantity, quality, sequence, and remedial and modification issues; (2) a critique of the program's utilization of computer capabilities, often involving a review of graphics, color, text, and sound; (3) a review of the instructional goals and objectives of software programs, entailing identifying intended learning objectives and determining if they are met; (4) consideration of software-presentation items such as lesson pacing, ability levels, ease of use, and material presentation; (5) a listing of software product information, such as publisher, title, and computer format; and (6) a review (sometimes to a lesser extent) of user manuals and documentation materials. Unfortunately, instructional software evaluation forms contain little uniformity with regard to evaluation criteria and procedural evaluation techniques and often vary dramatically when compared with one another.

The reader should note that few guidelines currently exist for developing and selecting the most appropriate software evaluation technique. A review of software-evaluation approaches indicates that these tools are often either too simplistic or much too sophisticated for teachers to use in classroom settings (Brownstein and Lerner, 1982; Flake, McClintock, and Turner, 1985; Shanahan and Ryan, 1984; and Wright and Forcier, 1985). However, the Educational Software Evaluation Consortium, a nonprofit software evaluation agency composed of state, regional, and local education agencies, has attempted to identify those criteria that are most critical to instructional software evaluation. In a questionnaire developed and completed by the consortium's 28 educational software evaluation agencies, a list of 22 criteria were identified and given a rank order. The results indicated a strong emphasis on content-related criteria and less attention on computer features such as graphics, animation, sound, and screen design (Bitter and Wighton, 1987). Despite the detailed checklists and evaluation criteria available to teachers, there is evidence that teachers still have difficulty discriminating between good and bad software features, and often teachers are strongly influenced by graphics and less likely to consider content material (Preece and Jones, 1985). Some research suggests that providing teachers with self-instructional guides that provide well-defined evaluation criteria and step-by-step evaluation procedures can assist the software-evaluation process (Chang and Osguthorpe, 1987). In addition, study results indicate that evaluators using self-instructional guides rated software more objectively and critically than did evaluators without the use of an instructional guide (Chang and Osguthorpe, 1987).

Software evaluation criteria can cover a wide range of instructional issues; moreover, there is also a wide variety of software-evaluation methods and techniques available for conducting evaluations. Therefore, given time and resource constraints, educators should consider closely what evaluation criteria are critical for learning activities, student populations, and overall curricular needs of the school.

Figures 5-9 and 5-10 show two different examples of evaluation forms. The content of these forms is not exhaustive, as such; they simply provide various ways for teachers to view the evaluation process. One software review form (Figure 5-9) represents a checklist for evaluating student behavior during the use of educational programs, while the other evaluation form (Figure 5-10) attempts to quantify instructional criteria for evaluating the potential effectiveness of instructional software programs. In conclusion, the breadth of information screening that these forms can accomplish is largely left up to the needs and creativity of teachers.

SUMMARY

The instructional software mentioned in this chapter will continue to evolve as software and hardware design improves. Moreover, to fully realize the potential of computer-based instruction, future educational software will have to concentrate on more effectively assimilating proven learning theory with capable computer hardware. Such a technological synthesis can produce more discerning and intelligent computer tools for learning. Indeed, many current software schemes provide inflexible computer-controlled learning environments. But new software-implementation approaches are moving

STUDENT COMPUTER BEHAVIOR FORM

STUDENT NAME: _____

SOFTWARE TITLE: _____

INSTRUCTIONAL SETTING: Individual / Group

DATE: _____

TIME ALLOTMENT: _____

from _____ am/pm to _____ am/pm

FIVE-MINUTE INTERVAL RECORDING

RATING SYSTEM: [0] POOR [1] FAIR [2] GOOD [3] EXCELLENT

ATTENDING TO TASK	Five-Minute Time Intervals					totals
	1	2	3	4	5	
[1] Eye contact and keying in appropriate responses.(active involvement)	0 1 2 3	0 1 2 3	0 1 2 3	0 1 2 3	0 1 2 3	
[2] Eye contact with video screen only. (passive involvement)	0 1 2 3	0 1 2 3	0 1 2 3	0 1 2 3	0 1 2 3	
[3] Eye contact with other computers.	0 1 2 3	0 1 2 3	0 1 2 3	0 1 2 3	0 1 2 3	
[4] Talking with students on other computers.	0 1 2 3	0 1 2 3	0 1 2 3	0 1 2 3	0 1 2 3	

SOCIAL INTERACTION

	Five-Minute Time Intervals					Totals
	1	2	3	4	5	
[1] Takes turns.	0 1 2 3	0 1 2 3	0 1 2 3	0 1 2 3	0 1 2 3	
[2] Discusses solutions to problems.	0 1 2 3	0 1 2 3	0 1 2 3	0 1 2 3	0 1 2 3	
[3] Dominates interaction.	0 1 2 3	0 1 2 3	0 1 2 3	0 1 2 3	0 1 2 3	
[4] Determines plan of action.	0 1 2 3	0 1 2 3	0 1 2 3	0 1 2 3	0 1 2 3	

AFFECT

	Five-Minute Time Intervals					Totals
	1	2	3	4	5	
[1] Shows enthusiasm.	0 1 2 3	0 1 2 3	0 1 2 3	0 1 2 3	0 1 2 3	
[2] Shows intense concentration.	0 1 2 3	0 1 2 3	0 1 2 3	0 1 2 3	0 1 2 3	
[3] Shows flat affect.	0 1 2 3	0 1 2 3	0 1 2 3	0 1 2 3	0 1 2 3	

Figure 5-9. Example of evaluation sheet for monitoring student-computer interaction behaviors.

SOFTWARE EVALUATION FORM

SOFTWARE TITLE: _____

NAME OF EVALUATOR: _____

DATE: _____

FINAL TOTAL SCORE: _____

DIRECTIONS: First, review the evaluation form criteria and select those that have specific relevance to the instructional objective. Then review the software package and its features. Use the rating scale (see below) to rate the software package based on each specified criterion. Total all criteria section scores to get an overall rating for the software package.

RATING SCALE: [0] NOT PRESENT [1] POOR [2] FAIR [3] GOOD [4] EXCELLENT [-] NOT APPLICABLE

INSTRUCTIONAL CONTENT

[0] Not present [1] Poor [2] Fair [3] Good [4] Excellent [-] Not Applicable

1. Defined instructional objective .... ____

2. Defined target student population .... ____

3. Content is both accurate and grammatically and syntactically correct .... ____

4. Content is oriented toward instructional objectives .... ____

5. Content is oriented toward target student population .... ____

6. Content is free of bias (race, sex, ethnic, etc.) .... ____

7. Teacher control over content modification .... ____

Total ☐

INSTRUCTIONAL DESIGN

[0] Not present [1] Poor [2] Fair [3] Good [4] Excellent [-] Not Applicable

1. Achieves the stated instructional objectives.................................
2. Provides various difficulty levels...
3. Sequences lesson appropriately..
4. Provides students with appropriate corrective feedback (content-related material)........
5. Provides students with appropriate feedback on program procedures (how to work the program).......
6. Provides lesson branching for individualized learning (accommodates student responses)......
7. Ability to test student performance.......................................
8. Ease of use...
9. Appropriate software documentation......................................

Total

PROGRAM MANAGEMENT

[0] Not present [1] Poor [2] Fair [3] Good [4] Excellent [-] Not Applicable

1. Availability of lesson record keeping......................................
2. Provides hard copy (printouts) of student performance......................
3. Provides the ability to save individual student lessons......................
4. Provides supplemental learning materials.................................

Total

Figure 5-10. Example of software evaluation form using a criteria rating technique.

closer toward transcending the limited boundaries of drill, tutorial, game, simulation, and problem-solving software. In fact, educational software programs are now incorporating instructional design techniques from traditionally distinct software-implementation approaches, making it more difficult to clearly distinguish between game, drill, tutorial, simulation, and problem-solving software.

In addition, authoring and productivity software tools provide teachers with many flexible devices for implementing classroom instruction. They support the development of CAI, and others augment planning and instructional materials development. Although many of these software programs can benefit the classroom, educators must provide a framework for gaining knowledge and information about these tools. Only cautious evaluation and review can distinguish appropriate applications from ineffective software tools. Hence, educators must provide clear and concise planning and evaluation methods if to adequately support school microcomputer-implementation efforts. Chapters 6, 7, and 8 provide educators with instructional software listings integrated into a sample reading, writing, and math curriculum respectively.

What follows are sample review questions and some follow-up activities students may wish to pursue. These activities can be used to further develop the concepts and practical applications presented in this chapter.

REVIEW QUESTIONS

1. Define drill and practice educational software.
2. Define tutorial software.
3. Explain the importance of branching to the instructional design of software tutorials.
4. Define educational simulation software.
5. Define educational problem-solving software.
6. Define the following terms, then explain the differences between them: editable software, authoring systems, and authoring languages.
7. Define the concept of integrated software packages.
8. Explain the importance of administrative roles in developing and supporting links to microcomputer information.
9. Explain the importance of evaluating instructional software.

SUGGESTED FOLLOW-UP ACTIVITIES

1. List some examples of drill software and game software. Explain the differences between these software approaches.
2. List some examples of simulation software. Describes the learning

approach and instructional objectives of simulation software. Evaluate the effectiveness of the design approach.

3. Locate some examples of software evaluation forms and compare the evaluation criteria of each form. Explain the evaluation focus or emphasis of each technique.

4. List some examples of authoring systems. Compare and evaluate the implementation approach of each system.

5. Develop a software evaluation form and use the form to evaluate a drill, game, tutorial, simulation, or problem-solving software package. Explain the benefits and limitations found in its classroom use.

6. Contact a school using educational software and identify the methods or techniques used by the school in the evaluation of its instructional software.

CHAPTER 6

*Microcomputer Reading
Applications in the Classroom*

INTEGRATING COMPUTERS
INTO THE READING CURRICULUM

The following sections introduce teachers to a wide variety of commercial software resources that may support instructional activities in both regular and special education classrooms. Specifically, the software resources in this chapter have been organized into a general reading curriculum covering the areas of vocabulary, literal comprehension, interpretive comprehension, and evaluative comprehension. Each curriculum area is outlined with specific instructional goals and matched with supporting educational software tools. The intent of this organization is to provide teachers with general examples and information on the types of software resources available to facilitate the integration of microcomputer instruction into the school's reading curriculum. To this end, the following sections will address: (1) goal specific instructional software titles; (2) a description of the software design approach; (3) the grade level of the target student population; (4) the names of the software publisher; (5) a description of the activities inherent in the software title; (6) a brief description of the teacher options and flexibility offered by the software title; and (7) a list of any special computer equipment necessary to implement the software title in the classroom.

In addition, this chapter will provide teachers with information on software productivity tools related to reading. This information is directed to specific software resources that aid teachers in developing reading materials for the classroom and in conducting testing and evaluation functions. Software title listings, publisher names, and brief descriptions of the tool's functions are included. The last section of the chapter will provide software publisher address information as well as a listing for mail-order software distributors.

The reader should note that this curriculum and its supporting software listing are examples. As such, they simply provide various ways to consider integrating current commercial educational software into the reading curriculum. Because children have different instructional needs and individual learning styles, software that works with one child may not work with another. Hence, teachers are encouraged to evaluate and test instructional software with their children before prescribing its use. To help facilitate this critical evaluation process many software publishers are now offering 30-day preview periods before purchasing educational software. The publisher resource listings at the end of this chapter identify those companies offering such services.

Finally, as an added help to those individuals primarily working with computers who may require a brief review of some of the basic terminology of reading, a reading glossary has been added to this chapter. It is in no way meant to be an all inclusive list, but it can serve as a way of familiarizing oneself with terms that are often used to promote the value of one software package over another.

COMPUTER READING INTEGRATION

CURRICULUM AREA: READING
VOCABULARY: ALPHABET RECOGNITION

SOFTWARE TITLE	SOFTWARE TYPE	GRADE LEVEL	SOFTWARE PUBLISHER
Letters and First Words	Drill and Practice	1–3	C & C Software

Activities: Drill upper- and lower-case letters, letter/picture associations, and letter/word associations. Teacher control over lesson difficulty, sound, instructions, and student performance.

| *Stepping Stones: Level I* | Drill and Practice | 1–3 | Compu-Teach |

Activities: Drill letters and words using letter-to-picture and word-to-picture associations. Teacher control over lesson level.

| *Stepping Stones: Level II* | Drill and Practice | 1–3 | Compu-Teach |

Activities: Drill letters and words using letter-to-picture and word-to-picture associations. Teacher control over lesson level.

| *First Letters and Words* | Drill | 1–3 | First Byte |

Activities: Introduce and practice upper and lower case letters, words, and sentences using synthesized speech. Teachers can modify lesson levels. Requires Apple IIgs, Macintosh, Amiga, or Atari ST computers.

| *Alphabet Express* | Drill and Practice | 1–3 | Gamco |

Activities: Drill alphabet sequence, upper-/lower-case letter matching, and picture/letter matching. Teacher control over number of lesson questions, sound, instruction display, and saving and printing student lesson records.

| *From ABC to XYZ* | Drill/Game | 1–4 | Hartley |

Activities: Drill the alphabetizing of letters, words, abbreviations, and initials. Teacher control over content material, lesson level, student lesson records.

| *Letter Recognition* | Drill and Practice | 4–7 | Hartley |

Activities: Drill and practice keyboard/letter location, and letter and number recognition. Teacher control over lesson difficulty level, upper- and lower-case letters, numbers, or mixed characters.

Pictures, Letters and Sounds	Game	1–3	Hartley

Activities: Animated graphic and sound game sequences provide practice on associating letter sound with pictures. Teacher control over lesson level.

Reading Skills Extender Series	Tutorial	3–8	Holt, Rinehart, & Winston

Activities: Supplements basal readers which introduce alphabetizing. The program also provides pre- and post-test evaluation, automatically generates individualized assignments, monitors student and class performance, and provides printouts of lesson materials.

Fun from A to Z	Drill/Game	1–3	MECC

Activities: Game and drill lessons provide practice on matching upper- and lower-case letters and alphabet sequence. Teachers can control lesson level and lesson content material.

Animal Alphabet and Other Things	Drill and Practice	1–2	Random House

Activities: Drill upper- and lower-case letters using letter/picture associations. Teacher control over speed and sound.

Alphabet, Sequence and Alphabetizing	Drill/Game	1–4	Random House

Activities: Alphabetizing letters and words. Teacher control over lesson difficulty level.

Alphabet Zoo	Drill/Game	1–4	Spinnaker

Activities: Drill letter recognition using letter/picture associations. Game sequences provides drill on matching letters to pictures. Teacher control over sound and lesson level.

Easy as ABC	Drill/Game	1–3	Springboard

Activities: Animated game sequences support drills on alphabetizing letters, matching upper- and lower-case letters, making letter/picture associations.

Getting Ready to Read and Add	Drill and Practice	1–3	Sunburst Communications

Activities: Drill upper- and lower-case letters and number and shape recognition. Teacher control over lesson level.

CURRICULUM AREA: READING
VOCABULARY: ALPHABET RECOGNITION

SOFTWARE TITLE	SOFTWARE TYPE	GRADE LEVEL	SOFTWARE PUBLISHER
Stickybear ABC	Drill and Practice	1–3	Weekly Reader Family Software

Activities: Drill and practice letter recognition using animated letter/picture associations.

CURRICULUM AREA: READING
VOCABULARY: SPELLING

SOFTWARE TITLE	SOFTWARE TYPE	GRADE LEVEL	SOFTWARE PUBLISHER
Spelling	Drill	4–6	American Educational Computer

Activities: Drill spelling with a list of the 4,233 most commonly used words in writing. Diagnostics and competency checks provide corrective feedback to students. Teachers can create their own word lists.

Spell It!	Drill/Game	2–5	Davidson & Associates

Activities: Review basic spelling rules, practices words, unscramble words, and use game situations to practice words. Teachers can add their own word lists.

Spellagraph	Drill	1–6	DesignWare

Activities: Drill spelling words are presented in sentence context. Word-picture puzzles (rebuses) are used as reinforcement. Teachers can create their own word lists and sentences and can control puzzle difficulty level.

Spellicopter	Drill/Game	1–6	DesignWare

Activities: Drill spelling words using anagram techniques or sentence context clues. Teachers can add their own spelling lists and sentences and can control game difficulty levels.

Spelling Mastery	Game	1–5	DLM

Activities: Drill spelling words using various spelling techniques. Teachers can add their own spelling lists and control game difficulty levels.

Compu-Spell	Tutorial	3–6	Britannica Software

Activities: Learn spelling words in sentence context. Program can automatically track misspelled words for remedial work. Program tracks student records. Spelling words are contained on six separate data disks.

Speller Bee	Drill	1–6	First Byte

Activities: Drill spelling words using synthesized speech. Teachers can add their own word lists and print out word lists. Requires Apple IIgs, Macintosh, Amiga, or Atari ST computers.

Spelling Speechware Series	Drill	1–6	Houghton Mifflin

Activities: Drill and practice spelling words using synthesized speech. Speech is used for lesson instructions, feedback, and spelling drills that utilize sentence context techniques. Teachers have control over lesson difficulty level and student performance tracking. Requires Echo II+ Speech Synthesizer (Apple II+, IIe, or IIgs) or Cricket speech synthesizer (Apple IIc).

Magic Spells	Drill	1–5	The Learning Company

Activities: Drill spelling words using anagram techniques. Teachers can add their own spelling lists and print out word lists.

Word Wizards	Drill/Game	2–6	MECC

Activities: Drill spelling words by unscrambling letters. Teachers can add their own word lists.

Spelling Rules	Tutorial	2–4	Micro Power & Light Co.

Activities: Provide spelling rule exercises for six rules: ie or ei; final e; adding y; final consonant; -sede, -ceed or cede; and final y.

Spelling Partner	Drill	4–6	Micro Power & Light Co.

Activities: Drill spelling words using recall, unscrambling, and supplying missing letters. Teachers can add word lists and print out word lists.

Stickybear Spellgrabber	Drill/Game	1–5	Weekly Reader Family Software

Activities: Drill spelling words using picture clues. Teachers can create their own spelling lists and adjust game difficulty levels.

CURRICULUM AREA: READING
VOCABULARY: PHONETIC AND STRUCTURAL ANALYSIS

SOFTWARE TITLE	SOFTWARE TYPE	GRADE LEVEL	SOFTWARE PUBLISHER
Learn About Sounds in Reading	Drill	1–3	AEC

CURRICULUM AREA: READING
VOCABULARY: PHONETIC AND STRUCTURAL ANALYSIS

			SOFTWARE
SOFTWARE TITLE	SOFTWARE TYPE	GRADE LEVEL	PUBLISHER

Activities: Introduce and review long and short vowel sounds and initial consonants. Teacher control over lesson level.

| *Stepping Stones Level I* | Drill | 1–3 | Compu-Teach |

Activities: Illustrations help drill word endings *-ar, -in,* and *-og.* Teacher has control over lesson level.

| *Stepping Stones: Level II* | Drill | 1–3 | Compu-Teach |

Activities: Illustrations help drill word endings *-ao, -od,* and *-ug.* Teacher has control over lesson level.

| *Stepping Stones: Level III* | Drill | 1–3 | Compu-Teach |

Activities: Illustrations help drill word endings *-ub, -ig,* and *-ow.* Teacher has control over lesson level.

| *Grammar Gremlins* | Drill/Game | 3–6 | Davidson & Associates |

Activities: Practice and reinforce rules for abbreviations, capitalization, contractions, and plurals. Teacher control over lesson content and game options.

| *Beamer: Prefixes, Base Words, Suffixes* | Game | 1–4 | Data Command |

Activities: Practice word recognition skills, identify root words, prefixes, and suffixes.

| *Arcademic Skill Builders: Word Man* | Drill/Game | 2–4 | DLM |

Activities: Practice building words using consonant-vowel-consonant and consonant-vowel-consonant-silent e patterns. Teachers can control game options like sound, lesson content, speed, game difficulty level, and/or joystick or keyboard control.

| *Construct-a-Word I* | Drill | 1–3 | DLM |

Activities: Graphics and synthesized speech introduce and review short and long vowels and initial consonants. Requires Echo+ speech synthesizer (Apple II+, IIe, or IIgs) Cricket speech synthesizer (Apple IIc), or Super-talker speech digitizer (by DLM).

Construct-a-Word　Drill　　　　　3–5　　　　　　DLM
　II

Activities: Graphics and synthesized speech introduce and review more difficult vowel-consonant combinations. Requires Echo+ speech synthesizer (Apple II+, IIe, or IIgs), Cricket speech synthesizer (Apple IIc), or Supertalker speech digitizer (by DLM).

Hint and Hunt I　Drill/Game　　　1–3　　　　　　DLM

Activities: Introduce and review five short vowel sounds and four vowel digraphs and diphthongs using synthesized speech. Requires Echo II+ speech synthesizer (Apple II+, IIe, or IIgs). Cricket speech synthesizer (Apple IIc), or Supertalker speech digitizer (by DLM).

Hint and Hunt II　Drill/Game　　　4–6　　　　　　DLM

Activities: Introduce and review three vowel digraphs and diphthongs using synthesized speech. Requires Echo II+ speech synthesizer (Apple II+, IIe, or IIgs), Cricket speech synthesizer (Apple IIc), or Supertalker speech digitizer (by DLM).

Syllasearch I　Drill　　　　　　1–2　　　　　　DLM

Activities: Use synthesized speech to introduce and review two-syllable words. Requires Echo+ speech synthesizer (Apple II+, IIe, or IIgs), Cricket speech synthesizer (Apple IIc), or Supertalker (by DLM).

Syllasearch II　Drill　　　　　　2–4　　　　　　DLM

Activities: Use synthesized speech to introduce and review two- and three-syllable words. Requires Echo+ speech synthesizer (Apple II+, IIe, or IIgs), Cricket speech synthesizer (Apple IIc), or Supertalker (by DLM).

Syllasearch III　Drill　　　　　　4–6　　　　　　DLM

Activities: Use synthesized speech to introduce and review two-, three-, and four-syllable words. Requires Echo+ speech synthesizer (Apple II+, IIe, or IIgs), Cricket speech synthesizer (Apple IIc), or Supertalker (by DLM).

Using Phonics in　Drill　　　　　3–5　　　　Educational
　Context　　　　　　　　　　　　　　　　　Activities

Activities: Drill initial and final consonants, digraphs, blends, short and long vowels, and irregular vowel patterns in sentence context. Program provides pretesting for identifying weaknesses and prescribing lessons. Program also tracks and saves student performance records.

Consonants　Drill　　　　　　　1–3　　　　　Hartley

Activities: Drill initial and final consonants using visual and auditory stimulus. Program also covers digraphs and blends. Teachers can create and modify their own lessons and save and print student performance records. Requires a cassette control device (by Hartley).

Multiple Skills　Drill　　　　　　1–6　　　　　Hartley

Activities: Use tape recorded voice to drill root words, compound words,

CURRICULUM AREA: READING
VOCABULARY: PHONETIC AND STRUCTURAL ANALYSIS

SOFTWARE TITLE	SOFTWARE TYPE	GRADE LEVEL	SOFTWARE PUBLISHER

plurals, and contractions. Teachers can create and modify lesson content and save and print student performance records. Requires a cassette control device to use tape-recorded voice (by Hartley).

Vowels	Drill	1–3	Hartley

Activities: Drill vowel sounds using visual and auditory stimulus. Program covers long and short vowel sounds, double vowels, diphthongs, schwa sounds, etc. Teachers can create their own lessons and save and print student performance records. Requires a cassette control device (by Hartley).

Vowel Tutorial	Tutorial	1–3	Hartley

Activities: Introduce and review long and short vowel sounds. Program incorporates both tape recorded voice and pictures when drilling vowel sounds. Program automatically stores student records and teachers can print records. Requires a cassette control device (by Hartley).

Word Families II	Drill	1–3	Hartley

Activities: Practice silent letters, digraphs, *i* blends, *r* blends, *s* blends, and *w* blends. Teachers can create and modify their own lessons and save and print student performance records.

Reading Rodeo: Consonants	Drill	1–3	Heartsoft

Activities: Review consonants with picture associations.

Reading Skills Extender Series	Tutorial	3–8	Holt, Rinehard & Winston

Activities: Teach suffixes and prefixes. The program also provides pre- and post-test evaluation, automatically generates individualized assignments, monitors student and class performance, and provides printouts of lesson materials.

Sound Ideas: Vowels	Drill	1–3	Houghton Mifflin

Activities: Graphics and synthesized speech are used for lesson instruction, reinforcement, and information feedback. Program covers short and long vowels. Teachers can control lesson level and student records management and can print out lesson material. Requires Echo+ speech synthesizer (Apple II+, IIe, or IIgs) or Cricket speech synthesizer (Apple IIc).

Sound Ideas: Consonants	Drill	1–3	Houghton Mifflin

Activities: Graphics and synthesized speech are used for lesson instruction, reinforcement, and information feedback. Program covers consonants. Teachers can control lesson level and student records management and can print out lesson material. Requires Echo+ speech synthesizer (Apple II+, IIe, or IIgs) or Cricket speech synthesizer (Apple IIc).

| *Starting with* | Drill | 1–3 | K-12 |
| *Phonics* | | | MicroMedia |

Activities: Use picture associations to practice vowel-consonant combinations.

| *Winning with* | Drill | 1–3 | K-12 |
| *Phonics* | | | MicroMedia |

Activities: Use picture associations to practice consonant blends and digraphs.

| *Reader Rabbit* | Drill | 1–3 | The Learning |
| | | | Company |

Activities: Drill 200 three-letter word families for vowels and consonants. Teacher control over lesson content and game options.

| *Reader Rabbit* | Drill | 1–3 | The Learning |
| *Apple IIgs* | | | Company |

Activities: Use synthesized speech to drill 200 three-letter word families for vowels and consonants. Teacher control over lesson content and game options. Requires Apple IIgs computer.

| *Consonant Combo* | Drill/Game | 1–3 | McCarthy- |
| | | | McCormack |

Activities: Animated graphics introduce and review 20 different consonant blends and the digraphs *ch, sh, th,* and *wh.*

| *Vowel Games* | Drill/Game | 1–3 | McCarthy- |
| | | | McCormick |

Activities: Drill long and short vowel sounds using picture associations.

| *Phonics Prime* | Drill/Game | 1–3 | MECC |
| *Time: Vowels* | | | |

Activities: Drill short and long vowels using picture associations and sentence context techniques. Teachers can control lesson levels and game options.

| *Words At Work:* | Drill/Game | 2–4 | MECC |
| *Prefix Power* | | | |

Activities: Review prefixes *bi-, dis-, in-, ex-, de-, re-,* and *un-.* Teachers can control lesson levels.

| *Words At Work:* | Drill/Game | 2–4 | MECC |
| *Suffix Sense* | | | |

Activities: Review suffixes *-th, -ful,* and *-less.* Teachers can control lesson levels.

CURRICULUM AREA: READING
VOCABULARY: PHONETIC AND STRUCTURAL ANALYSIS

SOFTWARE TITLE	SOFTWARE TYPE	GRADE LEVEL	SOFTWARE PUBLISHER
Vocabulary Skills: Prefixes, Suffixes, Root Words	Drill	2–4	Media Materials

Activities: Introduction and review of prefixes, suffixes, and root words. Teachers can control lesson content.

Reading: Instruction for Beginners	Drill	1–4	Microteacher

Activities: Use synthesized speech to introduce and review letter sounds, digraphs, and words. Requires Echo+ speech synthesizer (Apple II+, IIe, or IIgs) or Cricket speech synthesizer (Apple IIc).

Word Magic	Drill/Game	1–4	Mindscape

Activities: Drill initial consonants and consonant blends, prefixes, suffixes and compound words. Teachers can control lesson level and game options.

Reading Readiness	Drill	1–3	Orange Cherry Software

Activities: Use picture associations to drill phonograms or word families.

Vowel Sounds	Drill	1–3	Orange Cherry Software

Activities: Use picture associations to drill vowel sounds. Program provides student performance summary.

Word Pictures	Drill	1–3	Orange Cherry Software

Activities: Use picture associations to drill vowels and consonants.

CURRICULUM AREA: READING
COMPREHENSION: FACTUAL RECOGNITION AND RECALL

SOFTWARE TITLE	SOFTWARE TYPE	GRADE LEVEL	SOFTWARE PUBLISHER
Read 'n Roll	Drill/Game	3–6	Davidson & Associates

Activities: Practice recognizing facts from short reading passages. Teachers can create reading passages, store student records, and print lesson materials. Requires 128K Apple computer.

Our Weird and   Drill/Tutorial   3–6   Educational
  Wacky World   Activities
Activities: True-to-life newspaper and magazine stories develop literal comprehension skills using fill-ins, ordering, and cloze techniques. Teachers can change lesson levels.

Reading for   Drill/Game   4–6   Hartley
  Meaning:
Level 1
Activities: Develop recall of facts and details using fairy tales and rhymes. Teachers can modify lesson content and create questions. The program also provides student diagnostics and recordkeeping features.

First Words   Drill/Tutorial   1–3   Laureate
                                         Learning
                                       Systems
Activities: Introduce 50 sight words in ten categories (animals, body parts, clothes, common objects, food, utensils, toys, outside things, household items, and vehicles). The program utilizes synthesized speech and graphics to present content material. Teachers can control lesson content, modify lesson options, and store and print student performance records. The program also supports access by motor-impaired users. Requires Echo+ speech synthesizer (Apple II+, IIe, or IIgs) or Cricket speech synthesizer (Apple IIc). Optional equipment may include a touch window or switch interface with an adaptive switch.

First Words II   Drill/Tutorial   1–3   Laureate
                                         Learning
                                       Systems
Activities: Introduce and test students on 50 noun sight words in ten categories (animals, body parts, clothes, common objects, food, utensils, toys, outside things, household items, and vehicles). The program utilizes synthesized speech and graphics to present content material. Teachers can control lesson content, modify lesson options, and store and print student performance records. The program also supports access by motor-impaired users. Requires Echo+ speech synthesizer (Apple II+, IIe, or IIgs) or Cricket speech synthesizer (Apple IIc). Optional equipment may include a touch window or switch interface with an adaptive switch.

The Montana   Drill   2–6   PDI
  Reading
  Program
Activities: Introduce and develop mastery of the Dolch word list. Drill 220 sight words using sentence context clues. Teachers can control lesson level.

Kermit's   Game   1–2   Simon &
  Electronic   Schuster
  Storymaker

CURRICULUM AREA: READING
COMPREHENSION: FACTUAL RECOGNITION AND RECALL

SOFTWARE TITLE	SOFTWARE TYPE	GRADE LEVEL	SOFTWARE PUBLISHER

Activities: Allows children to create their own animated stories using graphic muppets as story actors. The computer presents open-ended sentences which students must complete with appropriate words. Sentences are presented with animated graphics. Requires a joystick.

SOFTWARE TITLE	SOFTWARE TYPE	GRADE LEVEL	SOFTWARE PUBLISHER
Memory: The First Step in Problem Solving	Drill	1–4	Sunburst Communications

Activities: Provide practice activities for picture recognition, recall, sequence, and matching. In addition, drill is provided for remembering parts of a whole and series of instructions. Teacher has control over lesson presentation features.

Now You See it, Now You Don't	Drill	1–4	Sunburst Communications

Activities: Drill picture recognition and recall skills. Teachers can control lesson difficulty level.

Memory Machine	Drill	2–6	Sunburst Communications

Activities: Practice factual recognition and recall skills using words to pictures, words to shapes, pictures to words, and pictures to shapes. Teachers can control lesson difficulty level.

CURRICULUM AREA: READING
COMPREHENSION: ORGANIZATION AND SEQUENCE SKILLS

SOFTWARE TITLE	SOFTWARE TYPE	GRADE LEVEL	SOFTWARE PUBLISHER
Reading Comprehension Skills 2	Drill	4–6	AEC

Activities: Practice sequencing story events using children's stories. Teachers can control lesson levels.

Read 'n Roll	Drill/Game	3–6	Davidson & Associates

Activities: Introduce and drill sequencing skills using 320 reading passages. Teachers can create stories, store student records, and print lesson material. Requires 128K Apple computer.

Kittens, Kids, and a Frog	Drill/Tutorial	1–3	Hartley

Activities: Sequence events using illustrated children's stories. Teachers can create and modify lesson stories and questions. The program also provides diagnostics and record-keeping features.

Scuffy and Friends	Drill/Tutorial	1–3	Hartley

Activities: Sequence events using illustrated children's stories. Teachers can modify stories, questions and lessons presentation features. The program also provides diagnostics and record-keeping features.

What's First? What's Next?	Drill and Practice	1–3	Hartley

Activities: Order sentences to match a paragraph and answer questions regarding story sequence. Teachers can change lesson content and store student records.

Chariots, Cougars and Kings	Drill/Tutorial	4–6	Hartley

Activities: Sequence events using illustrated stories. Teachers can modify lesson stories and questions. The program also provides diagnostics and record-keeping features.

Reading Skills Extender Series	Tutorial	3–8	Holt, Rinehart & Winston

Activities: Supplements basal readers in teaching word classification, following directions, indexing, recognizing word sequences, and outlining. The program also provides pre- and post-test evaluation, automatically generates individualized assignments, monitors student and class performance, and provides printouts of lesson materials.

First Categories	Tutorial	1–3	Laureate Learning Systems

Activities: Introduce and classify 60 nouns in six categories (animals, body parts, clothes, food, utensils, and vehicles). The program utilizes synthesized speech and graphics to present content material. Teachers can store student performance records, control lesson content, and modify lesson options. The program also supports access by motor-impaired users. Requires Echo+ speech synthesizer (Apple II+, IIe, or IIgs) or Cricket speech synthesizer (Apple IIc).

Word Bank	Drill/Game	1–4	Learning Well

Activities: Introduce and classify words by meaning. Teachers can change lessons and obtain student performance summaries.

Sequence What Comes First	Drill/Game	4–6	Learning Well

CURRICULUM AREA: READING
COMPREHENSION: ORGANIZATION AND SEQUENCE SKILLS

SOFTWARE TITLE	SOFTWARE TYPE	GRADE LEVEL	SOFTWARE PUBLISHER

Activities: Sequence scrambled words, sentences, paragraphs, and story topics in four subject areas. Teachers can change game options and lesson difficulty level and obtain student performance summaries.

Ace Detective	Drill/Game	2–8	MindPlay

Activities: This interactive program provides practice on sequencing events and organizing facts and information in order to solve mysteries. Teachers can create their own mysteries and modify game options.

Wordzzzearch	Drill/Game	3–8	MindPlay

Activities: Introduce and practice word recognition and categorization skills using word puzzles. Teachers can create word puzzles, modify game options, and obtain student performance summaries.

Ace Reporter	Drill/Game	2–6	MindPlay

Activities: This interactive program provides practice in organizing who, what, where, and why story facts in order to identify main ideas and develop descriptive stories. Teachers can change lesson stories, modify game options, and obtain performance summaries.

Sequence Courseware PLUS	Drill/Tutorial	2–4	Random House

Activities: Provides software and basal readers which introduce and drill story sequence skills. Teachers can obtain performance summaries and control lesson levels.

Hide 'n Sequence	Drill/Game	3–8	Sunburst Communications

Activities: Text story selections are presented to students for practicing sentence sequence skills. A built-in word processor allows users to enter their own stories.

Odd One Out	Drill/Game	1–3	Sunburst Communications

Activities: Practice classification skills using pictures, words, letters, and numbers. Teachers can create their own lesson content and customize lesson presentation and difficulty levels.

CURRICULUM AREA: READING
COMPREHENSION: INFERENTIAL THINKING SKILLS

SOFTWARE TITLE	SOFTWARE TYPE	GRADE LEVEL	SOFTWARE PUBLISHER
Regrouping	Drill	2–4	Sunburst Communications

Activities: Drill categorization and recall skills using pictures and words to organize household items, animals, nature etc. Teachers can control lesson presentation features.

Chariots, Cougars   Drill/Tutorial   4–6   Hartley
and Kings

Activities: Develop inferences from illustrated stories. Teachers can modify lesson stories and questions. The program also provides diagnostics and recordkeeping features.

Reading for   Drill/Game   4–6   Hartley
Meaning Level
2

Activities: Develop inferences using fairy tales and rhymes. Teachers can modify lesson content and questions. The program also provides student diagnostics and record-keeping features.

Scuffy and   Drill   1–3   Hartley
Friends

Activities: Develop inferential thinking skills using pictures, stories and questions. Teachers can modify lesson content and questions. The program also provides student diagnostics and record-keeping features.

Reading Skills   Tutorial   3–8   Holt, Rinehart &
Extender Series   Winston

Activities: Aids students in making inferences about story character motives and cause-and-effect relationships. The program also provides pre- and post-test evaluation, automatically generates individualized assignments, monitors student and class performance, and provides printouts of lesson materials.

Reading   Drill/Tutorial   1–4   Houghton
Comprehension   Mifflin

Activities: Develop inference skills through stories from children's literature. Synthesized speech is used for student questions and answers. Teachers can control lesson levels and student performance functions. Requires Echo + speech synthesizer (Apple II +, IIe, or IIgs) or Cricket speech synthesizer (Apple IIc).

The Gapper   Authoring   2–6   HRM
System

Activities: Develop text-based reading comprehension lessons utilizing cloze techniques. Program includes a teacher authoring system for creating lessons and questions, built-in reading analysis and record-keeping facilities, and print out features.

Inference School   Drill/Game   1–4   Learning Well
Days

Activities: Students develop inferences related to specific reading selections

CURRICULUM AREA: READING
COMPREHENSION: INFERENTIAL THINKING SKILLS

SOFTWARE TITLE	SOFTWARE TYPE	GRADE LEVEL	SOFTWARE PUBLISHER

which are based on student life in grammar school, junior high, high school and college. Teachers can select lesson levels and obtain student performance summaries.

Inference Courseware PLUS	Drill/Tutorial	2–4	Random House

Activities: Software and basal readers supplement this program in developing inferential thinking skills. Teachers can obtain performance summaries and control lesson levels.

Dragon's Keep	Game	2–6	Sierra On-Line

Activities: An adventure game develops reading comprehension by utilizing map reading, identifying details, making inferences and drawing conclusions. Teachers can control game options.

Tales from the Arabian Nights: Talking Version	Drill/Game	3–7	Unicorn Software

Activities: Interactive stories provide graphics and synthesized speech for developing reading comprehension skills. Program provides multiple choice and fill-in-the-blank questions. Built-in word processor allows students to create their own stories. An edit program allows teachers to create their own questions and answers. Requires an Apple IIgs computer.

Stickybear Reading Comprehension	Drill	3–6	Weekley Reader Family Software

Activities: Illustrated high-interest stories and questions test students on inferential thinking skills. Teachers can create their own stories, questions, and print out stories and answers.

CURRICULUM AREA: READING
COMPREHENSION: MAIN IDEA SKILLS

SOFTWARE TITLE	SOFTWARE TYPE	GRADE LEVEL	SOFTWARE PUBLISHER
Reading Comprehension Skills 1	Drill	1–4	AEC

Activities: Introduce and practice main idea skills using children's stories. Teachers can control lesson levels.

| *Read 'n Roll* | Drill/Game | 3–6 | Davidson & Associates |

Activities: Practice recognizing main idea facts from short reading passages. Teachers can create reading passages, store student records, and print lesson materials. Requires 128K Apple II computer.

| *Main Idea Gold Rush* | Drill/Game | 3–4 | Gamco |

Activities: Game simulates a journey west during the gold rush. Students advance west as they identify the main idea from a given paragraph. Teachers can control lesson levels and record and print student performance records.

| *Chariots, Cougars and Kings* | Drill/Tutorial | 4–6 | Hartley |

Activities: Develop main idea skills using illustrated stories. Teachers can modify lesson stories and questions. The program also provides diagnostics and record-keeping features.

| *Reading for Meaning Level 2* | Drill/Game | 4–6 | Hartley |

Activities: Develop main idea skills using graphics, fair tales and rhymes. Teachers can modify lesson content and questions. The program also provides student diagnostics and record-keeping features.

| *Scuffy and Friends* | Drill | 1–3 | Hartley |

Activities: Develop main ideas using pictures, stories and questions. Teachers can modify lesson content and questions. The program also provides student diagnostics and record-keeping features.

| *Reading Skills Extender Series* | Tutorial | 3–8 | Holt, Rinehart & Winston |

Activities: This software series develops skills for identifying main idea and supporting details. The program also provides pre- and post-test evaluation, automatically generates individualized assignments, monitors student and class performance, and provides print outs of lesson materials.

| *Reading Comprehension* | Drill/Tutorial | 1–4 | Houghton Mifflin |

Activities: Develop story main idea skills through children's stories. Synthesized speech is used for student questions and answers. Teachers can control lesson levels and student record-keeping functions. Requires Echo + speech synthesizer (Apple II +, IIe, or IIgs) or Cricket speech synthesizer (Apple IIc).

| *Getting the Main Idea Around the World* | Game | 1–4 | Learning Well |

CURRICULUM AREA: READING
COMPREHENSION: MAIN IDEA SKILLS

SOFTWARE TITLE	SOFTWARE TYPE	GRADE LEVEL	SOFTWARE PUBLISHER

Activities: Animated graphics introduce short reading selections and students must identify the sentence that best states the main idea of a given paragraph. Teachers can control game options.

Getting the Main Idea Around the World	Game	4–6	Learning Well

Activities: Animated game introduces short reading selections. Questions and answers test student comprehension skills during the course of the game.

Reading Comprehension I	Drill	3–6	Media Materials

Activities: Recognize and develop topic sentences, summarize main ideas, choose titles, and evaluate and list supporting details. Teachers can control lesson levels.

Main Idea Courseware PLUS	Drill/Tutorial	2–4	Random House

Activities: Software and basal readers are included in this program which introduces main idea skills. Teachers can obtain performance summaries and control lesson levels.

Stickybear Reading Comprehension	Drill	3–6	Weekly Reader Family Software

Activities: Illustrated stories and questions test students on main idea skills. Teachers can create their own stories, questions, and print out stories and answers.

CURRICULUM AREA: READING
COMPREHENSION:
PREDICTING AND GENERALIZATION SKILLS

SOFTWARE TITLE	SOFTWARE TYPE	GRADE LEVEL	SOFTWARE PUBLISHER
Reading for Meaning Level 2	Drill/Game	4–6	Hartley

Activities: Develop inferences using fairy tales and rhymes. Teachers can modify lesson content and questions. The program also provides student diagnostics and record-keeping features.

Little Riddles   Drill   1–3   Hartley
Activities: Illustrated riddles and questions are used for drawing conclusions and predicting outcomes. Teachers can modify riddles and questions. The program also provides student record-keeping features.

Reading Skills   Tutorial   3–8   Holt, Rinehart &
  Extender Series   Winston
Activities: Software exercises help students draw and support conclusions from reading passages. The programs also provide pre- and post-test evaluation, automatically generates individualized assignments, monitors student and class performance, and provides printouts of lesson materials.

Reading   Drill/Tutorial   1–4   Houghton
  Comprehension   Mifflin
Activities: Children's stories are animated with graphics and synthesized speech for instruction and practice in drawing conclusions. Synthesized speech is used for student questions and answers. Teachers can control lesson levels and student record-keeping functions. Requires Echo + speech synthesizer (Apple II +, IIe, or IIgs) or Cricket speech synthesizer (Apple IIc).

Drawing   Game   1–4   Learning Well
  Conclusions
Activities: Animated games allow students to analyze letters in order to draw conclusions about the meanings of words.

Drawing   Game   4–6   Learning Well
  Conclusions/
  Chief of
  Detectives
Activities: Practice drawing conclusions using chidren's stories and a bingo game to test reading comprehension. Teachers can obtain performance summaries and control game options and lesson level.

Predicting   Game   3–5   Learning Well
  Outcomes
Activities: Game situation introduces reading passages to students who must then predict outcomes. The program allows teachers to change lesson level, and game options and record student progress.

The Puzzler   Problem Solving 3–6   Sunburst
                                                                          Communications
Activities: Students make story predictions using syntactic, semantic and pragmatic language clues. Teachers can control lesson level.

CURRICULUM AREA: READING COMPREHENSION: PREDICTING AND GENERALIZATION SKILLS

SOFTWARE TITLE	SOFTWARE TYPE	GRADE LEVEL	SOFTWARE PUBLISHER
Stickybear Reading Comprehension	Drill	3–6	Weekly Reader Family Software

Activities: Students can practice drawing conclusions from 30 illustrated stories. Teachers can create their own stories and questions, modify lesson options, and print out stories and answers.

CURRICULUM AREA: READING COMPREHENSION: JUDGMENTAL THINKING SKILLS

SOFTWARE TITLE	SOFTWARE TYPE	GRADE LEVEL	SOFTWARE PUBLISHER
Fact or Opinion	Tutorial	4–6	Hartley

Activities: Introduce and review factual statements and opinions. Questions allow students to evaluate statements. Incorrect responses are supplemented with explanations of key words and statement concepts. Teachers may modify lesson content and store student records.

| *Reading Skills Extender Series* | Tutorial | 3–8 | Holt, Rinehart & Winston |

Activities: Drills and exercises aid students in distinguishing between fact and opinion and realism and fantasy. These programs also provide pre- and post-test evaluation, automatically generate individualized assignments, monitor student and class performance, and provide printouts of lesson materials.

| *Fact or Opinion* | Game | 1–4 | Learning Well |

Activities: Animation and graphics introduce fact and opinion questions to students about consumer shopping. Teachers can obtain performance summaries.

| *Fact or Opinion* | Game | 4–6 | Learning Well |

Activities: Animation and graphics introduce fact and opinion questions to students about consumer shopping. Teachers can obtain performance summaries.

SOFTWARE PRODUCTIVITY TOOLS FOR TEACHERS

SOFTWARE TITLE	SOFTWARE PUBLISHER
The Print Shop	Broderbund

Functions: A versatile printing tool that enables teachers to write, design, and print greeting cards, stationery, school letterhead, classroom signs, and bulletin board materials. The program includes various types styles, nine border designs, dozens of pictures, text editing features, and a built-in graphics editor for creating individualized logos and pictures. Printer is required.

Appleworks   Claris
Functions: This integrated software package includes (1) a data base to organize classroom information; (2) a word processor to write reports, documents, letters, articles, or memos; and (3) a spreadsheet for school budgets. Requires a 128K Apple computer. Printer is optional.

Classmate   Davidson & Associates
Functions: Track and maintain student grades, test scores, attendance records, and other daily classroom functions. This productivity tool can automatically compute final grades taking into account absences and incomplete work and produce class rankings, grade distributions, and class performance. The program can also print reports for teachers, students, and parents. Printer is optional.

Test Generator   Gamco
Functions: This authoring system tool allows teachers to design and create up to 500 test questions. The program accepts five types of questions: fill-in-the-blank, matching, multiple choice, true or false, and short answer. Test can include a mixture of question types.

Create–Lessons   Hartley
Functions: Write drills, tutorials or tests without programming experience. Teachers use frame-based methods to develop lessons. The program presents material using large letters, which is well-suite to elementary and special needs populations.

Create–Intermediate   Hartley
Functions: This authoring system allows teachers to easily write drills, tutorials or tests without programming experience. Teachers use frame-based methods to develop lessons. The program can record and print student performance records. Printer is optional.

Kalamazoo Teacher's Record Book   Hartley
Functions: Record and compute student grades. Print bar graphs, list point totals, list letter grades, calculate grades using various weighting methods, and adjust grade curves. The program can also print reports. Printer is optional.

Wordsearch   Hartley
Functions: This productivity tool allows teachers to create wordfind puzzles containing large elementary letters and up to 40 words. Program options include overlapping words, left to right only, top to bottom only, words

SOFTWARE PRODUCTIVITY TOOLS FOR TEACHERS

SOFTWARE TITLE　　　　　　　　　　　SOFTWARE PUBLISHER

printed backwards, and words printed diagonally. Teachers can add their own word lists, print them, and save them on disk. The program also generates word lists at the bottom of each puzzle and produces an answer sheet. Printer is required.

Super Wordfind　　　　　　　　　　　Hartley
Functions: This productivity tool allows teachers to create wordfind puzzles containing up to 250 words with sentence clues. Teachers can add their own word lists and save them on disk. The program also prints word lists and clues at the bottom of each puzzle and produces an answer sheet. Printer is required.

Test Writer　　　　　　　　　　　K-12 MicroMedia
Functions: Create tests using multiple choice, essays, true/false, fill-in-the-blank, and matching question formats. The tests can be saved and used by Appleworks (see above) or printed with answer keys.

Detroit Tests of Learning Aptitude　　　Psychological Assessment
(DTLA-2)　　　　　　　　　　　Resources Inc.
Functions: Converts raw scores into standard scores and percentile ranks; generates composite scores and compares composite performance within domains for significance; compares DTLA-2 performance and achievement test performance to assess intra-individual discrepancies; and provides a two-page printout for school records.

Detroit Tests of Learning Aptitude—　　Psychological Assessment
Primary (DTLA-P)　　　　　　　　Resources Inc.
Functions: Converts raw scores into standard scores and percentile ranks; generates composite scores and compares composite performance within domains for significance; compares DTLA-P performance and achievement test performance to assess intra-individual discrepancies; and provides a two-page printout for school records.

SuperPrint　　　　　　　　　　　Scholastic
Functions: Allows teachers to create signs, banners, posters, etc. This printing program contains hundreds of graphics, six type styles, and pre-designed borders. Graphics can be printed from sizes and from 1–55 inches. A built-in editor allows teachers to design, create and, mix an unlimited number of different graphics elements. Printer is required.

Certificate Maker　　　　　　　　　Springboard
Functions: This teacher tool provides the ability to choose from over 200 certificates in scholastic, sports, recreation, and other achievement categories. Teachers can enter their own messages, choose from sixteen borders, and change types styles. Printer is required.

The Professional Sign Maker   Sunburst Communications
Functions: A flexible tool for producing signs, handouts, banners, etc. Letters can be created in 1-, 2-, 4-, and 8-inch heights. Special patterns allow teachers to make a variety of borders for bulletin boards. Printer is required.

The Self-Instruction Management   Sunburst Communications
  System (SIMS)
Functions: This productivity tool, used in self-directed learning activities, helps students monitor and manage self-instructional projects. It includes assistance for planning, scheduling, recording daily progress and tracking learning behaviors. The program can also provide feedback to student users.

SOFTWARE PUBLISHERS

American Educational Computer, Inc.
  (AEC)
2450 Embarcadero Way
Palo Alto, CA 94303

Britannica Software
345 Fourth St.
San Francisco, CA 94107

Broderbund
17 Paul Drive
San Rafael, CA 94903

Claris
440 Clyde Ave.
Mountain View, CA 94043

C & C Software
5713 Kentford Circle
Wichita, KS 67220

Compu-Teach
78 Olive St.
New Haven, CT 06511

Data Command
P.O. Box 548
Kankakee, IL 60901

Davidson & Associates
3135 Kashiwa St.
Torrance, CA 90505

DesignWare
185 Berry St.
San Francisco, CA 94107

Developmental Learning Materials
  (DLM)
200 Bethany Drive
Allen, TX 75002

Educational Activities
P.O. Box 392
Freeport, NY 11520

First Byte
3333 East Spring St.
Long Beach, CA 90806

Gamco Industries
P.O. Box 1911
Big Spring, TX 79721
(Offers 30-day preview period.)

Hartley
133 Bridge St.
Dimondale, MI 48821
(Offers 30-day preview period.)

Heartsoft
P.O. Box 691381
Tulsa, OK 74169

Holt, Rinehart & Winston
1627 Woodland Ave.
Austin, TX 78741

Houghton Mifflin
Dept. 67
Mount Support Rd. CN9000
Lebanon, NH 03766-9000

HRM
175 Tompkins Ave.
Pleasantville, NY 10570
(Offers 30-day preview period.)

Learning Well
200 S. Service Rd.
Roslyn Heights, NY 11577

MECC
3490 Lexington Ave. North
St. Paul, MN 55126

McCarthy-McCormack
1440 Oak Hills Drive
Colorado Springs, CO 80919

Media Materials
2936 Remington Ave.
Baltimore, MD 21211

Micro Power & Light Co.
12820 Hillcrest Rd., Ste. 200A
Dallas, TX 75230

MindPlay
82 Montvale Ave.
Stoneham, MA 02180
(Offers 30-day preview period.)

Mindscape
3444 Dundee Rd.
Northbrook, IL 60062

Orange Cherry Software
P.O. Box 390
Pound Ridge, NY 10576-0390

Random House Media
400 Hahn Rd.
Westminster, MD 21157

Sierra On-Line
36575 Mudge Ranch Rd.
Coarsegold, CA 93614

Simon & Schuster
P.O. Box 2987
New York, NY 10185

Spinnaker
One Kendall Square
Cambridge, MA 02139

Springboard Software
7807 Creekridge Cir.
Minneapolis, MN 55435

Sunburst Communications
39 Washington Ave.
Pleasantville, NY 10570
(Offers 30-day preview period.)

The Learning Company
6493 Kaiser Drive
Fremont, CA 94555

Unicorn Software
2950 E. Flamingo Rd.
Las Vega, NV 89121

Weekly Reader Family Software
10 Station Place
Norfolk, CT 06058
(Offers 30-day preview period.)

SOFTWARE DISTRIBUTORS

Academic Software
1415 Queen Anne Rd.
Teaneck, NJ 07666

Alpha Resources Centers
P.O. Box 70647
Washington, D.C. 20024

American Micro Media, Inc.
19 N. Broadway
Red Hook, NY 12571
(30-day preview policy).

Cambridge Development Laboratory
42 4th Ave.
Waltham, MA 02154
(30-day preview policy)

Follett Library Book Company
4506 Northwest Highway
Crystal Lake, IL 60014

K-12 MicroMedia
6 Arrow Rd., Dept. C
Ramsey, NJ 07446

Learning Lab Software
8833 Reseda Blvd.
Northridge, CA 91324
(30-day preview policy)

Psychological Assessment Resources
Inc.
P.O. Box 998
Odessa, FL 33556-0998

National School Products
101 East Broadway
Maryville, TN 37801-2498
(30-day preview policy)

Scholastic
P.O. Box 7502
2931 East McCarty St.
Jefferson City, MO 65102

Opportunities for Learning, Inc.
20417 Nordhoff St., Dept. 6 AM
Chatsworth, CA 91311

READING GLOSSARY

The reading process is a complex one involving the interaction of its component parts. There parts include word recognition (vocabulary), comprehension (on a continuum of levels), functional skills (sometimes called basic skills) and organizational/study skills.

Each part of the reading process demands specialized instructional techniques that address the network of skills required for proficiency in reading, but these methods must also reflect the instructor's understanding of an sensitivity to the individual needs of the student.

A variety of techniques are mentioned for developing vocabulary. These include strategies for breaking words down for decoding (phonetic and structural analysis) or for learning the word as a single entity (whole word approach). Comprehension is also addressed at all its levels with an array of questioning techniques and activities.

Among the techniques currently available in many classrooms is the computer as an instructional tool. There are obvious merits to using a computer for reading instruction: pacing of material presentation, variety of material for presentation, the novelty of the presentation, the impersonal correction style of the machine, and the independence it affords the student. The computer is not a substitute for a teacher, but used appropriately, it can be a strong asset in supplementing instruction. Below are some of the major terms associated with reading.

Alphabet

the essential symbols of language, arbitrarily ordered.

**Auditory
  discrimination**

the act of distinguishing between and among sounds: beginning, medial, and ending; likenesses and differences; digraphs, diphtongs, vowels, and consonants.

Basals	programmed reading series that introduce vocabulary and concepts in a systematic order, progressing through a hierarchy of materials.
Cloze procedure	an instructional and assessment technique. The reader completes blanks spaced throughout text in order to demonstrate comprehension of words via contextual clues. Reader response indicates patterns of error as well as level of vocabulary development and general comprehension.
Comprehension	the presumed end product of the reading act; understanding of the message conveyed by the text; usually assessed through questioning (see Levels of Questioning).
Dictionary skills	the applications needed for locating words, pronouncing words, and determining the meaning of words.
Functional reading skills	the abilities necessary to function as an independent adult in society. The assessment of these skills is often part of the so-called minimum competency movement, and demonstration of these skills, as in completing forms, reading directions, using a map or chart, or locating information, are part of a functional battery.
Levels of comprehension	the components of the hierarchy of skills necessary to derive meaning from text. They include literal comprehension, interpretive comprehension, critical comprehension, and creative comprehension. Levels are assessed by means of a variety of questioning techniques (see Levels of Questioning).
Levels of questioning	a variety of types of questions designed to elicit information about the reader's understanding of the message of text. The levels include: *Literal* questions, requiring the reader to find facts within the text to answer basic questions from a selection. The answer is present in fact within the text.

Interpretive questions, requiring the reader to apply abstract concepts, make generalizations, screen relevant from irrelevant information, and draw conclusions. The answer is often "between the lines" and not explicitly stated.

Critical questions, requiring the reader to distinguish fact from opinion, determine validity of statements and recognize propaganda devices in selected readings.

Creative questions call upon the reader to use imagination to move from context to an abstract plane in order to solve problems or to expand on ideas presented in the text.

Morphology   the essential units of meaning in language.

Phonology   the essential sounds of language.

Semantics   the evolving meanings of words in language.

Structural analysis   the morphological examination of words and their parts, such as affixes, punctuation, inflectional endings, syllabication, and roots.

Study skills   sometimes called "functional skills of reading;" applications for the purpose of retrieval of previously learned information for use later. Skills include location of information, organization of information (classification and outlining), specialized vocabulary, interpretive skills, reading for speed, and summarization.

Syntax   the essential order of arrangement of words in language; the "grammar" of language.

VAKT approach   a multisensory instructional strategy used to tap all the senses in the course of a lesson. Material is introduced, reinforced, and remediated through visual, auditory, kinesthetic and tactile channels, depending on the relative strengths and weaknesses apparent in the reader.

Visual discrimination in reading, the act of distinguishing be-

	tween and among letter and word shapes: upper and lower case, manuscript and cursive, subtle orthographics (letters that go above and below the line) and symbols of punctuation and inflection.
Vocabulary	the basic unit of reading, accumulation of meaningful and expressive symbols with correlation in sound.
Whole word approach	method of developing sight vocabulary by memorizing the word as a single visual/sound correlate.
Word attack	methods of decoding words, either by sound (phonetic analysis), by composition (structural analysis), or by total configuration (whole word approach).

CHAPTER 7

*Microcomputer Writing
Applications in the Classroom*

INTEGRATING COMPUTERS INTO THE WRITING CURRICULUM

The following sections introduce teachers to a wide variety of commercial software resources that may support instructional activities in both regular and special education classrooms. Specifically, the software resources in this chapter have been organized into a general writing curriculum covering the areas of composition and functional writing. Each curriculum area is outlined with specific instructional goals and matched with supporting educational software tools. The intent of this organization is to provide teachers with general examples and information on the types of software resources available to facilitate the integration of microcomputer instruction into the school's writing curriculum. To this end, the following sections will address: (1) goal specific instructional software titles; (2) a description of the software design approach; (3) the grade level of the target student population; (4) the name of the software publisher; (5) a description of the activities inherent in the software title; (6) a brief description of the teacher options and flexibility offered by the software title; and (7) a list of any special computer equipment necessary to implement the software title in the classroom.

In addition, this Chapter will provide teachers with information on software productivity tools related to writing. This information is directed to specific software resources that aid teachers in developing writing materials for the classroom and in conducting testing and evaluation functions. Software title listings, publisher names, and brief descriptions of the tool's functions are included. The last section of the chapter will provide software publisher address information as well as a listing for mail-order software distributors.

Finally, the reader should note that this curriculum and its supporting software listing are examples. As such, they simply provide various ways to consider integrating current commercial educational software into the writing curriculum. Because children have different instructional needs and individual learning styles, software that works with one child may not work with another. Hence, teachers are encouraged to evaluate and test instructional software with their children before prescribing its use. To help facilitate this critical evaluation process, many software publishers are now offering 30-day preview periods before purchasing educational software. The publisher resource listings at the end of this chapter identifies those companies offering such services.

Finally, as an added help to those individuals primarily working with computers who may require a brief review of some of the basic terminology of writing, a writing glossary has been added to this chapter. It is not meant to be an all inclusive list, but it can serve as a way of familiarizing oneself with terms that are often used to promote the value of one software package over another.

COMPUTER WRITING INTEGRATION
CURRICULUM AREA: WRITING
COMPOSITION: PREWRITING

SOFTWARE TITLE	SOFTWARE TYPE	GRADE LEVEL	SOFTWARE PUBLISHER
Writer's Helper	Drill	8–12	Conduit

Activities: Provides practice in selecting topics, researching, brainstorming, choosing relevant details, clustering, and sequencing of ideas and concepts. The program links these lessons to popular word processing programs so students can draft and edit stories. Requires 80 column card and any word processor that uses standard DOS 3.3 Applesoft text files.

The Writing Adventure	Game	4–8	DLM

Activities: Students preview a graphic scenario representing a potential story. The program then poses who, what, where, when, and why questions in order to help students focus attention on story plots. Student responses to each scenario are saved on disk for later recall so students can expand, complete, and edit their stories. The program also includes some error diagnosis features.

Outlining Skills	Drill	4–12	Micro Power & Light Co.

Activities: Practice prewriting skills such as grouping related items, naming groups, arranging items in specific order, identifying main topics, reorganizing, and outlining. Teachers can individualize lessons.

Author! Author!	Game	1–10	MindPlay

Activities: Practice developing writing purpose, outlining ideas, and creating characters and story themes. Teachers can customize game options and print out stories and outlines.

Ace Reporter	Problem solving	1–10	MindPlay

Activities: Practice developing story details and story sequence and clustering relevant details. Teachers can select from 60 stories and control game options for each story.

Ace Detective	Problem solving	1–10	MindPlay

CURRICULUM AREA: WRITING
COMPOSITION: PREWRITING

SOFTWARE TITLE	SOFTWARE TYPE	GRADE LEVEL	SOFTWARE PUBLISHER

Activities: Practice data collection techniques for stories. These skills include observation, information organization, and sequencing. Teachers can control sound, lesson level, text speed, and story selection game options. In addition, teachers can obtain student performance summaries.

Prewrite I   Problem solving   3–6   Mindscape
Activities: Interactive question sessions between the computer and student help define the writing process. This interactive format helps the student develop and identify main ideas, relevant details, and sources of information and select a target audience. Teachers can enter their own questions.

Prewrite II   Problem solving   6–12   Mindscape
Activities: Interactive question sessions between the computer and student help define the writing process. This interactive format helps the student develop and identify main ideas, relevant details, and sources of information and select a target audience. Teacher can enter their own questions.

First Draft   Productivity tool 6–12   Scholastic
Activities: Helps students brainstorm lists of ideas and provides outlining and word processing features to structure student ideas. Outlines can be printed with automatic numbering of composition headings. The program saves each outline file as standard Pro DOS text files so students can load their outlines directly into popular word processing programs. Requires 64K Apple computer and a 128K MS DOS computer. Printer is recommended.

Success With   Productivity tool 7–12   Scholastic
  Writing
Activities: Provides students with two prewriting modules. These activities help students develop prewriting skills involving brainstorming, developing ideas, clustering and sequence activities. In addition, the program provides word processing features for arranging and organizing logical story outlines. Teachers can print student work. Requires 128K Apple IIe or 256K Apple IIgs computer. Printer is recommended.

Homework Helper- Productivity tool 7–12   Spinnaker
  Writing
Activities: Guides students through prewriting activities such as brainstorming and outlining. The program also includes a word processor for composing, editing, and printing student compositions. Printer is recommended.

Snooper Troops Problem solving 4–8   Spinnaker
  #1
The Granite Point
  Ghost

Activities: Using an interactive mystery story setting, students practice note-taking, classifying and organizing information. Graphics are used to enhance the story.

Snooper Troops #2	Problem Solving	4–8	Spinnaker

The Disappearing Dolphin

Activities: Using an interactive mystery story setting, students practice note taking, classifying and organizing information. Graphics are used to enhance the story.

CURRICULUM AREA: WRITING
COMPOSITION: COMPOSING AND POSTCOMPOSING

SOFTWARE TITLE	SOFTWARE TYPE	GRADE LEVEL	SOFTWARE PUBLISHER
The Writing Adventure	Game	4–8	DLM

Activities: Students preview graphic "adventure story" scenarios representing a potential story. The program then poses who, what, where, when, and why questions in order to help students focus attention on story plots. Students take notes, solve problems, observe details, and draft and edit their stories based on the picture scenario. Teachers can print stories.

Kidtalk	Productivity tool	3–6	First Byte

Activities: This word processor uses synthesized speech for writing and editing stories. The program allows the teacher to change between male and female voices and change speech tone, speed, and volume. The program can easily be set to speak letters, words, sentences, paragraphs, or whole stories. Stories can be saved on disk. Requires an Apple IIgs or Macintosh computer.

Dr. Peet's Talk Writer	Productivity tool	1–3	Hartley

Activities: This word processor uses a 20 column screen display and synthesized speech for writing and editing compositions. An exploratory disk with talking alphabet and phrase activities introduces children to the computer keyboard and introductory word processing. Requires Echo speech synthesizer (Apple II+ and Apple IIe) or Cricket speech synthesizer (Apple IIc). Printer is recommended.

My Words	Productivity tool	1–3	Hartley

Activities: This word processor uses synthesized speech for writing and editing stories. The program generates a talking word list from the story so students can hear each word and use the word list for writing additional stories. Teachers can print stories in small and large text. Requires Echo

CURRICULUM AREA: WRITING
COMPOSITION: COMPOSING AND POSTCOMPOSING

SOFTWARE TITLE	SOFTWARE TYPE	GRADE LEVEL	SOFTWARE PUBLISHER

speech synthesizer (Apple II+ and Apple IIe) or Cricket speech synthesizer (Apple IIc). Printer is recommended.

Proof It	Drill	4–8	Merry Bee Communications

Activities: Presents stories to students. Students must then find the errors in each story. The program uses large screen text for stories. Feedback and help screen are included.

That's My Story	Drill	3–12	Mindscape

Activities: Encourages creative writing with the use of "starter sentences" and "what if" suggestions. The program also provides "branching" so that students can select different story suggestions and create their own individualized stories. Built-in word processing functions help students in the story creation process.

Text Tiger	Game/tool	2–6	MindPlay

Activities: This word processor offers basic word processing features, large screen characters, and options to move, copy, print, save, load, and erase files. In addition, the program includes nine lessons for introducing keyboard skills and games for typing in words, using the cursor, and editing screen text. Teachers can change game options, adjust lesson difficulty level, and obtain student performance records. Printer is recommended.

Story Writer	Productivity tool	4–8	Mindscape

Activities: A combination of graphics and word processing features allows students to write and illustrate their own stories. This writing tool includes 40 pictures covering fable, adventure, nature, and social themes.

Creative Writing Series: Creation	Productivity tool	2–8	Pelican

Activities: Animated story building tool allows students to design, write, and print their own story books. Contains a large group of children's graphics. Stories can be created with graphic scenes and animated characters. A built-in text processor is included for student writing. Teachers can print stories in color and in five different sizes. Printer is recommended.

Creative Writing Series: Dinosaur Days	Game	2–8	Pelican

Activities: Introduce students to prehistoric creatures and plant life. An animated story-building tool is included so that students can design, write, and print their own dinosaur story books. Contains a large group of prehistoric creature and background graphics. Stories can be created with graphic scenes and characters. A built-in text processor is included for student writing. Teachers can print stories in color and in five different sizes. Printer is recommended.

Creative Writing Series: Jumbled Jungle	Game	2–8	Pelican

Activities: Introduce students to jungle animals. An animated story building tool is included so that students can design, write, and print their own animal story books. Contains a large group of animal body part graphics. Students mix and match animal parts to create their own animals. A built-in text processor is included so students can write stories about their creations. Teachers can print stories in color and in five different sizes. Printer is recommended.

Creative Writing Series: Monsters and Make Believe	Productivity tool	2–8	Pelican

Activities: Animated story building tool allows students to design, write, and print their own monster and myth story books. Contains a large group of creature body parts and background graphics. Stories can be created with graphic scenes and characters. A built-in text processor is included for student writing. Teachers can print stories in color and in five different sizes. Printer is recommended.

Creative Writing Series: Transportation Transportation	Productivity tool	2–8	Pelican

Activities: Animated story building tool allows students to design, write, and print their own story books about unusual transportation vehicles. Contains a large group of vehicle parts and background graphics. Students invent their own vehicles and write stories about their creations. A built-in text processor is included for student writing. Teachers can print stories in color and in five different sizes. Printer is recommended.

Story Starter	Drill	2–4	Random House

Activities: Offers students a selection of open-ended sentences. After the student selects and completes the sentence, the program uses connecting words (*because, when,* and *then*) to prompt writers to expand the sentence. Teachers can print and save stories.

Story Builder	Drill	3–6	Random House

Activities: Offers a selection of over 4,000 sentence elements from which students may select and combine in order to make syntactically correct

CURRICULUM AREA: WRITING
COMPOSITION: COMPOSING AND POSTCOMPOSING

			SOFTWARE
SOFTWARE TITLE	SOFTWARE TYPE	GRADE LEVEL	PUBLISHER

stories. Graphics are utilized to enhance concepts. Teachers can control lesson levels, print and save stories.

| *MasterType's Writer* | Productivity tool | 3–8 | Scarborough |

Activities: This word processor helps students with prewriting, composing, and postcomposing activities. The prewriting features help students develop outlines, arrange and number notes, and sort information. The writing tool incorporates 20, 40, 55, 70 or 80 column screens. The program incorporates help screens and a tutorial to assist the user. Printer is recommended.

| *Bank Street Writer III* | Productivity tool | 2–12 | Scholastic |

Activities: This word processor helps facilitate writing, revising, editing, and proofreading. The program includes pull-down menus that provide access to all writing functions. The writing tool accommodates 20, 40, and 80 column screen displays. An integrated spelling checker (60,000 word dictionary) and an on-line thesaurus (50,000 words) are included for editing and proofreading. A tutorial program is included to help teachers introduce the word processing tool to students. Requires 128K Apple or MS DOS computer. Printer is recommended.

| *Story Tree* | Productivity tool | 4–12 | Scholastic |

Activities: This productivity tool allows students to write "interactive" text stories. The program, utilizing story "branching" features, provides students with the ability to control the way a story unfolds, offering unique story twists and multiple story endings. Built-in word processing features support editing, revising, reorganizing, and printing functions. Stories can be read on the computer screen or printed on paper.

| *Multiscribe* | Productivity tool | 3–12 | Scholastic |

Activities: This word processor uses pull-down menus to access all word-processing functions. Advanced editing features include a ruler-based "floating format" which automatically centers text, adjusts line spacing, and sets tabs, margins, and page breaks. The program includes a variety of type styles and sizes. A built-in spelling checker (50,000 words) aids proofreading activities. This writing tool also uses a picture manager that allows students to incorporate graphics for desktop publishing activities. Teachers can also import documents from many popular word processing programs that save files such as ASCII text files. Requires 128K Apple IIe or IIc. Mouse is optional. Printer is recommended.

Multiscribe IIGS Productivity tool 3–12 Scholastic
Activities: This word processor uses pull-down menus to access all word-processing functions. Advanced editing features include a ruler-based "floating format" which automatically centers text, adjusts line spacing, and sets tabs, margins, and page breaks. The program includes a variety of type styles and sizes. A built-in spelling checker (50,000 words) aids proofreading activities. This writing tool also uses a picture manager that allows students to incorporate graphics for desktop publishing activities. The program can print in color and print documents on a laser printer. Teachers can also import documents from many popular word processing programs that save files such as ASCII text files. Requires 512K Apple IIgs and mouse. Printer is recommended.

Success with Productivity tool 7–12 Scholastic
Writing
Activities: This writing tool, in addition to outlining features, incorporates a word-processing program to help students turn ideas and notes into compositions. The program also provides editing/evaluation features that help students review their writing. A built-in style checker proofreads the text for correct grammar and style. Teachers can print student work. Requires 128K Apple IIe or 256K Apple IIgs computer. Printer is recommended.

Talking Text Productivity tool 1–6 Scholastic
Writer
Activities: This word processor includes synthesized speech to provide sound-symbol correspondence during writing, revising, editing, and proofreading activities. The program includes basic word-processing features for editing, inserting, moving, copying, deleting, and saving text. Requires 128K Apple with Echo speech synthesizer or Cricket speech synthesizer (Apple IIc). Apple IIgs and 256K MS DOS Computers do not require a speech synthesizer. Printer is recommended.

Story Maker Productivity tool 3–6 Scholastic
Activities: Allows students to mix both text and graphics for illustrated stories. The program includes 8 type styles, a gallery of 66 pictures, and drawing tools for illustrating stories. Students can read stories on the computer or print them on paper. The program uses icons (pictures that represent writing functions—i.e., a typewriter icon for typing text) to simplify the writing process for students. Requires a joystick, mouse, or koala pad. Printer is recommended.

Homeword Productivity tool 3–8 Sierra On-Line
Activities: This word processor uses "icons," or picture symbols, to represent word processing functions. The program uses a 40 column screen and includes a 28,000-word spelling checker for editing and proofreading functions. An audio cassette is included for tutorial lessons. Requires 64K Apple computer. Printer is recommended.

CURRICULUM AREA: WRITING
COMPOSITION: COMPOSING AND POSTCOMPOSING

SOFTWARE TITLE	SOFTWARE TYPE	GRADE LEVEL	SOFTWARE PUBLISHER
Homeword Plus	Productivity tool	3–8	Sierra On-Line

Activities: This word processor uses "icons," or picture symbols, to represent word processing functions. The program uses an 80 column screen and includes a 28,000-word spelling checker for editing and proofreading functions. An audio cassette is included for tutorial lessons. Requires 128K Apple computer. Printer is recommended.

Kidwriter	Productivity tool	1–4	Spinnaker

Activities: Incorporates simple word processing features and includes 99 graphics for creating illustrated stories. Graphics include background scenes, letters, numbers, shapes, characters, and objects that can change color and size. Text is added in separate text windows. Stories can be printed or saved on disk and viewed in sequence as computerized story books. Printer is optional.

Story Machine	Game	1–4	Spinnaker

Activities: Utilizes graphics, sound, and animation to encourage students to write simple sentences, paragraphs, and stories. Students use a predefined list of nouns, verbs, prepositions, and other parts of speech during writing activities. The computer acts out the content of each sentence with animated characters.

II Write	Productivity tool	4–12	Random House

Activities: This word processor uses a graphics-oriented approach to word processing with pull-down menus, rulers, and icons to access word-processing features. The program provides multiple windows for editing up to four documents at a time. The writing tool supports a variety of fonts, type styles, and type sizes. The word processor works with keyboard or mouse. Requires 128K Apple Computer. Printer is recommended.

CURRICULUM AREA: WRITING
COMPUTER KEYBOARDING

SOFTWARE TITLE	SOFTWARE TYPE	GRADE LEVEL	SOFTWARE PUBLISHER
Type!	Drill	7–12	Broderbund

Activities: Introduces typing exercises involving letters, numbers, words, and sentences. Diagnostics provides teachers with information on typing speed and accuracy. This program also provides typing tests with student performance summaries.

Superkey	Drill	3–8	Bytes of Learning

Activities: Introduces students to correct body and hand positions. Ten lessons introduce the "home row" and other hand positions. The program also includes a skill check so students can practice typing and measure speed and accuracy.

Keyboard Cadet   Drill   3–12   Mindscape
Activities: On-screen graphics show students correct fingering. The program includes lessons for timed typing of letters, words, sentences, and paragraphs. Teachers can control lesson levels.

MasterType   Game   4–12   Scarborough
Activities: Arcade game drills touch-typing skills. Teachers can create their own lessons. The program includes 17 built-in typing levels for practicing individual keys, words, and sentences. Teachers can control game options and obtain student performance summaries.

Typing Tutor IV   Drill   7–12   Simon &
                                                           Schuster
Activities: Includes sequential lessons on letters, words, and full keyboard speed tests. The program gives feedback on student strengths and weaknesses. Teachers can control lesson levels.

Alphabetic   Tutorial   6–12   Southwestern
   Keyboarding   Publishing
Activities: Animated graphics introduce 18 lessons on typing letters, numbers, and words. Illustrations show students which fingers should strike which keys. Teachers can change lesson levels.

MicroType   Game   2–6   Southwestern
                                                           Publishing
Activities: Drills alphabet and numbers. Teachers can change lesson difficulty. Correct hand positioning is reinforced with animated illustrations.

Stickybear Typing   Game   2–6   Weekly Reader
                                                              Family
                                                              Software
Activities: Three games are used to teach students keyboard skills. Teachers can control lesson difficulty levels.

CURRICULUM AREA: WRITING
FUNCTIONAL WRITING

SOFTWARE TITLE	SOFTWARE TYPE	GRADE LEVEL	SOFTWARE PUBLISHER
Filling out Job Applications	Tutorial	9–12	Microcomputer Educational Programs

CURRICULUM AREA: WRITING
FUNCTIONAL WRITING

SOFTWARE TITLE	SOFTWARE TYPE	GRADE LEVEL	SOFTWARE PUBLISHER

Activities: Takes students through the process of filling out their own application forms. The program provides explanations of the various components of a job application. Student responses are stored and are printed with the application form. Printer is required.

Resumes Made Easy	Productivity tool	9–12	Microcomputer Educational Programs

Activities: Helps students organize and develop their own resumes. Questions and answers help format and automatically create functional and chronological resumes. Students can also print their resumes. Printer is recommended.

Notetaking	Drill	5–9	LRC

Activities: Focuses on writing skills necessary to write a report. Students must determine important facts, condense information, take notes, label and categorize notes, and collect information for footnotes and bibliographies. The program includes word processing features.

CURRICULUM AREA: WRITING
HANDWRITING

SOFTWARE TITLE	SOFTWARE TYPE	GRADE LEVEL	SOFTWARE PUBLISHER
Touch 'n Write	Drill	1–3	Sunburst Communications

Activities: Provides 21 lessons designed to teach the Palmer Method of manuscript handwriting. Students practice forming strokes, letters and words on the screen. Teachers can change lesson levels and create their own lessons. A touch-screen is required.

SOFTWARE PRODUCTIVITY TOOLS FOR TEACHERS

SOFTWARE TITLE	SOFTWARE PUBLISHER
Bank Street Speller	Broderbund

Functions: This spelling checker works with the Bank Street Writer word processor. Teachers can add their own dictionary words.

Show Off	Broderbund

Functions: This productivity tool allows teachers to create multimedia presentations including overhead transparencies, slide shows, posters, and handouts. The program can also control 35-mm slide projectors. The program includes 380 graphics, 140 borders, and a variety of text types, styles and sizes. Teachers can use a graphics editor to create their own pictures. Requires an Apple IIgs computer. Printer is recommended.

The Print Shop   Broderbund
Functions: This printing tool enables teachers to write, design, and print greeting cards, stationery, school letterhead, classroom signs, and bulletin board materials. The program includes various type styles, nine border designs, dozens of pictures, text-editing features, and a built-in graphics editor for creating individualized logos and pictures. Printer is required.

Appleworks   Claris
Functions: This integrated software package includes: (1) a data base to organize classroom information; (2) a word processor to write reports, documents, letters, articles, or memos; and (3) a spreadsheet for school budgets. Requires a 128K Apple computer. Printer is optional.

HomeWorker   Davidson & Associates
Functions: This student productivity tool contains six integrated programs: a word processor, outliner, flash card maker, calendar, grade keeper, and calculator. The program includes on-screen tutorials. Printer is optional.

Kalamazoo Teacher's Record Book   Hartley
Functions: Record and compute student grades. Print bar graphs, list point totals, list letter grades, calculate grades using various weighting methods, and adjust grade curves. The program can also print reports. Printer is optional.

Test Writer   K-12 MicroMedia
Functions: Create tests using multiple choice, essay, true/false, fill-in-the-blank, and matching question formats. The test can be saved and used by Appleworks (see above) or printed with answer keys.

Principal's Assistant   Learning Well
Functions: This productivity tool allows teachers and students to create certificates, greeting cards, letters, awards, and newsletters. Printer required.

Sensible Grammar Checker   Sensible Software
Functions: This grammar checker can identify misused English phrases that include informal, cliche, vague, wordy, and repetitive phrases. The program also identifies punctuation, capitalization, and other typographical errors. Requires 128K Apple computer.

Sensible Speller   Sensible Software
Functions: This spelling checker includes 80,000 words from the Random House Dictionary. Adds, ignores, looks up, suggests, and replaces words. Two versions are available for either Apple DOS or ProDOS.

SOFTWARE PRODUCTIVITY TOOLS FOR TEACHERS

SOFTWARE TITLE   SOFTWARE PUBLISHER

SuperPrint   Scholastic
Functions: This printing program allows teachers to create signs, banners, posters etc. The program contains hundreds of graphics, six type styles, and predesigned borders. Graphics can be printed from sizes ranging from 1–55 inches. A built-in editor allows teachers to design, create and, mix an unlimited number of different graphic elements. Printer is required.

Webster's New World Spelling Checker   Simon & Schuster
Functions: This spelling checker contains 100,000 words. The program can suggest and replace words. Teachers can add words to an auxiliary dictionary. The program works with both Apple DOS and ProDOS.

Certificate Maker   Springboard
Functions: This teacher tool provides the ability to choose from over 200 certificates in scholastic, sports, recreation, and other achievement categories. Teachers can enter their own messages, choose from sixteen borders, and change type styles. Printer is required.

Springboard Publisher   Springboard
Functions: Provides desktop publishing including page layout, word processing, and graphics. Requires 128K Apple.

The Professional Sign Maker   Sunburst Communications
Functions: A flexible tool for producing signs, handouts, banners etc. Letters can be created in 1-, 2-, 4- and 8-inch heights. Special patterns allow teachers to make a variety of borders for bulletin boards. Printer is required.

SOFTWARE PUBLISHERS

American Educational Computer, Inc.
  (AEC)
2450 Embarcadero Way
Palo Alto, CA 94303

Broderbund
17 Paul Drive
San Rafael, CA 94903

Bytes of Learning
150 Consumers Rd.
Suite 202
Willowdale, Ontario, Canada M2J1P9

Claris
440 Clyde Ave.
Mountain View, CA 94043

Conduit
University of Iowa
Oakdale campus
Iowa City, IA 52242

Compu-Teach
78 Olive St.
New Haven, CT 06511

Data Command
P.O. Box 548
Kankakee, IL 60901

Davidson & Associates
3135 Kashiwa St.
Torrance, CA 90505

Developmental Learning Materials
 (DLM)
200 Bethany Drive
Allen, Texas 75002

First Byte
3333 East Spring St.
Long Beach, CA 90806

Hartley
133 Bridge St.
Dimondale, MI 48821
(Offers 30-day preview period)

Learning Well
200 S. Service Rd.
Roslyn Heights, NY 11577

Merry Bee Communications
815 Crest Drive
Omaha, NE 68046

Microcomputer Educational
 Programs
157 S. Kalamazoo Mall
Suite 250
Kalamazoo, MI 49007

Micro Power & Light Co.
12820 Hillcrest Rd., Ste. 200A
Dallas, TX 75230

MindPlay
82 Montvale Ave.
Stoneham, MA 02180
(Offers 30-day preview period)

Mindscape
3444 Dundee Rd.
Northbrook, IL 60062

Pelican
c/o Learning Lab Software
8833 Reseda
Northridge, CA 91324

Random House Media
400 Hahn Rd.
Westminster, MD 21157

Scarborough
25 N. Broadway
TarryTown, NY 10591

Sensible Software
335 E. Big Beaver, Suite 207
Troy, MI 48083

Sierra On-Line
P.O. Box 485
Coarsegold, CA 93614

Simon & Schuster
P.O. Box 2987
New York, NY 10185

Southwestern Publishing
5101 Madison Rd.
Cincinnati, OH 45227

Spinnaker
One Kendall Square
Cambridge, MA 02139

Springboard Software
7807 Creekridge Cir.
Minneapolis, MN 55435

Sunburst Communications
39 Washington Ave.
Pleasantville, NY 10570
(Offers 30-day preview period)

Weekly Reader Family Software
10 Station Place
Norfolk, CT 06058
(Offers 30-day preview period)

SOFTWARE DISTRIBUTORS

Academic Software
1415 Queen Anne Rd.
Teaneck, NJ 07666

Alpha Resources Centers
P.O. Box 70647
Washington, D.C. 20024

American Micro Media, Inc.
19 N. Broadway
Red Hook, NY 12571
(30-day preview policy)

Cambridge Development Laboratory
42 4th Ave.
Waltham, MA 02154
(30-day preview policy)

Follett Library Book Company
4506 Northwest Highway
Crystal Lake, IL 60014

K-12 MicroMedia
6 Arrow Rd. Dept. C
Ramsey, NJ 07446

Learning Lab Software
8833 Reseda Blvd.
Northridge, CA 91324
(30-day preview policy)

National School Products
101 East Broadway
Maryville, TN 37801-2498
(30-day preview policy)

Opportunities for Learning, Inc.
20417 Nordhoff St., Dept. 6 AM
Chatsworth, CA 91311

Psychological Assessment Resources
Inc.
P.O. Box 998
Odessa, FL 33556-0998

Scholastic
P.O. Box 7502
2931 East McCarty St.
Jefferson City, MO 65102

WRITING GLOSSARY

It is futile to study writing in isolation. Students read constantly while they write (Calkins, 1983). The sounds of language determine what is written about and how the written product will proceed. Writing, like reading, is an evolving process that has component levels and functions.

Writing is among the last language skills acquired since the progression of language acquisition is from auditory receptive (listening) to auditory expressive (speaking) to visual receptive (reading), and finally to visual skills. It is a difficult skill to acquire and evolves from a complex network of skills that include spoken language, organization of thoughts, knowledge of language conventions (grammar and usage) and graphomotor control.

The process of instruction in written language is enhanced by using the computer in the classroom. From the use of graphics tablets for development of graphomotor skills to the sue of the word processor for development of functional and expository written products, one can find a variety of uses for the computer in the course of instruction. Below are some of the major terms associated with writing.

Dictation skills   application of ability to write information that is heard.

Drafting   a four stage (starting, writing, reformulating, stopping) process of free flow exposition within a noncritical framework to get

	ideas on paper. Later refinement and editing will streamline the written product.
Graphic quality	components of the written product which relate to legibility, visual clarity, spacing and size.
Orthographic quality	components of the written product which relate to spelling.
Phonologic quality	components of the written product which relate to proper oral interpretation of that product (i.e., words that run together, non-phonetic spellings, etc.)
Prewriting	the systematic preparation of the writer for composition. This process involves the clarification of the topic, the audience, and the format for the ultimate written product.
Revising	the process of reviewing a written product for semantic and syntactic quality.
Semantic quality	components of the written product which relate to meaning (i.e., coherence, sequence of ideas, use of idioms, etc.).
Syntactic quality	components of the written product which relate to grammar (i.e., subject-verb agreement, punctuation, etc.)
Transcription skills	application of ability to write information that is seen from either a near or distant vantage point.

CHAPTER 8

*Microcomputer Math
Applications in the Classroom*

INTEGRATING COMPUTERS
INTO THE MATH CURRICULUM

The following sections introduce teachers to a wide variety of commercial software resources that may support instructional activities in both regular and special education classrooms. Specifically, the software resources in this chapter have been organized into a general math curriculum covering the areas of basic concepts, operations, and applications. Each curriculum area is outlined with specific instructional goals and matched with supporting educational software tools. The intent of this organization is to provide teachers with general examples and information on the types of software resources available to facilitate the integration of microcomputer instruction into the school's math curriculum. To this end, the following sections will address: (1) goal specific instructional software titles; (2) a description of the software design approach; (3) the grade level of the target student population; (4) the name of the software publisher; (5) a description of the activities inherent in the software title; (6) a brief description of the teacher options and flexibility offered by the software title; and (7) a list of any special computer equipment necessary to implement the software title in the classroom.

In addition, this chapter will provide teachers with information on software productivity tools related to math. This information is directed at specific software resources that aid teachers in developing math materials for the classroom and conducting testing and evaluation functions. Software title listings, publisher names, and brief descriptions of the tool's functions are included. The last section of the chapter will provide software publisher address information as well as a listing for mail-order software distributors.

Finally, the reader should note that this curriculum and its supporting software listing are examples. As such, they simply provide various ways to consider integrating current commercial educational software into the math curriculum. Because children have different instructional needs and individual learning styles, software that works with one child may not work with another. Hence, teachers are encouraged to evaluate and test instructional software with their children before prescribing its use. To help facilitate this critical evaluation process, many software publishers are now offering 30-day preview periods before purchasing educational software. The publisher resource listings at the end of this chapter identifies those companies offering such services.

Finally, as an added help to those individuals primarily working with computers who may require a brief review of some of the basic terminology of mathematics, a math glossary has been added to this chapter. It is not meant to be an all inclusive list, but it can serve as a way of familiarizing oneself with terms that are often used to promote the value of one software package over another.

COMPUTER MATH INTEGRATION

CURRICULUM AREA: MATH
BASIC CONCEPTS: NUMERATION

SOFTWARE TITLE	SOFTWARE TYPE	GRADE LEVEL	SOFTWARE PUBLISHER
Math and Me	Drill	1–2	Davidson & Associates

Activities: Introduce math readiness skills involving shape, number, and pattern recognition. The program also includes single-digit addition. Teachers can select lesson levels.

Number Farm	Game	1–2	DLM

Activities: Six animated games introduce students to number recognition, number/word recognition, numerical ordering, counting skills, and *greater than* and *less than* number concepts. Teachers can select lesson levels.

Webster's Numbers	Game	1–2	Britannica Software

Activities: Animated graphics introduce students to shape and number recognition, pattern development, and counting skills. Teachers can select lesson levels.

First Numbers	Game	1–3	First Byte

Activities: Animated graphics and synthesized speech provide instruction and feedback in number recognition, counting, and simple addition and subtraction. Teachers can control game options and lesson levels. Requires Apple IIgs or Macintosh computer.

Number Sea Hunt	Game	1–2	Gamco

Activities: Animated graphics introduce numerals, grouping objects, matching, finding the missing number, and 1–10 addition and subtraction. Teachers can change lesson levels. The program can store up to 200 student performance records.

Expanded Notation	Drill	2–4	Hartley

Activities: Introduce and practice place value and writing numerals in a variety of expanded forms. Teachers can change or create their own lessons. The program tracks student performance.

Number Words Level 1	Drill	1–2	Hartley

Activities: Practice matching numerals to the appropriate number words. The program includes a keyboard graphic to help identify correct answers. Lessons include numbers from 0 to 99. The program can print and store student performance records.

| *Number Words* | Drill | 3–6 | Hartley |
| *Level II* | | | |

Activities: Practice matching numerals to the appropriate number words. Lessons include numbers from 100 to millions. The program can print and store student performance records.

| *Math Rabbit* | Game | 1–2 | The Learning Company |

Activities: Practice number recognition, counting, and matching objects to numbers. The program also includes addition and subtraction activities involving one- and two-digit numbers. Teachers can select lesson levels.

| *Counting &* | Game | 1–3 | Micro Power & |
| *Ordering* | | | Light Co. |

Activities: Animated games drill students on number recognition, sequence, and counting. Teachers can select lesson levels.

| *Charlie Brown's* | Drill | 1–2 | Random House |
| *1,2,3s* | | | |

Activities: Animated graphics introduce students to number recognition and keyboard. The program also provides practice in counting objects.

| *Stickybear* | Drill | 1–2 | Weekly Reader |
| *Numbers* | | | Software |

Activities: Practice counting and number recognition. Animated graphics and sound help reinforce number and counting skills.

CURRICULUM AREA: MATH
BASIC CONCEPTS: GEOMETRY AND SYMBOLS

SOFTWARE TITLE	SOFTWARE TYPE	GRADE LEVEL	SOFTWARE PUBLISHER
Trap-a-Zoid	Game	6–8	DesignWare

Activities: Practice identifying geometric shapes and learn basic concepts using an animated game. Teachers can change lesson difficulty level. The program also includes a dictionary of geometry terms.

| *Bumble Games* | Game | 3–5 | The Learning Company |

Activities: Introduce students to the principles of numbers and geometry. Six games introduce and provide practice on number lines, number pairs, and graph plotting. Students can also draw pictures using X–Y coordinate grids.

CURRICULUM AREA: MATH
BASIC CONCEPTS: GEOMETRY AND SYMBOLS

SOFTWARE TITLE	SOFTWARE TYPE	GRADE LEVEL	SOFTWARE PUBLISHER
Bumble Plot	Game	3–5	The Learning Company

Activities: Introduce students to coordinate geometry. Five games introduce and provide practice on number-plotting skills using negative and positive numbers.

Elastic Lines	Problem solving	2–8	Sunburst Communications

Activities: Simulates a "geoboard" in which electronic rubber bands are stretched over pegs. Students manipulate bands on the geoboard creating different patterns, sizes, and types of geometric shapes. The program also allows students to rotate and flip geoboards for studying geometric concepts.

The Geometric preSupposer	Problem solving	7–12	Sunburst Communications

Activities: Introduce beginning high school geometry concepts including congruence, similarity and parallelism, geometric shapes, and measurements.

Geometry Concepts	Drill	7–12	Ventura

Activities: Introduce geometric figures including circles, triangles, angles, lines, planes, area, perimeter, planar figures, solids, and constructions. The program provides practice in identifying and spelling geometrical terms and a data bank for storing information and facts about terms and concepts.

Coordinate Geometry	Tutorial	7–12	Ventura

Activities: Introduce students to the cartesian plane and coordinate geometry. The program also includes a graphic equation processor that allows students to define equations which the computer automatically graphs. The program can generate random quiz problems from topic material.

Geoart	Drill	7–12	Ventura

Activities: Students are introduced to concepts of geometry and art. The program drills students on the names and characteristics of common geometrical figures, perimeters, and area problems. A drawing program allows students to draw a figure and then rotate, reflect and transform the figure.

CURRICULUM AREA: MATH
OPERATIONS: ADDITION, SUBTRACTION,
MULTIPLICATION, AND DIVISION

SOFTWARE TITLE	SOFTWARE TYPE	GRADE LEVEL	SOFTWARE PUBLISHER
Success with Algebra: Equations	Tutorial	8–11	CBS

Activities: Introduce and practice AX + B = C equations, where A, B, and C are integers. All solutions are integer values. Students solve each equation step-by-step. All errors, including incorrect use of algebraic axioms, are highlighted and explained.

Success with Algebra: Equations II	Tutorial	8–11	CBS

Activities: Introduce and practice AX + B = CX + D equations, where A, B, C, and D are integers. All solutions are integer values. Students solve each equation step-by-step. All errors, including incorrect use of algebraic axioms, are highlighted and explained.

Success with Algebra: Equations III	Tutorial	8–11	CBS

Activities: Introduce and practice AX + B (CX + D) = EX + F or AX + B = CX + D (EX + F) equations. All coefficients, constants, and problem solutions are integers. Students solve each equation step by step in any number of correct solution paths. All errors, including incorrect use of algebraic axioms, are highlighted and explained. Teachers can generate printed tests with answer sheets for classroom use.

Arthimagic: Addition	Drill	1–2	Compu-Teach

Activities: Animated graphics introduce students to addition and counting skills using single digit numbers. Teachers can change lesson levels.

Arthimagic: Subtaction	Drill	1–2	Compu-Teach

Activities: Animated graphics introduce students to subtraction skills using single digit numbers. Teachers can change lesson levels.

Alge-Blaster	Tutorial	7–12	Davidson & Associates

Activities: Contains over 600 problems in five subject areas: positive/negative numbers; monomials; polynomials; factoring; and solving both equations and systems of equations. A tutorial is included for describing a systematic approach to solving algebra problems.

CURRICULUM AREA: MATH
OPERATIONS: ADDITION, SUBTRACTION,
MULTIPLICATION, AND DIVISION

SOFTWARE TITLE	SOFTWARE TYPE	GRADE LEVEL	SOFTWARE PUBLISHER
Math Blaster Plus!	Drill	1–6	Davidson & Associates

Activities: Contains over 700 problems in seven skill areas: addition, subtraction, multiplication, division, fractions, decimals, and percents. The program includes student performance summaries. Teachers can add their own math problems.

Decimal Discovery	Game	4–7	DLM

Activities: Seven games involve comparing, adding, subtracting, multiplying and dividing decimals, comparing place value, and equivalency. The program offers three different response modes: fill-in, matching, and scanning for special-needs students. Teachers can create their own lessons, select lesson difficulty levels, or change game options. The program records student responses and contains a worksheet generator for printing practice worksheets.

Algebra 1–6	Tutorial	7–12	Britannica Software

Activities: This algebra series is made up of six independent software volumes that comprise a first-year course in algebra. Content material is presented in four learning styles; working sample problems; reading explanations of concepts; watching the computer solve equations step-by-step; or reviewing rules that govern an algebra operation. Students manage the learning process by selecting their preferred learning styles.

EduWare Decimals	Tutorial	4–8	Britannica Software

Activities: Tutorial lessons provide pretest, instruction, practice, and posttest on decimals. Seven learning units cover conversion, addition of decimals, subtraction of decimals, rounding off of decimal numbers, multiplication of decimals, division of decimals, and percentages. Teachers can change lesson options.

EduWare Fractions	Tutorial	4–8	Britannica Software

Activities: Tutorial lessons provide pretest, instruction, practice, and posttest on fractions. Six learning units cover definitions and parts of fractions, denominators, addition, subtraction, multiplication, and division of fractions. Teachers can change lesson options.

Building TENS   Drill   1–3   Hartley
  Strategy
Activities: Animated graphic lessons provide students with activities involving dot counting, pattern recognition, and addition of two-digit numbers. The program incorporates math strategies in which students "build tens" as they do addition problems. The program allows teachers to change lesson levels and do student record keeping.

Math Talk   Drill   1–6   First Byte
Activities: Synthesized speech and graphics are used for practicing addition, subtraction, multiplication, and division. Speech capabilities are utilized with instructions and feedback. Teachers can enter their own math problems and obtain student performance summaries. Requires Apple IIgs or Macintosh computer.

Math Talk   Drill   3–8   First Byte
  Fractions
Activities: Synthesized speech and animated graphics are used to drill fractions, decimals, and percents. Speech capabilities are utilized with instructions and feedback. Teachers can enter their own math problems and obtain student performance summaries. Requires Apple IIgs or Macintosh computer.

Whole Numbers: Drill   2–6   Gamco
  Addition and
  Subtraction
Activities: Practice addition, subtraction, and mixed operations with whole numbers. Addition activities involve problems with two addends (with no regrouping) to four addends (with multiple regrouping). Subtraction problems may involve no regrouping to multiple regrouping. The program also includes a student record management system that tracks, views, prints, or deletes student files.

Fractions: Drill   4–9   Gamco
  Addition and
  Subtraction
Activities: Provides practice in addition and subtraction of fractions. Lessons include problems with like or unlike denominators and regrouping mixed numbers with like or unlike denominators. Students control the pace of lessons. Teachers can select number of problems in lessons and can save, print, and delete student performance records.

Fractions: Drill   4–9   Gamco
  Multiplication
  and Division
Activities: Provides practice in multiplication and division of fractions (with or without canceling) and multiplication or division of whole numbers and mixed numbers. Teachers can select number and level of problems in

CURRICULUM AREA: MATH
OPERATIONS: ADDITION, SUBTRACTION,
MULTIPLICATION, AND DIVISION

SOFTWARE TITLE	SOFTWARE TYPE	GRADE LEVEL	SOFTWARE PUBLISHER

lessons. Student record Keeping allows teachers to save, print, and delete student performance records. The program also includes a game for student reward.

Electric Chalkboard	Drill	1–4	Heartsoft

Activities: Animated graphics are used to motivate students with drill operations involving addition, subtraction, multiplication, and division of whole numbers. Problems are randomly generated. Teachers can change lesson difficulty levels.

Milt's Math Drills	Drill	1–4	Hartley

Activities: Large screen letters and graphics provide a diagnostic/prescriptive drill and practice for addition, subtraction, multiplication, and division. The program can test students and generate a detailed list of recommended math lessons. Teachers can change lessons levels, record student performance, and print student worksheets.

Kindermath II	Drill	1–3	Houghton Mifflin

Activities: Graphics and synthesized speech introduce students to 90 math skill objectives in number identification, counting, addition, subtraction, multiplication, and division. Lessons are interactive and self-paced. Teachers can select lesson difficulty levels, monitor student progress, and print lesson scores. Requires Apple IIe or Apple IIgs and Echo speech synthesizer.

Talking Math Tutor	Tutorial	1–4	Intrinsic Systems

Activities: Synthesized speech is utilized for introducing students to addition, subtraction, multiplication, and division problems. Instructions and feedback are spoken for each math problem. Teachers can select lesson levels. Requires Echo speech synthesizer.

Conquering Whole Numbers	Drill	3–6	MECC

Activities: Practice using whole numbers in addition, subtraction, multiplication and division. The drill activities involve regrouping and using numbers with up to five digits. Teacher options include selecting lesson difficulty level, control over game options, and student record keeping.

Mixed Numbers	Drill	6–8	Media Materials

Activities: Includes a readiness mode for drilling addition, subtraction, multiplication, and division of mixed numbers. An instruction mode gives students step-by-step instructions on the correct operations and procedures for problems. A records management system allows teachers to obtain student performance records and prepare tests and activity sheets.

Division Skills   Drill   6–8   Media Materials
Activities: The program includes a readiness mode for drilling 90 facts. Students use one- and two-digit divisors, whole number remainders, fractional remainders, and decimal remainders. An instruction mode gives students step-by-step instructions on the correct operations and procedures for problems. Teachers can save student records, generate pre- and post-tests, and develop activity sheets.

Decimal Skills   Drill   6–8   Media Materials
Activities: Includes a readiness mode for drilling addition, subtraction, multiplication, and division of decimals. An instruction mode gives students step-by-step instructions on the correct operations and procedures for problems. A records management system allows teachers to store student performance records, give pre- and post-tests, and prepare activity sheets.

Ratios and   Drill   6–8   Media Materials
  Proportions
Activities: The program includes a readiness mode in which students, using raw data, write ratios and proportions. An instruction mode gives students step-by-step instructions on the correct operations and procedures for problems. A records management system allows teachers to keep student performance records, prepare pre- and post-tests, and develop activity sheets.

Percents   Drill   6–8   Media Materials
Activities: Includes a readiness mode for drilling percents. The program includes activities for expressing equations and solving for percentage, base, and rate. An instruction mode gives students step-by-step instructions on the correct operations and procedures for problems. A records management system allows teachers to save student performance records, develop pre- and post-tests, and make activity sheets.

Fractions   Drill   7–10   Micro Power &
                                                          Light
Activities: Review and practice arithmetic operations involving fractions; converting improper to mixed and mixed to improper fractions; finding equivalent fractions and common denominators; and reducing fractions. Teachers can change lesson difficulty levels.

Math Sequence   Drill   2–11   Milliken
  Series   Publishing
Activities: This six-disk series provides drill and practice in six mathematical operations: addition, subtraction, multiplication, division, fractions, and percents. Teachers can change lesson levels.

CURRICULUM AREA: MATH
OPERATIONS: ADDITION, SUBTRACTION, MULTIPLICATION, AND DIVISION

SOFTWARE TITLE	SOFTWARE TYPE	GRADE LEVEL	SOFTWARE PUBLISHER
Math Magic	Game	1–4	MindPlay

Activities: Graphics and animation introduce counting, addition, and subtraction skills to students. The program also provides practice with carry and borrow operations using single- and double-digit numbers. Teachers have comprehensive control over game features and have have the ability to create their own math problems. The program also stores student performance summaries.

RoboMath	Game	2–7	MindPlay

Activities: Graphics and animation introduce multiplication and division skills to students. The program also provides practice with regrouping whole numbers and decimals. Math operations use 1-, 2-, 3-, 4-, and 5-digit numbers. Teachers have comprehensive control over game features and have the ability to add their own math problems. The program also stores student performance summaries.

Galaxy Math, Vol. 1: Basic Math Facts	Game	2–4	Random House

Activities: This game provides students with drill and practice exercises in addition, subtraction, multiplication, and division of single-digit whole numbers. Teachers can change lesson difficulty levels.

Galaxy Math, Vol. 2: Fractions	Game	4–7	Random House

Activities: Provides students with drill and practice exercises in addition, subtraction, multiplication, and division of fractions. In addition, students compare fractions using *less than*, *more than*, and *equal to* concepts. Teachers can change lesson difficulty levels.

Building Your Math Skills	Drill	3–4	Random House

Activities: Drill and practice addition, subtraction, multiplication, division, number concepts, fractions, decimals, percents, and geometry. Teachers can select lesson difficulty levels.

Galaxy Math, Vol. 3: Decimals	Game	5–8	Random House

Activities: Provides students with drill and practice exercises in addition, subtraction, multiplication, and division of decimals. Teachers can change lesson difficulty levels.

Galaxy Math, Vol.   Game   6–8   Random House
   4: Integers
Activities: Provides students with drill and practice exercises in addition, subtraction, multiplication, and division of positive and negative whole numbers. Teachers can change lesson difficulty levels.

Snoopy to the   Game   3–5   Random House
   Rescue
Activities: Students drill addition facts in an animated adventure game involving the Snoopy and Woodstock characters.

Math Shop   Game   6–8   Scholastic
Activities: Practice problem solving skills using addition, subtraction, multiplication, division, fractions, decimals, percents, ratios, binary numbers, estimation, money, measurements, factors, inequalities, and remainders. Teachers can adjust lesson levels.

Fraction Factory   Drill   5–9   Springboard
Activities: Students practice describing fractions, finding equal values with different denominators, multiplying whole numbers with a fraction and fractions with fractions, and subtracting fractions from fractions. Teachers can select lesson difficulty levels.

Challenge Math   Game   2–6   Sunburst
                                              Communications
Activities: Practice addition, subtraction, multiplication, and division problems using whole numbers and decimals. In addition, students practice finding the addend and product using single- and two-digit numbers. Teachers can modify lesson difficulty levels.

Fraction Action   Game   3–9   Unicorn
                                            Software
Activities: Multi-screen arcade adventure with synthesized speech drills fraction skills. The program covers addition, subtraction, multiplication, and division of fractions. Instructions and feedback use synthesized speech. Teachers can change lesson difficulty levels. Requires Apple IIgs or Macintosh computer.

Decimal Dungeon   Game   4–8   Unicorn
                                            Software
Activities: Using an adventure game theme and synthesized speech, students practice adding, subtracting, multiplying, and dividing decimals. Lessons also allow students to convert decimals to fraction or percents. Teachers can change lesson difficulty level. Requires Apple IIgs or Macintosh computer.

Math Wizard   Game   5–9   Unicorn
                                            Software
Activities: Synthesized speech is used for drill and practice activities in

CURRICULUM AREA: MATH
OPERATIONS: ADDITION, SUBTRACTION,
MULTIPLICATION, AND DIVISION

SOFTWARE TITLE	SOFTWARE TYPE	GRADE LEVEL	SOFTWARE PUBLISHER

addition, subtraction, multiplication, and division of whole numbers. The program also includes a word problems module. Teachers can change lesson difficulty levels. Requires Apple IIgs computer.

Stickybear Math I	Drill	1–3	Weekly Reader Family Software

Activities: Animated graphics introduce addition and subtraction problems to students. The program can generate horizontal or vertical math problems utilizing single-digit to four-digit numbers. Teachers can add their own math problems and store student performance records.

Stickybear Math II	Drill	3–6	Weekly Reader Family Software

Activities: Animated graphics introduce multiplication and division problems to students. The program can generate horizontal or vertical math problems utilizing single-digit to four-digit numbers. Teachers can add their own math problems and store student performance records.

CURRICULUM AREA: MATH
APPLICATIONS: TIME AND MONEY

SOFTWARE TITLE	SOFTWARE TYPE	GRADE LEVEL	SOFTWARE PUBLISHER
Telling Time	Drill	2–6	Gamco

Activities: This drill and practice program offers four different lesson types: typing digital time when shown a clock face, typing digital time when given time in words, setting clock hands when given digital time, or setting clock hands when given time in words. Each lesson has four difficulty levels: hours, half-hours, quarter-hours, and 5 minutes. An arcade-style game is included for student reinforcement. Teacher management system allows teachers to select the number of questions, change game options, and store student records.

The Calendar	Drill	3–6	Gamco

Activities: Picture calendars and randomized multiple-choice or fill-in-the-blank question formats are used to drill students on days and months, seasons, special days, holidays, and general use of the calendar. The program also includes an arcade game for student reinforcement. The program allows teachers to select the number of questions per lesson, choose multiple-choice or fill-in-the-blank question formats, change game options, and manage student record-keeping functions.

Money!Money!   Drill   3–5   Hartley
Activities: Graphics help students count coins and bills and make change. Students also practice solving simple word problems, determining amounts in coins and bills, and drilling the concepts *more* and *less*. The program includes student record keeping. Teachers can change or create new lessons.

Using a Calendar   Drill   3–5   Hartley
Activities: On-screen picture calendars, along with information and questions, provide students with drill and practice activities involving calendar skills. Level 1 lessons cover calendar reading skills. Level 2 includes word problems that require students to use information on calendars. Level 3 provides practice on learning calendar facts, special dates, and holidays. Teachers may change or create new lessons. The program can print and store student performance records.

Mackids   Drill   2–6   Nordic Software
   Coinworks
Activities: Practice identifying and counting coins and making change. Teachers can change lesson difficulty levels and obtain printouts. Requires Macintosh computer.

The Coin Changer   Drill   1–4   Heartsoft
Activities: Introduce and practice identifying coins, coin values, and counting money. High resolution graphics are used to represent coins. Teachers can control lesson difficulty level.

Tommy the Time   Tutorial/drill   2–4   Heartsoft
   Telling Turtle
Activities: This two-disk series introduces students to telling time. The first disk provides a tutorial on reading clocks. Lessons are sequenced to teach 1-hour, 30-minute, 15-minute, 5-minute, and 1-minute time intervals. Each lesson concludes with a quiz. The second disk provides drill and practice activities of setting the clock to match the given time.

Money Matters   Drill   2–5   MECC
Activities: High resolution graphics introduce students to identifying and counting coins and bills and making change with coins and bills. The program provides error analysis to help students identify counting errors. Teachers can track and print student performance summaries and give students pre- and post-tests.

Clock Works   Drill   1–5   MECC
Activities: Four animated lessons in color drill students in telling time with

CURRICULUM AREA: MATH
APPLICATIONS: TIME AND MONEY

SOFTWARE TITLE	SOFTWARE TYPE	GRADE LEVEL	SOFTWARE PUBLISHER

analog and digital clocks. Lesson activities include reading time on an analog clock, setting the hands on an analog clock, setting the time on a digital clock, and setting a clock alarm. Teachers may select alternate clock faces, change lesson difficulty levels, and change lesson presentation options.

The Magic Cash Register	Drill	1–8	Avant-Garde

Activities: Practice counting change (bills and coins) using a simulated cash register. The program can provide information on setting up money problems, demonstrating correct change making, and giving correct answers to money problems. The program can also track a student's net gain or loss for a day's sales. Teachers can select difficulty levels.

The Boars' Store	Drill	2–5	Random House

Activities: This program features an animated store with high-resolution graphics in which students may choose from over 100 objects to purchase. Students go the cash register to total their purchases where they either pay with the exact amount of money or determine how much change they should receive.

The Boars Tell Time	Drill	1–3	Random House

Activities: Practice telling time with animated high-resolution graphic analog and digital clocks. Lessons require students to indicate the digital time that corresponds to a given clock time or to move the hands on a clock to match a given digital time. Lesson difficulty varies from hour to five-minute time-telling intervals.

Timekeeper	Drill	1–4	Personal Touch Corp.

Activities: Drill and practice setting an analog clock face and digital clock. Lessons also provide practice in matching analog and digital time to time in words. Teachers can control time increments (1 hour, ½ hour, 15 minutes, and 5 minutes). Touch-screen optional.

Money & Time Adventures	Drill	1–4	SVE

Activities: Animation and high resolution graphics introduce students to counting coins, finding the value of a group of coins, finding the value of a collection of coins and bills, using money, and counting change. A second disk drills students on setting time by hours, setting time by hours and minutes, setting the hands of a clock, and setting the time on a digital clock.

CURRICULUM AREA: MATH
APPLICATIONS: WORD PROBLEMS AND PROBLEM SOLVING

SOFTWARE TITLE	SOFTWARE TYPE	GRADE LEVEL	SOFTWARE PUBLISHER
Collamore Castle I & II	Game	3–6	D.C. Heath & Company

Activities: Introduce students to problem-solving techniques by focusing on eight common strategies and presenting practice problems for each technique. Examples of these strategies include making tables, pattern recognition, organizing, and acting out. Teachers can select lesson difficulty levels.

Math 1: The Mechanics of Word Problems	Tutorial	3–6	Decision Development Corporation

Activities: Teach students to a six-step method for solving word problems using addition, subtraction, multiplication, and division. Word problems introduce "key word" clues and contain randomly generated numbers through the number twelve.

Math 2: Building on Word Problems	Tutorial	3–6	Decision Development Corporation

Activities: Students solve word problems using numbers 1 through 999,999 with an expanded list of key word clues. Lessons include addition, subtraction, multiplication and division. Word problems also introduce extraneous clues to develop problem-solving skills. Student record keeping is included.

Sailing Through Story Problems	Game	3–6	DLM

Activities: Practice one- and two-step math problems. Twelve content areas include addition, subtraction, multiplication, division, and solving randomly generated problems. The program also includes a built-in calculator. Teachers can control lesson levels and obtain student performance summaries.

LEGO Logo	Programming language	1–12	LEGO Systems, Inc.

Activities: Using LEGO logo, students can build machines with LEGO blocks, gears, and motors and then connect these machines to the computer. Students can control the machines by programming with the LEGO Logo language. Requires Apple II computer.

Logo	Programming language	1–12	Terrapin

Activities: Develop programming principles, problem-solving, and critical thinking skills. Computer language offers turtle graphics and program primitives.

CURRICULUM AREA: MATH
APPLICATIONS: MEASUREMENT AND ESTIMATION

SOFTWARE TITLE	SOFTWARE TYPE	GRADE LEVEL	SOFTWARE PUBLISHER
Fish Scales	Drill	1–3	DLM

Activities: Six different activities introduce height, length, and distance, and how to make measurements to compare sizes and distances. Multiple player games are included. Teachers can change game options and select lesson levels.

Introduction to Counting	Drill	1–3	Britannica Software

Activities: Animated graphics introduce students to the concepts of counting, addition, subtraction, height, weight, shape discrimination, and measurement. Teachers can select the number of problems, lesson difficulty level, and lesson presentation features. The program also includes student record keeping.

Estimation	Game	1–3	Lawrence Hall of Science

Activities: Three games introduce students to estimating volume (how many things fit in a jar), estimating rate (speed and distance an object travels), and estimating and comparing lengths of objects.

Estimation	Drill	6–9	MECC

Activities: Animated graphics introduce students to estimation skills using whole numbers and decimals. Estimation problems involve estimating money in a shopping situation.

Bake and Taste	Simulation	1–6	MindPlay

Activities: Learn to follow directions and practice measuring skills in cooking exercises. Measurement skills involve cup, tablespoon, teaspoon, ingredients, and oven setting activities. Teachers can change difficulty levels and print baking recipes.

Campaign Math	Simulation/game	4–9	MindPlay

Activities: This election simulation provides math drills and word problems involving practice with fractions, percentages, and ratios. Each of these math activities is intertwined in election campaign activities involving surveys, interviews, and advertising by phone, newspaper, radio, and TV. Teachers have comprehensive control over game features and have the ability to add their own content material.

Homework Helper	Tutorial	7–12	Spinnaker

Activities: Teaches a step-by-step method for doing word problems. The solver section allows students to add their own homework word problems and develop solution equations. A built-in calculator helps students solve word problems.

Blockers and   Problem solving   4–9   Sunburst
   Finders II   Communications
Activities: Using a 4-by-4 grid, students collect and organize visual data in an attempt to locate hidden obstacles that cause their objects to deviate from their original course. The program exercises visual perception, coordination, data collection, and the evaluation of ambiguous information. Teachers can select four lesson difficulty levels to investigate.

The Pond   Problem solving   3–9   Sunburst
                                                 Communications
Activities: Using an animated frog, lost in a pond of lily pads, students must recognize patterns and articulate patterns into a solution in order to guide the frog off the lily pond. Teachers can select lesson difficulty levels.

The Super Factory   Problem solving   6–9   Sunburst
                                                 Communications
Activities: Using color graphics and animation, this problem solving environment challenges students to duplicate three-dimensional geometric objects. Students must use spatial geometry, visual discrimination, sequence, and logic to develop strategies for research and design duplicate objects. Teachers can select lesson difficulty levels.

Stickybear Word   Problem solving   4–8   Weekly Reader
   Problems   Family
                                                 Software
Activities: Animated graphics reinforce word problems in addition, subtraction, multiplication, and division. Teachers can add their own word problems, change lesson difficulty levels, and print student records and practice problems.

Math Word   Problem solving   5–9   Weekly Reader
   Problems   Family
                                                 Software
Activities: Students practice word problems in addition, subtraction, multiplication, and division. The program highlights incorrect operations and then displays the operations in correct order. The program also has a built-in calculator. Teachers can add their own word problems and change lesson difficulty levels.

SOFTWARE PRODUCTIVITY TOOLS FOR TEACHERS

SOFTWARE TITLE   SOFTWARE PUBLISHER

KeyMath-R ASSIST   AGS
Functions: This software program is designed to report KeyMath-R scores and summarize the student's performance quickly and accurately. The program reports standard scores, age and grade equivalents, and percentile ranks. For total test scores, stanines and normal curve equivalents are given.

SOFTWARE PRODUCTIVITY TOOLS FOR TEACHERS

SOFTWARE TITLE   SOFTWARE PUBLISHER

Subtest performance is reported by mean scaled scores and percentile ranks. Requires a 128K computer.

Worksheet Wizard I   EduSoft
Functions: This teacher tool prints individual worksheets or class worksheets on whole numbers. All new worksheets are different. The worksheet generator covers addition, subtraction, multiplication, and division operations. Teachers are provided with answer keys. Printer required.

Worksheet Wizard II   EduSoft
Functions: This teacher tool prints individual worksheets or class worksheets on fractions. All new worksheets are different. The worksheet generator covers addition, subtraction, multiplication, and division operations. Teachers are provided with answer keys. Printer required.

Worksheet Wizard III   EduSoft
Functions: This teacher tool prints individual worksheets or class worksheets on decimals. All new worksheets are different. The worksheet generator covers addition, subtraction, multiplication, and division operations. Teachers are provided with answer keys. Printer required.

Fact Sheets   Hartley
Functions: This productivity tool is a worksheet generator that allows teachers to create math problems in addition, subtraction, multiplication, or division. All worksheets are unique, provide date, subject, and student identification, and provide answer sheets for each worksheet. Printer required.

Number Fact Sheets   Gamco
Functions: This productivity tool randomly generates worksheets and corresponding answer keys containing 1 to 40 number problems. Operations include addition, subtraction, multiplication, division, and mixed operations. Requires Printer.

Math Assistant I   Scholastic
Functions: This productivity tool provides error analysis in addition and subtraction. Teachers can use this tool for pinpointing student errors in remedial work. The program offers sample tests, create-your-own-test features, and automatic scoring with records of error type by class, group, and individual. The program prints test and answer sheets for desk work. Printer optional.

Math Assistant II   Scholastic
Functions: This productivity tool provides error analysis in multiplication and division. Teachers can use this tool for pinpointing student errors in remedial math work. The program tests for errors in regrouping, pro-

cedures, place value, remainders, etc. The program includes create-your-own-test features, automatic scoring with records of error type by class, group, and individual, and a print feature that generates a printout of each test and supporting answer sheet. Printer optional.

SOFTWARE PUBLISHERS

AGS
Publishers Building
Circle Pines, Minnesota 55014-1796

Avant-Garde
P.O. Box 30160
Eugene, OR 97403

Britannica Software
345 Fourth St.
San Francisco, CA 94107

Compu-Teach
78 Olive St.
New Haven, CT 06511

Davidson & Associates
3135 Kashiwa St.
Torrance, CA 90505

D.C. Heath & Company
125 Spring St.
Lexington, MA 02173

DesignWare
185 Berry St.
San Francisco, CA 94107

Developmental Learning Materials
(DLM)
200 Bethany Drive
Allen, Texas 75002

EduSoft
P.O. Box 2560
Berkeley, CA 94702

First Byte
3333 East Spring St.
Long Beach, CA 90806

Gamco Industries
P.O. Box 1911
Big Spring, TX 79721
(Offers 30-day preview period)

Hartley
133 Bridge St.
Dimondale, MI 48821
(Offers 30-day preview period)

Heartsoft
P.O. Box 691381
Tulsa, OK 74169

Houghton Mifflin Company
Department 67
Mount Support Rd.
Lebanon, NH 03766-9000

Intrinsic Systems
P.O. Box 103
Bronx, N.Y. 10470

Lawrence Hall of Science
University of California
Math/Computer Education Project
Berkeley, CA 94025

LEGO Systems, Inc.
555 Taylor Rd.
Enfield, CT 06082

MECC
3490 Lexington Ave. North
St. Paul, MN 55126

Media Materials
2936 Remington Ave.
Baltimore, MD 21211

Micro Power & Light Co.
12820 Hillcrest Rd. Ste. 200A
Dallas, TX 75230

Milliken Publishing
1100 Research Blvd.
P.O. Box 21579
St. Louis, MO 63132-0579

MindPlay
82 Montvale Ave.
Stoneham, MA 02180
(Offers 30-day preview period)

Nordic Software
3939 North 48th
Lincoln, NE 68504

Personal Touch Corporation
4320 Stevens Creek Blvd., #290
San Jose, CA 95129

Random House Media
400 Hahn Rd.
Westminster, MD 21157

Spinnaker
One Kendall Square
Cambridge, MA 02139

Springboard Software
7807 Creekridge Cir.
Minneapolis, MN 55435

Sunburst Communications
39 Washington Ave.
Pleasantville, NY 10570
(Offers 30-day preview period)

SVE
Department VK
1345 Diversey Parkway
Chicago, IL 60614-1299

Terrapin, Inc.
376 Washington St.
Malden, MA 02148

The Learning Company
6493 Kaiser Drive
Fremont, CA 94555

Unicorn Software
2950 E. Flamingo
Las Vegas, NV 89121

Ventura Educational Systems
3440 Brokenhill St.
Newbury Park, CA 91320

Weekly Reader Family Software
10 Station Place
Norfolk, CT 06058
(Offers 30-day preview period)

SOFTWARE DISTRIBUTORS

Academic Software
1415 Queen Anne Rd.
Teaneck, NJ 07666

Alpha Resources Centers
P.O. Box 70647
Washington, D.C. 20024

American Micro Media, Inc.
19 N. Broadway
Red Hook, NY 12571
(30-day preview policy)

Cambridge Development Laboratory
42 4th Ave.
Waltham, MA 02154
(30-day preview policy)

Follett Library Book Company
4506 Northwest Highway
Crystal Lake, IL 60014

K-12 MicroMedia
6 Arrow Rd., Dept. C
Ramsey, NJ 07446

Learning Lab Software
8833 Reseda Blvd.
Northridge, CA 91324
(30-day preview policy)

National School Products
101 East Broadway
Maryville, TN 37801-2498
(30-day preview policy)

Opportunities for Learning, Inc.
20417 Nordhoff St., Dept. 6 AM
Chatsworth, CA 91311

Psychological Assessment Resources
 Inc.
P.O. Box 998
Odessa, FL 33556-0998

Scholastic
P.O. Box 7502
2931 East McCarty St.
Jefferson City, MO 65102

MATH GLOSSARY

The ability to reason mathematically and perform arithmetic operations may be just as language-based as the ability to listen, speak, read or write (Cohen, 1971). Such concepts as *number, more,* and *less* are symbolic in nature. Any student who has difficulty with symbols is likely to be equally disabled in mastery of mathematics.

Readiness for each stage of development is crucial (Piaget, 1953; Copeland, 1974). Especially at the concrete operational stage, many experiences should be provided with manipulatives to facilitate mastery of basic operations. Similarly, frequent assessment must be conducted because children do not always arrive at their developmental stages at the same ages.

Both the theoretical and practical aspects of instruction in mathematics can be reinforced by careful selection and usage of computer software. Many programs allow children to correct mistakes by letting students know if the solution is right or wrong. The classroom can only be richer when mathematics software is an integrated part of a creative program. Below are some of the major terms associated with mathematics.

Decimal   any numeral based on 10; a fraction with an unwritten denominator of 10 or some power of 10, indicated by a point before the numerator (Example: .5 = 5/10).

Digit   any one of ten different symbols used to write numerals (0,1,2,3,4,5,6,7,8,9)

Equation   a number sentence that contains the phrase "is equal to" (often expressed symbolically by =).

Estimate   a general calculation of size, value, etc.

Fraction   a rational number expressing one or more of the equal parts of a whole; a comparison or ratio; an indicated division.

Graph   a type of drawing designed to picture relationships among the elements of two or more sets.

Integer
any positive or negative whole number or zero.

Measurement
a comparison process by which numbers are assigned to concrete objects (includes heights, lengths, weights, sizes, temperatures, containers, capacity, time, and money).

Metric system
a system of units of measure based on the decimal system (includes meter, gram, and liter).

Number
a mathematical abstraction showing how many or which one in a series (examples: 1,2; 1st, 2nd).

Numeral
one name for a number.

Numeration
a system of numbering or counting; the act of reading in words numbers expressed by figures.

Operations
addition, subtraction, multiplication, or division.

Percent
a hundredth part.

Rational number
any number that can be named by a fraction in the form a/b, where a and b are integers with the restriction that b cannot equal 0.

Set
a collection of points, numbers, or other objects.

BIBLIOGRAPHY

Alessi, S.M., and Trollip, S.R. (1985). *Computer-based instruction: Methods and development.* Englewood Cliffs, NJ: Prentice Hall.

American national standard for human factors engineering of visual display terminal workstations: Review draft. Santa Monica, CA: Human Factors Society, 1986.

Anderson, R.E. (1983). Innovative microcomputer games and simulations. *Simulations and Games, 14,* 3–8.

AT&T Bell Laboratories (1984). *Video display terminals: Preliminary guidelines for selection, installation & use.* Indianapolis, IN: AT&T Technologies.

Baker, R., and Schutz, R. (Eds.). (1971). *Instructional product development.* New York, NY: Van Nostrand Reinhold.

Bandura, A. (1978). Social learning theory of aggression. *Journal of Communication, 128(3),* 12–29.

Bardwell, R. (1981). Feedback: How does it function? *Journal of Experimental Education, 50,* 4–9.

Bass, G.M. and Perkins, H.W. (1984). Teaching Critical Thinking Skills with CAI. *Electronic Learning, 4(2),* 32–34, 96.

Bean, H.C. (1983). Computerized word-processing as an aid to revision. *College Composition and Communication, 34,* 146–148.

Becker, H. (1983). *How schools use microcomputers: Reports from a national survey.* Baltimore: Johns Hopkins University, Center for Social Organization of Schools.

Bender, M., and Church, G. (1984). Developing a computer-applications training program for the learning disabled. *Learning Disabilities, 3(8),* 99–102.

Berman, P., and McLaughlin, M.W. (1975). *Federal programs supporting educational change.* Vol. 1, *Model of Educational change.* Santa Monica, CA: The Rand Corporation.

Beverstock, C. (1984). *Computer using educators.* Paper presented at the Arizona State University Conference, Tempe, AZ

Bitter, G. (1984). Hardware and software selection and evaluation. *Computers in the schools, 1(1),* 13–28.

Bitter, G., and Wighton, D. (1987). The most important criteria used by the eduational software evaluation consortium. *The Computing Teacher, 14(6),* 7–9.

Bloom, B.S. (Ed.). (1956). *Taxonomy of educational objectives.* New York, NY: McKay.

Boegehold, B.D. (1984). *Getting ready to read,* The Bank Street College of Education Child Development Series, New York, NY: Ballantine Books, 130.

Bowman, R.F. (1982). A "Pac-Man" theory of motivation: Tactical implications for classroom instruction. *Educational Technology, 22,* 14–16.

Bowman, B. (1983). *Do computers have a place in preschools?* ERIC Publication, ED 321 504.

Bozeman, W. (1984). Strategic planning for computer-based educational technology. *Educational Technology, 24(5),* 23–27.

Bracey, G.W. (1982). Computers in education: What the research shows. *Electronic Learning, 2(3),* 51–54.

Bright, G.W., Harvey, J.G., and Wheeler, M.M. (1980s). Varying manipulative game constraints, Player verbalizations, and mathematics learning. *Journal of Experimental Education, 49,* 52–55.

Bright, G.W., Harvey, J.G., and Wheeler, M.M. (1980b). Using games to maintain multiplication basic facts. *Journal for Research in Mathematics Education, 11,* 379–385.

Bright, G.W., Harvey, J.G., and Wheeler, M.M. (1985). Learning and mathematics games. *Journal for Research in Mathematics Education.* Monograph Number 1. Reston, VA: National Council of Teachers of Mathematics.

Browning, P., Zambrosky-Barkin, P., Nave, G., and White, W. (1985). *Computer technology for the handicapped in special education and rehabilitation: A resource guide.* Vol. II. Eugene, OR: International Council for Computers in Education.

Brownstein, I., and Lerner, N.B. (1982). *Guidelines for evaluating and selecting software packages.* New York, NY: The Productivity Group, Inc.

Bruwelheide, J.H. (1982). Teacher competencies for microcomputer use in the classroom: A literature review. *Educational Technology, 22(10),* 29–31.

Budoff, M., and Hutton, L.R. (1982). Microcomputers in special education: Promises and Pitfalls. *Exceptional Children, 49(2),* 123–128.

Bunch, G.B. (1984). Special education in Canada: An overview. In D.D. Hammill, N.R. Bartel, and G.G. Bunch, *Teaching children with learning and behavior problems.* Toronto, Ontario: Allyn & Bacon.

Burton, J.K., and Merrill, P.F. (1977). Needs assessment: Goals, needs, and priorities. In L.J. Briggs (Ed.), *Instructional design: Principals and applications.* Englewood Cliffs, NJ: Educational Technology Publications.

Cacha, F.B. (1983). Glamorizing and legitimizing violence in software: A misuse of the computer. *Educational Technology, 23(3),* 7–9.

Calkins, L.M. (1983). Making the reading-writing connection. *Learning,* Sept. 1983, 82–86.

Campanazzi, J.A. (1978). The effects of locus of control and provision of overviews in a computer-assisted instruction sequence. *AEDS Journal, 12,* 12–30.

Carnegie Quarterly. (1985). From drill sergeant to intellectual assistant: Computers in the schools, *30(3), 30(4).*

Carter, J. (1984). Instructional learner feedback: A literature review with implications for software development. *The Computing Teacher, 12(2),* 53–55.

Chaffin, J.D. (1983). Motivational Features of Video Arcade Games. In C. Gutman, *Video games and human development: A research agenda for the 80s, 49,* 54–56. Cambridge, MA: Harvard Graduate School of Education.

Chaffin, J.D., Maxwell, B., and Thompson, B. (1983). ARC-ED curriculum: The application of video game formats to educational software. *Exceptional Children, 49,* 173–178.

Chang, L., and Osguthorpe, R. (1987). An evaluation system for educational software: A self-instructional approach. *Educational Technology, 27(6),* 15–19.

Church, G., and Bender, M. (1985). School Administration and technology: Planning educational roles. *Educational Technology, 25(6),* 21–24.

Clements, D.H., and Gullo, D.F. (1984). Effects of computer programming on young children's cognition. *Journal of Educational Psychology, 76,* 1051–1058.

Cohen, R. (1971). Arithmetic and learning disabilities. In H.R. Myklebust (Ed.), *Progress in learning disabilities.* Vol. 2. New York, NY: Grune & Stratton.

Cohen, V. (1983). Criteria for the evaluation of microcomputer courseware. *Educational Technology, 23(1),* 9–14.

Cohen, V.B. (1985). A reexamination of feedback delay on retention of computer-based instruction: Implications for instructional design. *Educational Technology, 25(1)* 33–37.

Copeland, R.W. (1974). *How children learn mathematics: Teaching implications of Piaget's research.* New York, NY: Macmillan.

Csapo, M., and Goguen, L. (Eds.). (1980). *Special education across Canada.* Vancouver, British Columbia: Center for Human Development and Research.

Daiute, C.A. (1982). Word processing: Can it make good writers better? *Electronic Learning, 1,* 29–33.

Dauite, C.A. (1983). The computer as stylus and audience. *College composition and communication, 34,* 134–145.

DeClercq, B., and Gennaro, E. (1986). *The effectiveness of supplementing the teaching of the volume displacement concept with use of an interactive computer simulation.* Paper presented at the 59th Annual Conference of the National Association for Research in Science Teaching, San Francisco, CA.

Demeter, L. (1951). "Accelerating the local use of improved educational practices in school systems." Ph.D. diss., Teachers College, Columbia University.

Dennis, R.J., Muiznieks, V.J., and Stewart, J.T. (1979). Instructional games and the computer-using teacher. Urbana, IL; Department of Secondary Education, University of Illinois, ERIC Document Reproduction Service No. ED 183 189.

Dick, W., and Carey, L. (1985). The systematic design of instruction. 2d ed. Glenview, IL: Scott, Foresman, & Company.

Diem, R.A. (1984). Preparing for the technological classroom: Will we meet the challenge? *Educational Technology, 24(3),* 13–15.

Dreyfus, H.L., and Dreyfus, S.E. (1984). Putting computers in their proper place: Analysis vs. intuition in the classroom. *Teachers College Record, 85,* 578–601.

Driskell, J.E., and Dwyer, D.J. (1984). Microcomputer video game-based training. *Educational Technology, 24(2),* 11–16.

Egan, D.E., Bowers, C., and Gomez, L.M. (1981). Learner characteristics that predict success in using a text-editor tutorial. *Association for Computing Machinery, Fall, 1981,* 337–340.

Eisele, J.E. (1985). Instructional computing: What's new in computing? Educational Technology, *25(8),* 24–25.

Fellmy, W.R., and Nicholson, E.W. (1985). School priorities in the information society. *Educational Technology, 25(11),* 48–50.

Finley, F.N. (1986). *Learning from science computer simulations.* Paper presented at the 59th Annual Conference of the National Association for Research in Science Teaching, San Francisco, CA.

Fisher, G. (1983). Word processing: Will it make all kids love to write? *Instructor, February, 1983.*

Flake, J.L., McClintock, C.E., and Turner, S.V. (1985). *Fundamentals of computer education.* Belmont, CA: Wadworth Publishing.

Futrell, M.K., and Geisert, P. (1984). The well-trained computer. Englewood Cliffs, NJ: Educational Technology Publications.

Foster, D. (1984). Computer simulation in tomorrow's schools. *Computers in the Schools, 1(3),* 81–89.

Gentner, D., and Norman, D. (1984). The typist's touch. *Psychology Today, 18(3),* 67–72.

Gillingham, M., Murphy, P., Cresci, K., Klevenow, S., Sims-Tucker, B., Slade, D., and Wizer, D. (1986). An evaluation of computer courseware authoring tools and a corresponding assessment instrument for use by instructors. *Educational Technology, 25(9),* 7–15.

Gilman, D.A. (1969). The effects of feedback on learners' certainty of response and attitude toward instruction in a computer-assisted instruction program for teaching science concepts. *Journal of Research in Science Training, 6,* 171–184.

Goodlad, J. (1975). *The dynamics of educational change: Toward responsive schools.* New York, NY: McGraw-Hill.

Gorman, H., and Bourne, L.E. (1983). Learning to think by learning logo: Rule learning in Third Grade Computer Programmers. Bulletin of the Psychonomic Society, *21,* 165–167.

Gorton, R. (1980). *School administration and supervision.* Dubuque, IA: Wm. C. Brown Company Publishers.

Grabe, M. (1986). Drill and practice's bad rep. *Electronic learning. 5(5),* 22–23.

Greenfield, P.M. (1984). *Mind and media: the effects of television, video games, and computers.* Cambridge, MA: Harvard University Press.

Griswold, P.A. (1983). Some determinants of computer awareness among education majors. *AEDS Journal, Winter, 1983,* 92–101.

Gross, N., Mason, W.S., and McEachern, A.W., (1958). *Explorations in role analysis: Studies of the school superintendency role.* New York, NY: Wiley.

Hasselbring, T.S., and Cavanaugh, K.J. (1986). Applications for the mildly handicapped. In

C.K. Kinzer, R.D. Sherwood, J.D. Bransford (Eds.), *Computer strategies for education: foundations and content area applications.* Columbus, OH: Merrill Publishing Company.

Hencley, S. (1960). The conflict pattern of school superintendents. *Administrator's Notebook, 7*, 9.

Hennings, D.G. (1981). Input: Enter the word processing computer. *Language Arts, 58*, 18–22.

Hennings, D.G. (1983). Words processed here: Write with your computer. *Phi Delta Kappan, 65*, 122–123.

Hofmeister, A., and Thorkildsen, R. (1981). Videodisc technology and the preparation of special education teachers. *Teacher Education and Special Education, 4(3)*, 34–39.

Hoth, E.K. (1985). Debunking myths about computer literacy for teachers. *Educational Technology, 25(1)*, 37–39.

IBM (1984). Human factors of workstations with visual displays. San Jose, CA: IBM Corporation Human Factors Center.

Icabone, D., and Hannaford, A. (1986). A comparison of two methods of teaching unknown reading words to fourth-graders: Microcomputer and tutor. *Educational Technology, 26(5)*, 36–39.

Jamison, D., Suppes, P., and Wells, S. (1974). The effectiveness of alternative instructional media: A survey. *Review of Educational Research, 44*, 1–67.

Jay, T. (1983). The cognitive approach to computer courseware design and evaluation. *Educational Technology, 23(1)*, 22–26.

Jensen, C.B. (1982). *The enhanced CAI tutorial.* In proceedings of the National Educational Computing Conference, Kansas City, KS.

Jesen, J. (1982). A Taxonomy of microcomputer authoring systems. *NSPI Journal, 21(6)*, 50–52.

Johnson, J. (1984). Evaluating do-it-yourself computer inservice training packages: Methods and some findings. *The Computing Teacher, (3)*, 65–66.

Kandaswamy, S. (1980). Evaluation of instructional materials: A synthesis of models and methods. *Educational Technology, 20(6)*, 19–26.

Karoff, P. (1983). Computerized head start. *Teaching, Learning, Computing,* November, 44–50.

Kaufman, J.E. and Hayes, H. (Eds.). (1981). *IES lighting handbook: Reference volume.* New York, NY: Illumination Engineering Society of North America.

Kaufman, R. (1977). Needs assessment: Internal and external. *Journal of Instructional Development, 1(1)*, 5–8.

Kaufman, R. (1979). Achieving useful results: Beyond performance and instruction. *NSPI Journal, 18(10)*, 4–8.

Kaufman, R., and English, F. (1979). Needs assessment: Concept and applications. Englewood Cliffs, NJ: Educational Technology Publications.

Kaufman, R. (1980). The passion for the practical: Are educational technologists losing their idealism? *Educational Technology, 20(1)*, 22–28.

Kaufman, R. (1982). Identifying and solving problems: A system approach. 3rd ed. San Diego, CA: University Associates Publishers.

Kaufman, R. (1983). A holistic planning model. *Performance and Instructional Journal, 22(8)*, 3–12.

Kaufman, R. (1984). Improving organizational impact. *Performance and Instructional Journal, 23(8)*, 11–5.

Kisner, E. (1984). Keyboarding: A must for tomorrow's world. *The Computing Teacher, 11(6)*, 21–22.

Kraus, W.H. (1981). Using a computer game to reinforce skills in addition to basic facts in second grade. *Journal for Research in Mathematics Education, 12*, 152–155.

Kulhavy, R. (1977). Feedback in written instruction. *Review of Educational Research, 47*, 211–232.

Kulhavy, R.W. and Anderson, R.C. (1972). Delay-retention effect with multi-choice tests. *Journal of Educational Psychology, 63,* 505–512.

Kulik, J.A., Bangert, R., and Williams, G. (1983). Effects of computer-based college teaching in secondary school teaching. *Journal of Educational Psychology, 75,* 19–26.

Kulik, J.A., Kulik, C.C. and Cohen, P.A. (1980). Effectiveness of computer-based college teaching: A meta-analysis of the findings. *Review of Educational Research, 50,* 525–544.

Lahey, G.F. (1978). Learner control of computer-based instruction: A comparison to guided instruction. Paper presented at the Association for the Development of Computer-Based Instructional Systems, Dallas, TX.

Lasoff, E.M. (1981). The effects of feedback in both computer-assisted instruction and programmed instruction on achievement and attitude. *Dissertation Abstracts International, 42,* 1553A. (University Microfilms No. 81-21,115).

Lathrop, A., and Goodson, B. (1983). *Courseware in the classroom: Selecting, organizing, and using educational software.* Menlo Park, CA: Addison-Wesley.

Levin, E. (1982). They zap, crackle, and pop, but video games can be powerful tools for learning. *People Weekly,* May 31, 74–79.

MacArthur, A., and Shneiderman, B. (1986). Learning disabled students' difficulties in learning to use a word processor: Implications for instruction and software evaluation. *Journal of Learning Disabilities, 19(4),* 248–253.

Malone, T.W. (1983). What makes things fun to learn? In M.C. Gutman (Ed.), *Video games and human development: A research agenda for the 80s.* Cambridge, MA: Harvard Graduate School of Education, 49–53.

Mandal, A.C. (1982). The correct height of school furniture. *Human Factors, 24,* 257–269.

McFarlan, F.W., and McKenney, K.L. (1983). *Corporate information systems management.* Homewood, IL: Richard D. Irwin, Inc.

McLeod, A. (1983). *Computers in language arts.* ERIC Document Reproduction System No. ED 128010.

Metzger, M. (1983). *Learning disabled students and computers: A teachers guidebook.* ERIC Document Reproduction System No. ED 242015.

Moore, M.L. (1984). Preparing teachers to teach about computers and computing. *The Monitor, 23(5,6),* 19–21.

Moskowitz, J., and Birman, B. (1985). Computers in the schools: Implications of change. *Educational Technology, 25(1),* 7–14.

Mourant, R.R., Lakshmanan, R., and Chantadisai, R. (1981). Visual fatigue and cathode ray tube display terminals. *Human Factors, 23,* 529–540.

Nadler,G. (1981). *The planning and design approach.* New York, NY: John Wiley and Sons.

Nolan,R.L., and Gibson, F.C. (1974). Managing the four stages of EDP Growth. *Harvard Business Review,* January/February, 1974, 76.

Overton, V. (1981). Research in instructional computing and mathematics education. *Viewpoints in Teaching and Learning, 57(2),* 23–26.

Papert, S. (1980). *Mindstorms: Children, computers, and powerful ideas.* New York, NY: Basic Books.

Pattison, L. (1985). Software writing made easy. *Electronic Learning,* March, 30–36.

Pea, R.D., and Kurland, D.M. (1984). On the cognitive effects of learning computer programming. *Journal of New Ideas Psychology, 2,* 137–168.

Pepin, M., and Leroux, Y. (1984). Modele de creation de jeux educatifs sur micro-ordinateurs. In L'Agence de l'Informatique (Ed.), *EA084: 1er colloque scienfique fracophone sur l'enseignement assiste par ordinateur* (pp. 265–288). Lyon: Ecole Superieure de Commerce.

Piaget, J. (1953). How children form mathematical concepts. *Scientific American, 189,* 74–89.

Preece, J., and Jones, A. (1985). Training teachers to select educational computer software. *British Journal of Educational Technology, 16(1),* 9–20.

Rankin, R., and Trepper, T. (1978). Retention and delay of feedback in a computer-assisted instructional task. *Journal of Experimental Education, 46,* 67–70.

Robin, A.L. (1978). The timing of feedback in personalized instruction. *Journal of Personalized Instruction, 3(2),* 81–88.

Robinson, G.E., and Protheroe, N. (1985). The teachers speak out. *Principal, 65(3),* 58–64.

Roblyer, M. (1981). When is it "good courseware?" Problems in developing standards for microcoputer courseware. *Educational Technology, 21(10),* 47–54.

Roblyer, M.D. (1986). Courseware: A practical revolution. *Educational Technology, 26(2),* 34–35.

Rogers, J.B., Moursand, D.G., and Ence, G.L. (1984). Preparing precollege teachers for the computer age. *Communications of the ACM, 1984,* 195–200.

Roper, W.J. (1977). Feedback in computer-assisted instruction. *Journal of Programmed Learning and Educational Technology, 14(1),* 43–47.

Rostron, A., and Sewell, D. (1984). Microtechnology in special education. Baltimore, MD: The Johns Hopkins University Press.

Sandoval, H.F. (1984). Teacher training in computer skills: A call for a redefinition. *Educational Technology, 24(10),* 29–31.

Scheffler, I. (1986). Computers at school? *Teachers College Record, 67(4),* 513–528.

Schmidt, J., and Jones, B. (1983). Keyboarding instruction: Elementary school options. *Business Education Forum, 37(7),* 11–12.

Schmidt, J., and Stewart, J. (1983). Microcomputer typewriting in business education. *Business Education Forum, 37(6),* 23–32.

Schmuck, R.A., and Runkel, P.J. (1985). *The handbook of organizational development in schools.* Palo Alto, CA: Mayfield Publishing Company.

School district uses of computer technology, Arlington, VA: Educational Research Services, Inc., 1982.

Schwartz, H. (1984). Teaching writing with computer aids. *College English, 46,* 239–247.

Shanahan, D., and Ryan, A.W. (1984). A tool for evaluating educational software. *ASCD Yearbook,* 242–246.

Shaw-Nickerson, E., and Kisker, K. (1984). Computer-based simulations in evaluating registered nurse students in a baccalaureate program. *Journal of Educational Technology Systems, 13,* 107–113.

Sheingold, K., Kane, J.H., and Endreweit, M.E. (1983). Microcomputer use in schools: Developing a research agenda. *Harvard Educational Review,* November.

Slattow, G. (1977). Demonstration of the PLATO IV computer-based education system. Urbana, IL: University of Illinois Computer-Based Educational Research Laboratory, ERIC Document Reproduction System No. ED 158 767.

Sleeman, D., and Brown, J.S. (1982). *Intelligent tutoring systems,* New York, NY: Academic Press.

Stammerjohn, L.W., Jr., Smith, M.J., and Cohen, B.G.F. (1981). Evaluation of work station design factors in VDT operations. *Human Factors, 23,* 401–412.

Stein, A.H., (1981). The effects of TV action and violence on children's social behavior. *The Journal of Genetic Psychology, 138.* 183–191.

Steinberg, E.R. (1983). Reviewing the instructional effectiveness of computer courseware. *Educational Technology, 23(1),* 17–19.

Steiner, G.A. (1979). Strategic planning: What every manager must know. New York, NY: Free Press.

Stephenson, B., and deLandsheere, G. (1985). Excerpts from the international conference on education and new information technologies. *Peabody Journal of Education, 62(2),* 75–92.

Stevens, D.J. (1982). Educators' perceptions of computers in education: 1979 and 1981. *AEDS Journal, Fall, 1982.*

Stevens, S.M. (1985). Surrogate laboratory experiments: Interactive computer/videodisc lessons and their effect on students' understanding of science. Paper presented at the

58th Annual Conference of the National Association for Research in Science Teaching, French Lick, IN.

Stewart, J., and Jones, B. (1983). Keyboarding instruction: elementary school options. *Business Education Forum, 37(7),* 11–12.

Stromberg, L., and Kurth, R. (1984). *Using word processing to teach revision in written composition.* Paper presented at the Annual Meeting of the National Reading Conference, Austin, TX.

Struges, P.T. (1972). Information delay and retention: Effect of information in feedback and tests. *Journal of Educational Psychology, 63,* 32–43.

Tennyson, R.D., Christensen, D.L., and Park, S.I. (1984). The Minnesota adaptive instructional system: An intelligent CBI system. *Journal of Computer-Based Instruction, 11(1),* 2–13.

Thomas, D.B. (1979). The effectiveness of computer assisted instruction in secondary schools. *AEDS Journal, 12,* 103–116.

Torgesen, J.K. (1984). Instructional uses of microcomputers with elementary aged mildly handicapped children. In R.E. Bennett and C.A. Maher (Eds.), *Microcomputers and exceptional children.* New York, NY: Hawthorn Press.

Truett, C. (1984). The search for quality micro programs: Software and review sources. *School Library Journal, 30(1),* 35–37.

Vetter, E. (1976). Coping with the demands: Role pressure and the school principal. *NASSP Bulletin,* November.

Welton, J., Weddell, K., and Vorhaus, G. (1984). *Meeting special education needs.* London: Heinemann Education Books Ltd.

Wheeler, F. (1985). Can word processing help the writing process? *Learning,* March.

Whithey, M. (1983). The computer and writing. *English Journal, 72,* 24–31.

Wilcox, W.C. (1978). *Learner control of number of instances in a rule-using task.* Report of a project funded by the National Science Foundation, Washington, D.C. ERIC Document Reproduction Service No. ED 201 531.

Womble, G. (1984). Process and processor: Is there room for a machine in the English classroom? *English Journal, 73,* 34–37.

Wright, E.B., and Forcier, R.C. (1985). *The computer: A tool for the teacher.* Belmont, CA: Wadworth Publishing.

Ziajka, A. (1983). Microcomputers in early childhood education? *Young Children, 38(5),* 61–67.

Zietsman, A.I. and Hewson, P.Q. (1986). Effects of instruction using microcomputer simulations and conceptual change strategies on science learning. *Journal of Research in Science Teaching, 23(1),* 27–39.

Zuk, D.A., and Stillwell, W.E. (1984). Taming the beast: A comprehensive model for the implementation of microcomputers in education. *Education, 104(4),* 377–384.

Index